Teaching English, Language and Literacy

Second edition

Dominic Wyse and Russell Jones
With a contribution from
Helen Bradford

Routledge
Taylor & Francis Group

LONDON AND NEW YORK

First published 2001 by Routledge
Reprinted 2002 (twice), 2003 (three times), 2004 (twice), 2005
This edition published 2008 by Routledge
2 Park Square, Milton Park, Abingdon, Oxon OX14 4RN.

Simultaneously published in the USA and Canada
by Routledge
270 Madison Ave, New York, NY 10016

Routledge is an imprint of the Taylor & Francis Group,
an informa business

© 2001, 2008 Dominic Wyse and Russell Jones

Typeset in Sabon by
RefineCatch Limited, Bungay, Suffolk
Printed and bound in Great Britain by
TJ International, Padstow, Cornwall

British Library Cataloguing in Publication Data
A catalogue record for this book is available from the British Library

Library of Congress Cataloging-in-Publication Data
A catalog record for this book has been requested

ISBN10: 0-415-39979-3 (hbk)
ISBN10: 0-415-39980-7 (pbk)

ISBN13: 978-0-415-39979-1 (hbk)
ISBN13: 978-0-415-39980-7 (pbk)

Teaching English, Language and Literacy
Second edition

'*The book is comprehensive, up-to-date, critical and authoritative. It is also, above all, well written. It will undoubtedly become standard reading for the next generation of teachers in training and practising teachers will also learn a great deal from dipping into its contents.*' **David Wray**, Professor of Literacy Education, University of Warwick

Are you looking for one book that covers every aspect of the teaching of English at primary level?

This fully updated second edition of *Teaching English, Language and Literacy* is an essential introduction for anyone learning to teach English at primary school level. Designed for students on initial teacher training courses, but also of great use to those teachers wanting to keep pace with the latest developments in their specialist subject, the book covers the theory and practice of teaching English, language and literacy and includes comprehensive analysis of the Primary National Strategy (PNS) Literacy Framework.

Each chapter has a specific glossary to explain terms and gives suggestions for further reading. This second edition covers key areas that students, teachers and English co-ordinators have to manage, and includes advice on:

- developing reading, including advice on choosing texts, and the role of phonics
- improving writing skills, including advice on grammar and punctuation
- planning and assessing speaking and listening lessons
- working effectively with pupils who are multilingual
- understanding historical developments in the subject
- the latest thinking in educational policy and practice
- the use of multimedia
- maintaining good home-school links
- gender and the teaching of English language and literacy.

All these chapters include clear examples of practice, coverage of key issues, analysis of research, and reflections on national policy to encourage the best possible response to the demands of the National Curriculum.

Dominic Wyse is Senior Lecturer in Early Years and Primary Education and Fellow of Churchill College at the University of Cambridge.

Russell Jones is Senior Lecturer in Primary Education at Manchester Metropolitan University.

They have worked as primary teachers and subject leaders and have substantial experience of working with students and teachers.

Dominic and Russell would like to thank the many students, teachers and colleagues who have shown appreciation for their work critically reflecting on government policy on the teaching of English, language and literacy.

Russell would like to dedicate this book to Emily and Hayley.

Contents

Figures

Tables

Foreword

Books about literacy and language teaching serve many different purposes. Some present original research into an aspect of teaching and learning; some focus on a particular issue; others attempt to summarise what is currently known in this field, drawing out the major implications for teachers and teachers in training.

Books of the last type are difficult to write well, demanding as they do an almost encyclopaedic knowledge of this vast area and it is perhaps not surprising that a few such books come to dominate reading lists for long periods. During the 1980s the key book of this type was Diana Hutchcroft's *Making Language Work*, but in the 1990s this was largely replaced as the standard text by our own *Literacy and Language in the Primary Years*.

With the publication of *Teaching English, Language and Literacy*, Dominic Wyse and Russell Jones could well have produced the standard text for the 2000s. The book is comprehensive, up-to-date, critical and authoritative. It is also, above all, well written. It will undoubtedly become standard reading for the next generation of teachers in training and practising teachers will also learn a great deal from dipping into its contents. As the co-author of the book it will replace, I was less than ecstatic at the arrival of this volume: as a student, researcher and teacher of literacy and language education, I am delighted to have this book on my shelf.

Comment on the second edition

How do you improve on an already excellent book? This is probably one of the toughest questions for all authors. After working so hard to produce what you think is the definitive work in the field, a couple of years later the publishers then ask you to produce a second edition – to make it even better! Well, here's one instance where the authors have actually achieved what must have seemed to them the impossible. Dominic Wyse and Russell Jones have clearly kept up to date with a rapidly moving field and produced a second edition which is genuinely better than the first. They have added new material, and tackled some issues in slightly different ways. The result is a really refreshing new take on the perennially interesting (and vitally important) topic of language and literacy teaching in the primary school. An impressive achievement!

David Wray
Director of Teacher Education
Professor of Literacy Education
Institute of Education
University of Warwick

Preface

The words 'second edition' perhaps only hint at the extensive changes we have made to our book. One important feature of this has been as a result of our reading and critically evaluating most of the texts that make up the Primary National Strategy (PNS) Literacy Framework which was published online in October 2006. The first edition was, to our knowledge, the first book to offer a comprehensive critical evaluation of the National Literacy Strategy (NLS). This second edition has the same relationship with the PNS Literacy Framework.

An example of the extent of our changes is a completely new chapter called 'Gender and the teaching of English', a subject we feel should have been in the first edition. Although most of the chapters were in the first edition, there have been substantial changes to nearly all of them. The four longer chapters are good examples of this process with the outcomes of new research interpreted in order to inform the reader about implications for practice and policy. The material from some chapters from the first edition has been moved to improve the structure and logic of the text. The chapter called 'Information and communication technologies (ICTs) and multimedia' is an example of this. Two previous chapters have been merged to result in a more sustained consideration of these related topics.

The hallmarks of our text remain its comprehensive coverage and its critically reflective approach to practice, research, theory and policy. We were very grateful for the many positive comments both in person and via email that we received from students and tutors about the first edition. We hope that you enjoy the second edition as much!

English is one of the most fascinating, controversial and challenging subjects of the school curriculum. The fact that English is the language we speak also makes it a subject that is closely linked with our identities, which is one of the reasons that it often engenders passionate views. Another reason that it is important is that all teachers have to be teachers of English because learning takes place through talking, reading and writing. In the early years and primary curriculum great stress is put on English because it is a bridge to all other learning.

This book is a comprehensive introduction to the ideas, concepts and knowledge that are part of the study of English teaching. *Teaching English, Language and Literacy* is written for all primary education students and their teachers. The established partnerships between providers of teacher education and schools have maintained the need for a book that offers a comprehensive overview of the subject to enable teacher mentors to update their professional knowledge in specific areas when appropriate. It is designed as a reader that will enhance and consolidate the learning in core English programmes and as an essential guide to the teaching of English.

The book is divided into five parts: 'Introduction'; 'Reading'; 'Writing'; 'Speaking and listening', and 'General issues'. The bulk of the book consists of short chapters that cover the variety of aspects that make up the English curriculum. All these chapters include clear examples of practice, coverage of key issues, analysis of research, and reflections on national policy. The short chapters are complemented by four longer ones that begin Parts I to IV. The first of these addresses the important subject of the history of English and English teaching. The other three look at children's development in reading, writing and langauge and relate this development to teaching approaches. The structure of the longer chapters allowed us to tackle some of the most important aspects of the English curriculum in depth and at a higher level. Part V is made up of issues that tend to be applicable to all three modes of reading, writing, and speaking and listening. The exception to this structure is 'Theories of learning' which is located in the introduction because of our view that learning theories underpin your understanding of the curriculum as a whole.

One of the innovative features of the book is its comprehensive nature. The subject of English is an area that boasts an impressive array of scholarship and practice. While there are many books that have addressed the modes of reading, writing, and speaking and listening separately, there are very few which address the complete subject area. By doing this we have accepted that inevitably some parts of the subject are only touched on briefly. In recognition of this you will find more than ninety descriptions of recommended books and papers for further reading which appear in the 'annotated bibliographies' for every chapter. A novel feature of these bibliographies is a system of coding which allows you to judge the reading level and the balance between theory and practice:

*   Mainly focused on classroom practice
**   Close balance between theory and practice
*** Research and theory based

L1   Introductory reading
L2   Intermediate reading
L3   Advanced reading

We are fully in support of the idea that teaching should be an evidence-informed activity. Each chapter in the book is underpinned by our reading of research. Most chapters include references to 'peer-reviewed' journals (a process which contributes to a higher quality of research), not just books. The academic standard of some books needs to be questioned, particularly those that are not subject to a rigorous review process. However, the fact that books and their ideas often communicate to a wider audience is important, and for that reason we have carefully selected references to both books and papers. So, in addition to the annotated bibliographies, each chapter contains its own reference list which includes a range of texts that we think are worthy of further study.

In addition to our inclusion of papers, books and official publications we also make reference to a range of websites. This is always a tricky business. This revision of the book took many months to complete and in that time information and communications technology (ICT) has continued to develop. In the light of this we have chosen sites that we hope will stand the test of time.

The most important part of reading a book like this is that it will enable you to become a better teacher. No book can offer a magic solution to becoming an effective teacher. Teaching skills and knowledge – like most learning – requires practical engagement with the subject in partnership with experienced professionals. However, in order to establish direct and explicit links with practice we use case studies, analysis of resources, reflections on children's work, teachers' thoughts, examples of teaching, and each chapter concludes with 'practice points' which have been written to focus attention on some of the most important practical ideas of which you should be aware.

This book covers a wide range of essential knowledge. If we consider technical vocabulary alone, there are hundreds of definitions supplied in the 'glossaries' that are a feature of every chapter. So if you are unsure about the meaning of a particular word as you are reading, you do not need to reach for a dictionary because most of the key words are defined for you at the end of the chapter. Another aspect of knowledge that has been played down in recent years is the knowledge of issues. It is the knowledge of these key issues that are vital to both effective teaching and success in the education profession. In order to maintain the tradition of English as a vibrant subject we hope teachers will continue to fully engage with the issues and ideas that are explored in this book.

Note

Throughout this book the following icons are used to assist the reader:

➡ Recommends the reader looks at another chapter in the book.
☞ These words are included in the glossaries at the end of each chapter.

Part I

Introduction

Chapter 1

The history of English, language and literacy

One of the important aspects of historical knowledge is that it enables us to better understand the present. This chapter briefly examines three important historical angles: the history of English as a language; the history of the teaching of English; and the history of national initiatives to improve the teaching of English. We conclude in the present by looking at the Primary National Strategy Literacy Framework.

The three words 'English', 'Language' and 'Literacy' in the title of this book are significant because they are central to many of the debates that have raged about the teaching of English in primary schools. During the 1970s and 1980s the teaching of 'language' was the focus. The job of primary schools was to foster the development of children's language through reading, writing and, to a lesser extent, talking. This focus included the need to support multilingual children's development in English and other languages. The teachers who coordinated the subject were known as 'language coordinators'. The teaching of language in primary schools was seen as different in many respects from the teaching of English that secondary schools carried out.

With the coming of the Education Reform Act 1988, 'English' was re-established as the main focus for primary education, however, this was still to be concerned with the teaching of the three language modes of reading, writing and talking. 'Speaking and Listening' became of equal importance to Reading and Writing for the first time, and this was prescribed by the National Curriculum. Coordinators were now to be called 'English' coordinators. The advent of the National Literacy Strategy in 1997 resulted in a heavy focus on 'Literacy'. You will probably have guessed that subject leaders were renamed 'literacy coordinators'.

The first part of this chapter looks at some of the historical aspects of the subject that have shaped its development. It is vital that all teachers have a historical perspective on their work, at the very least this can give you a means to critically examine modern initiatives and to check how 'new' they really are.

We start with a brief look at some of the significant moments in the development of the English language and reflect on their continuing relevance to classroom teaching. This is followed by reflections on the history of the *teaching* of English. We conclude with an outline of some of the major national projects that have been undertaken and finish right up-to-date with a look at the Primary National Strategy.

The English language

English, like all languages, is constantly changing. When the editor of the *Oxford English Dictionary* was interviewed in 1998, he commented on the fact that 'phwoarr' had recently been included in the dictionary, defined as an exclamation of sexual attraction. Each time publishers produce new editions of dictionaries, new words – and new meanings for old words – are added in recognition that language is always changing. The *Oxford English Dictionary* has a large team of people who are constantly searching for new uses and new additions to the language. The online version of the dictionary has resulted in a spectacular resource. For teachers, the idea that language is always changing is an important one. If we place too heavy an emphasis on absolute and fixed 'rules', we may be teaching in a linguistically inaccurate or inappropriate way. Modern teaching needs to recognise those features of the language that are stable and those that are subject to constant change.

The increasing standardisation of the language has altered the pace and nature of change. Dictionaries themselves play a major role in the standardisation of the language, and it is interesting to note that standard American English is represented by *Webster's Third New International Dictionary* but Standard (English) English is represented by the *Oxford English Dictionary* or *Chambers Dictionary* for many things. The significant influence of publishing has also resulted in standard reference works that lay down particular conventions. So if you have ever wondered how to reference properly using the *Author–Date* method, try *The American Psychological Association (APA) 5th Style* (or for a simplified version try *The Good Writing Guide for Education Students*, Wyse (2007)).

If we look back in time we can see that this process of change is by no means a recent phenomenon. During the fifth century, the Anglo-Saxons settled in England and, as always happens when people settle, they bring changes to the language, which was at that time 'Old English'. The few texts that have survived from this period are in four main dialects (☞): West Saxon, Kentish, Mercian, and Northumbrian. The last two are sometimes grouped together and called Anglian. West Saxon became the standard dialect at the time but is not the direct ancestor of modern Standard English (☞), which is mainly derived from an Anglian dialect (Barber, 1993). If you take the modern word 'cold' as an example, the Anglian 'cald' is a stronger influence than the West Saxon version, 'ceald'.

In the ninth century the Vikings brought further changes to the language. Placenames were affected: 'Grimsby' meant Grim's village and 'Micklethwaite' meant large clearing. The pronunciation of English speech was also affected, and it is possible to recognise some Scandinavian-influenced words because of their phonological form (☞). It is suggested that 'awe' is a Scandinavian word and that this came from changes of pronunciation to the Old English word 'ege'. One of the most interesting things about Scandinavian loanwords (☞) is that they are so commonly used: sister, leg, neck, bag, cake, dirt, fellow, fog, knife, skill, skin, sky, window, flat, loose, call, drag and even 'they' and 'them' (Barber, 1993).

In more recent times words from a range of countries have been borrowed. Here are a small selection of examples: French – elite, liaison, menu, plateau; Spanish and Portuguese – alligator, chocolate, cannibal, embargo, potato; Italian – concerto, balcony, casino, cartoon; Indian – bangle, cot, juggernaut, loot, pyjamas, shampoo; African languages – banjo, zombie, rumba, tote. However, for many of these words it is difficult to attribute them to one original country. To illustrate the complexities consider the word 'chess':

> 'Chess' was borrowed from Middle French in the fourteenth century. The French word was, in turn, borrowed from Arabic, which had earlier borrowed it from Persian 'shah' 'king'. Thus the etymology (☞) of the word reaches from Persian, through Arabic and Middle French, but its ultimate source (as far back as we can trace its history) is Persian. Similarly, the etymon of 'chess', that is, the word from which it has been derived, is immediately 'esches' and ultimately 'shah'. Loanwords have, as it were, a life of their own that cuts across the boundaries between languages.
>
> (Pyles and Algeo, 1993: 286)

The influence of loanwords is one of the factors that has resulted in some of the irregularities of English spelling. David Crystal (1997) lists some of the other major factors. Above we referred to the Anglo-Saxon period; at that time there were only 24 graphemes (letter symbols) to represent 40 phonemes (sounds). Later 'i' and 'j', 'u' and 'v' were changed from being interchangeable to having distinct functions and 'w' was added but many sounds still had to be signalled by combinations of letters.

After the Norman conquest, French scribes – who had responsibility for publishing texts – respelled a great deal of the language. They introduced new conventions such as 'qu' for 'cw' (queen), 'gh' for 'h' (night) and 'c' before 'e' or 'i' in words such as 'circle' and 'cell'. Once printing became better established in the West this added further complications. William Caxton (1422–91) is often credited with the 'invention' of the printing press but that is not accurate. During the seventh century the Chinese printed the earliest known book *The Diamond Sutra*, using inked wooden relief blocks. By the beginning of the fifteenth century the process had developed in Korea to the extent that printers were manufacturing bronze type sets of 100,000 pieces. In the West, Johannes Gutenberg (1390s–1468) is credited with the development of moveable metal type in association with a hand-operated printing press.

Many of the early printers working in England were foreign (especially from Holland) and they used their own spelling conventions. Also, until the sixteenth century, line justification (☞) was achieved by changing words rather than by adding spaces. Once printing became established, the written language did not keep pace with the considerable changes in the way words were spoken, resulting in weaker links between sound and symbol.

Samuel Johnson's dictionary published in 1755 was another important factor in relation to English spelling. His work resulted in dictionaries becoming more authoritarian and used as the basis for 'correct' usage. Noah Webster, the first person to write a major account of American English, compared Johnson's contribution to Isaac Newton's in mathematics. Johnson's dictionary was significant for a number of reasons. Unlike dictionaries of the past that tended to concentrate on 'hard words', Johnson wanted a scholarly record of the whole language. It was based on words in use and introduced a literary dimension drawing heavily on writers such as Dryden, Milton, Addison, Bacon, Pope and Shakespeare (Crystal, 1997: 109). Shakespeare's remarkable influence on the English language is not confined to the artistic significance of his work, many of the words and phrases of his plays are still commonly used today:

> He coined some 2,000 words – an astonishing number – and gave us countless phrases. As a phrasemaker there has never been anyone to match him. Among his inventions: one fell swoop, in my mind's eye, more in sorrow than in anger, to be in a pickle, bag and baggage, vanish into thin air, budge an inch, play fast and loose, go down the primrose path, the milk of human kindness, remembrance of things past, the sound and fury, to thine own self be true, to be or not to be, cold comfort, to beggar all description, salad days, flesh and blood, foul play, tower of strength, to be cruel to be kind, and on and on and on and on. And on. He was so wildly prolific that he could put two in one sentence, as in Hamlet's observation: 'Though I am native here and to the manner born, it is custom more honoured in the breach than the observance.' He could even mix metaphors and get away with it, as when he wrote: 'Or to take arms against a sea of troubles.'
>
> (Bryson, 1990: 57)

Crystal (2004) makes the point that although spelling is an area where there's more agreement about what is correct than in other areas of language, there's still considerable variation. Greenbaum's (1986) research looked at all the words beginning with A in a medium-sized desk dictionary which were spelled in more than one way; he found 296. When extrapolating this to the dictionary as a whole, he estimated 5000 variants altogether, which is 5.6 per cent. If this were to be done with a dictionary as complete as the *Oxford English*

Dictionary, it would mean many thousands of words where the spelling has not been definitively agreed. Crystal gives some examples including: accessory/accessary; acclimatize/acclimatise; adrenalin/adrenaline; aga/agha; ageing/aging; all right/alright.

Many of Greenbaum's words were pairs but there were some triplets, for example, aerie/aery/eyrie. And there were even quadruplets: anaesthetize/anaesthetise/anesthetize/anesthetise. Names translated from a foreign language compound the problems, particularly for music students: Tschaikovsky/Tchaikovsky/Tschaikofsky/Tchaikofsky/Tshaikovski.

The teaching of English

The establishment of state education as we know it can be conveniently traced back to the 1870 Elementary Education Act. Before that, the education of working-class children in this country was largely in the hands of the voluntary sector: church schools, factory schools, and, in the earlier part of the nineteenth century, schools run by the oppositional Chartist and Owenite Co-operative movements. The 1870 Act led to the establishment of free educational provision in elementary schools for all children from the age of 5 up to the age of 12. Education up to the age of 10 was compulsory, but if children had met the standards required they could be exempted from schooling for the final years. State schools and voluntary sector schools existed side by side from that date, a distinction that is still found today. Class differences were firmly established: the elementary and voluntary schools were schools for the labouring classes and the poor. The middle and upper classes expected to pay for the education of their children; secondary education in the form of the grammar and public schools was not available to the bulk of the population.

The curriculum in the voluntary schools and later in the elementary schools was extremely limited. Writing meant copying or dictation (DES, 1967: 5601). Oral work involved such things as the children learning by heart from the Book of Common Prayer, which included: 'To order myself lowly and reverently to all my betters' and 'to do my duty in that state of life, unto which it shall please God to call me' (Williamson, 1981: 79).

The elementary schools emerged at a time when the government exerted considerable control over the curriculum through the 'Revised Code' established in 1862 (➡ Chapter 11), better known as 'payment by results'. This was administered through frequent tests in reading, writing and arithmetic – the three Rs. If the children failed to meet the required standards, the grant was withdrawn and the teachers did not get paid. Under such conditions curriculum development was impossible because schools had to focus so much on the tests in order to get paid (Lawson and Silver, 1973).

Though the code was abolished in 1895, and the statutory control of the curriculum relinquished in 1902, the effects lasted well into the twentieth century, leading one inspector to comment that 30 years of 'code despotism' meant that 'teaching remained as mechanical and routine ridden as ever' (Holmes, 1922). Despite these criticisms, however, the introduction of universal compulsory education meant that literacy rates climbed steadily.

'English' as a subject, 1900–39

At the start of the twentieth century the term 'English' referred to grammar. Reading and writing were not even seen as part of 'English'. The emergence of English as a school subject in its own right occurred in the first years of the twentieth century. A major landmark in the development of the subject was the Newbolt Report on 'The Teaching of English in England' (Board of Education, 1921). Sampson, a member of the Newbolt committee, writing in the same year (1921), had identified the following 'subjects' still being taught in elementary schools across the land: 'oral composition, written composition, dictation, grammar, reproduction, reading, recitation, literature, spelling, and handwriting' (Shayer, 1972: 67). The Newbolt Report sought to change that and to bring together:

> under the title of English, 'taught as a fine art', four separate concepts: the universal need for literacy as the core of the curriculum, the developmental importance of children's self expression, a belief in the power of English literature for moral and social improvement, and a concern for 'the full development of mind and character'.
>
> (Protherough and Atkinson, 1994: 7)

This was how English became established as a subject in the secondary curriculum, and placed at the centre of the curriculum for all ages. Famously the Newbolt Report suggested, of elementary teachers, that 'every teacher is a teacher of English because every teacher is a teacher in English' (Shayer, 1972: 70). The committee recommended that children's creative language skills should be developed. They recommended the study of literature in the elementary schools. In addition they recommended the development of children's oral work, albeit in the form of 'speech training', which they saw as the basis for written work. Finally they challenged the nineteenth-century legacy of educational class division, placing English at the centre of an educational aim to develop the 'mind and character' of all children.

Change on the ground was slow to occur but it was happening. The old practice of reading aloud in chorus was disappearing, silent reading was being encouraged and, in the 1920s, textbooks were published that encouraged children's free expression and that questioned the necessity for formal grammar teaching. However, although within the pages of the Newbolt Report there was evidence of the uselessness of grammar teaching, the committee had the strong feeling that self-expression could go too far, and that the best way for children to learn to write was to study grammar and to copy good models.

The Hadow Reports

The years 1926, 1931 and 1933 saw the publication of the three Hadow Reports on secondary, primary and infant education respectively, the second (Board of Education, 1931) focused on the 7–11 age range. It had a number of specific recommendations about the curriculum in general and English in particular. Famously, it stated: 'We are of the opinion that the curriculum of the primary school is to be thought of in terms of activity and experience rather than of knowledge to be acquired and facts to be stored' (Board of Education, 1931: 139).

In English, oral work was seen as important, with an emphasis on speaking 'correctly', and including 'oral composition', getting the child to talk on a topic of their choice or one of the teacher's. 'Reproduction' involved getting the child to recount the subject matter of the lesson they had just been taught. Class libraries were encouraged, and silent reading was recommended, though not in school time except in the most deprived areas. And the aim? 'In the upper stage of primary education the child should gain a sense of the printed page and begin to read for pleasure and information' (ibid.: 158).

As for writing, children's written composition should build on oral composition and children should be given topics that interested them. Spelling should be related to the children's writing and reading: 'Any attempt to teach spelling otherwise than in connection with the actual practice of writing or reading is beset with obvious dangers' (ibid.: 160). The abstract study of formal grammar was rejected, though some grammar was to be taught. Bilingualism was addressed in the Welsh context, and teaching in the mother tongue was recommended. Welsh-speaking children were expected to learn English and, strikingly, English-speaking children were expected to learn Welsh.

The third Hadow Report (Board of Education, 1933) drew on ideas current at the time to suggest that formal instruction of the three Rs traditionally started too early in British schools, and recommended that for infant and nursery children: 'The child should begin to learn the 3 Rs when he [sic] wants to do so, whether he be three or six years old' (ibid.: 133).

The report noted three methods of teaching reading that were used at the time: 'look and say', 'phonics' and more contextualised meaning-centred 'sentence' methods. It recommended that teachers should use a mix of the three as appropriate to the child's needs. Writing should start at the same time as reading, and children's natural desire to write in imitation of the adult writing they saw around them at home or at school should be encouraged. The child should have control over the subject matter and his or her efforts should be valued by the teacher as real attempts to communicate meaning.

The report emphasised the importance of imaginative play, and noted, 'Words mean nothing to the young child unless they are definitively associated with active experience' (ibid.: 181) and, 'Oral lessons should be short and closely related to the child's practical interests' (ibid.: 182). While 'speech training' was important, drama work was recommended for the development of children's language, and nursery rhymes and game songs were encouraged alongside traditional hymns. Stories should be told and read to the children.

The Hadow Reports read as remarkably progressive documents for their time, and the principles of child-centred education that are explicit in many of their recommendations continued to inform thinking in primary language teaching for the next 50 years.

Progressive education (☞), 1931–75

The central years of the twentieth century can perhaps be characterised as the years of progressive aspiration so far as primary language was concerned. The progressive views of the Hadow Reports began to be reflected in the Board of Education's regular guidelines, and teachers were on the whole free to follow them as they pleased. The 1944 Education Act itself offered no curriculum advice, except with regard to religious education, and central guidance on the curriculum ended in 1945. The primary curriculum in particular came to be regarded as something of a 'secret garden' to quote Lord Eccles, Tory minister of education in 1960 (Gordon *et al.*, 1991: 287).

The 1944 Education Act finally established primary schools in place of elementary schools, though it would be another 20 years before the last school that included all ages of children closed. At secondary level a three-layered system of grammar, technical, and secondary modern schools was established, and a new exam, the 11+, was devised to decide which children should go where. Like the scholarship exam before it, the 11+ continued to restrain the primary language curriculum, particularly with the older children, in spite of the fact that more progressive child-centred measures were gaining ground with younger children. With the reorganisation of secondary schools along comprehensive lines in the 1960s (encapsulated in circular 10/65), the 11+ was abolished and the primary curriculum was technically freed from all constraint.

In retrospect, the Plowden Report on primary education (DES, 1967) can be seen as centrally representative of the progressive aspiration of 'child-centred education'. Its purpose was to report on effective primary education of the time, and it was concerned to see to what extent the Hadow recommendations had been put into effect. It functioned as much to disseminate effective practice as it did to recommend future change. The child was central: 'At the heart of the educational process lies the child' (ibid.: para. 9); and language was crucial: 'Spoken language plays a central role in learning' (ibid.: para. 54) and 'The development of language is, therefore, central to the educational process' (ibid.: para. 55).

Like its predecessors, the report emphasised the importance of talk; like its predecessors, it emphasised the fact that effective teachers of reading used a mix of approaches. Drama work and story telling were to be encouraged, the increased importance of fiction and poetry written for children and the development of school libraries were all emphasised. The report applauded wholeheartedly the development of personal 'creative' writing (➡ Chapter 11) by the children, characterising it as a dramatic revolution (1967: para. 60.1). On spelling and punctuation the committee was more reticent, noting only that when inaccuracy impeded communication then steps should be taken to remedy the deficiencies (1967: para. 60.2). Knowledge about language was seen as an interesting new area but 'Formal study of grammar will have little place in the primary school' (1967: para. 61.2).

The Plowden Report was followed by the Bullock Report on English (DES, 1975). So far as primary age children were concerned, this spelt out in more detail much of what was already implicit in Plowden. Central to both the reports was an emphasis on the 'process' of language learning. From such a perspective children's oral and written language would best develop in meaningful language use. A couple of quotes from the Bullock Report will illustrate the point. Of the development of oral language it suggested: 'Language should be learned in the course of using it in, and about, the daily experiences of the classroom and the home' (ibid.: 520). Where writing was concerned: 'Competence in language comes above all through its purposeful use, not through working of exercises divorced from context' (ibid.: 528).

So far as bilingual children and children from the ethnic minorities were concerned, the Plowden Report had already recognised the contribution that such children could make to the classroom, and the Bullock committee was concerned that such children should not find school an alien place:

> No child should be expected to cast off the language and culture of the home as he [sic] crosses the school threshold, nor to live and act as though home and school represent two totally separate and different cultures which have to be kept firmly apart. The curriculum should reflect many elements of that part of his life which a child lives outside school.
>
> (ibid.: para. 20.5)

Increasing political control, 1976 onwards

The ideas of progressive education remained important – despite increasingly frequent attacks – until the 1970s when things started to change. Britain was declining in world economic importance and the oil crisis of the early 1970s was followed by an International Monetary Fund (IMF) loan which saw the Labour government of the time having to cut back on public spending. Effective child-centred education is teacher-intensive and requires small classes, and the previous decades had seen reductions in class size. That was no longer compatible with the financial constraints of the time and class sizes began to increase again. A more regulated curriculum is easier to cope with in such circumstances.

The National Curriculum itself was established by the 1988 Education Reform Act, which in the process gave the Secretary of State considerable powers of direct intervention in curriculum matters. Following the Act, curriculum documents were drawn up for all the major subject areas. In line with the recommendations of the TGAT Report (DES, 1987: S227), attainment in each subject was to be measured against a ten-level scale and tested at ages 7, 11, 14 and 16. As the curriculum was introduced into schools it became clear that each subject group had produced documents of considerable complexity. Discontent in the profession grew and a slimmed-down version was introduced in 1995.

The original English document was prepared by a committee under the chairmanship of Brian Cox (DES, 1989, 1990; Cox, 1991). English was to be divided up into five 'attainment targets': Speaking and Listening, Reading, Writing, Spelling, and Handwriting. These were reorganised into three in Sir Ron Dearing's 1995 rewrite, as Spelling and Handwriting were incorporated into Writing (DFE, 1995). In 1998, the National Literacy Strategy (NLS) (☞) Framework for Teaching (DfEE, 1998) was introduced and primary teachers found themselves confronted with their third major change in eight years.

During the mid to late 1980s a number of large-scale projects were undertaken which aimed to improve the teaching and learning of English. The Schools Council, a body responsible for national curriculum development, had been replaced by the School Curriculum Development Committee (SCDC); the SCDC initiated the National Writing Project. This was in two phases: the development phase took place from 1985 to 1988 and the implementation phase from 1988 to 1989, although the Education Reform Act 1988 and the resulting National Curriculum and testing arrangements changed the focus of implementation.

One of the key problems of the time was that many children were being turned off by writing, something confirmed by some evidence from the Assessment of Performance Unit (APU). The APU found that as many as four in ten children did not find writing an enjoyable experience and 'not less than one in ten pupils [had] an active dislike of writing and endeavour[ed] to write as little as possible' (APU, 1988: 170). Somewhat later the National Writing Project gathered evidence that many children, particularly young children, tended to equate writing with transcription skills rather than composition.

The National Writing Project involved thousands of educators across the country. One of the main messages from the project was that writers needed to become involved in writing for a defined and recognisable audience, not just because the teacher said so. Connected to these ideas was the notion that writing should have a meaningful purpose. With these key concepts in place teachers began to realise that writing tasks which were sequentially organised in school exercise books and consisting of one draft – or at best 'rough copy/neat copy' drafts – were not helping to address the audiences and purposes that needed to be generated.

The National Oracy Project was also initiated by SCDC and partly overlapped with the National Writing Project. During the period from 1987 to 1991, 35 local education authorities were involved in the oracy project. The recognition that oracy, or speaking and listening as it came to be called, needed a national initiative was in itself significant. Since the late 1960s a number of enlightened educators had realised that talking and learning were very closely linked and that the curriculum should reflect that reality. But these people were in a minority and most educators continued to emphasise reading and, to a lesser extent, writing. The major achievement of the oracy project was to secure recognition that talk was important and that children could learn more if teachers understood the issues, and planned activities to support the development of oracy. As Wells pointed out: 'The centrality of talk in education is finally being recognised. Not simply in theory – in the exhortations of progressive-minded academics – but mandated at all levels and across all subjects in a national curriculum' (Wells, 1992: 283).

The other large national project that we will touch on is the Language in the National Curriculum (LINC) project (➡ Chapter 16). In 1987, a committee of inquiry was commissioned to make recommendations about the sort of knowledge about language that it would be appropriate to teach in school. The Kingman Report, as it was known (DES, 1988), disappointed the right-wing politicians and sections of the press when it failed to advocate a return to traditional grammar teaching. The Cox Report (DES, 1989) ran into similar problems for the same reason, but both the 1990 and the 1995 orders for English in the National Curriculum (DES, 1990; DFE, 1995) contented themselves with general recommendations to use grammatical terms where and as the need arose. Between 1989 and 1992 most schools in England were involved with the LINC project. Its main aim was to acquaint teachers with the model of language presented in the Kingman Report. Kingman's work reaffirmed the idea that children and teachers should have sufficient 'knowledge about language' or 'KAL' if they were to become successful language users.

One of the strong features of the materials that were produced by the LINC project was that they were built on an explicit set of principles and theories:

Principles:

1   Teaching children should start positively from what they can already do.
2   The experience of using language should precede analysis.
3   Language should be explored in real purposeful situations not analysed out of context.
4   An understanding of people's attitudes to language can help you understand more about values and beliefs.

Theories:

1   Humans use language for social reasons.
2   Language is constantly changing.
3   Language is a cultural phenomenon.
4   There are important connections between language and power.

5   Language is systematically organised.
6   The meanings of language depend on negotiation.

It may have been that some of these philosophies resulted in the politicians of the time refusing to publish the materials. In spite of this the materials were photocopied and distributed widely and various publications independent of government were produced, e.g. Carter (1990).

The National Literacy Project (☞) was developed between 1996 and 1998. The project's main aim was to raise the standards of literacy in the participating schools so that they raised their achievements in line with national expectations. The project established for the first time a detailed scheme of work with term-by-term objectives that were organised into text-level, sentence-level and word-level. These were delivered through the use of a daily literacy hour with strict timings for the different sections. The project was supported by a national network of centres where literacy consultants were available to support project schools.

The National Literacy Project was important because it was claimed that its success was the reason that the National Literacy Strategy adopted the ideas of a Framework for Teaching and a prescribed literacy hour. However, it should be remembered that the schools who were involved in the project were schools who had identified weaknesses in their literacy teaching and this has to be taken into account when any kind of evaluation is made about the success of the project. The other important point to bear in mind is that it was originally conceived of as a five-year project; after that time, evaluations were to be carried out. One of the features of these evaluations was that they were supposed to measure the success of the three years of the programme when schools were no longer *directly* involved in the project. In the event, the approaches of the National Literacy Project were adopted as part of the National Literacy Strategy in 1998. This occurred *before* any independent evaluation had been carried out and long before the planned five-year extent of the National Literacy Project.

The only *independent* evaluation of the project carried out by the National Foundation for Educational Research (INFER) found that:

> The analyses of the test outcomes have indicated that, in terms of the standardised scores on reading tests, the pupils involved in Cohort 1 of the National Literacy Project have made substantial gains. All three year groups showed significant and substantial increases in scores from the beginning to end of the project.
>
> (Sainsbury *et al.*, 1998: 21)

This outcome illustrates definite progress in the fairly restricted parameters of standardised reading tests. It is not possible to conclude that the specific approach of the National Literacy Project was more beneficial than other approaches as this variable was not controlled. It is possible that the financial investment, extra support and a new initiative were the dominant factors in improved test scores rather than the particular characteristics of the recommended teaching methods. One area of concern about the findings from the evaluation was that pupils eligible for free school meals, pupils with special educational needs, pupils with English as an additional language (EAL) at the 'becoming familiar with English stage', and boys, made less progress than other groups.

It seems particularly regrettable, though not surprising, that no serious attempt were made to evaluate what pupils thought of the project. Sainsbury *et al.* admitted that:

> The reading enjoyment findings are less easy to interpret. The survey showed that children do, on the whole, enjoy their reading, with substantial majorities of both age groups expressing favourable attitudes both before and after involvement in the project. These measures, however, did not change very much, indicating that the systematic introduction of different text types that was a feature of the project did not have any clearly apparent effect on children's enjoyment of reading these varied text types. In the absence of a control group, however, it is difficult to draw any more definite conclusions.
>
> (ibid.: 27)

The National Literacy Strategy, 1997–2006

The Literacy Task Force was established on 31 May 1996 by David Blunkett, then Shadow Secretary of State for Education and Employment. It was charged with developing, in time for an incoming Labour government, a strategy to substantially raise standards of literacy in primary schools over a five- to ten-year period (Literacy Task Force, 1997: 4).

The Literary Task Force produced a final report that suggested how a National Literacy Strategy could be implemented. The recommendations heralded some of the most profound changes to English teaching. The single most important driving force behind the strategy was the introduction of target-setting: specifically that by 2002, 80 per cent of 11-year-olds should reach the standard expected for their age in English (i.e. Level 4) in the Key Stage 2 National Standard Assessment Tasks (SATs). Despite all the many changes to the curriculum since 1997, target-setting, and the associated publication of league tables, remain in place and now have an even more dominant effect on the curriculum and children's daily lives.

Earlier in this chapter we mentioned the important contribution of Brian Cox in relation to developing the guidance for the subject of English in the National Curriculum, a document that achieved a remarkable consensus in such a contentious area. His views on the National Literacy Strategy in his book *Literacy Is Not Enough* have much to offer our thoughts today. He did not mince his words: the policy on reading 'is too prescriptive, authoritarian and mechanistic', there should be 'more emphasis on motivation, on helping children to enjoy reading' (Cox, 1998: ix). Other contributors to the book were equally critical: Margaret Meek (1998: 116) criticised the 'repeated exercises in comprehension, grammar and spelling' and Bethan Marshall (1998: 109) suggested that 'the bleak spectre of utilitarianism ☞ hangs over our schools like a pall'. The words of an inspector in 1905 quoted by Marshall should cause all concerned to think very carefully about the potential impact of the latest Primary National Strategy literacy framework:

> A blackboard has been produced, and hieroglyphics are drawn upon it by the teacher. At a given signal every child in the class begins calling out mysterious sounds: 'Letter A, letter A' in a sing-song voice, or 'Letter A says Ah, letter A says Ah', as the case may be. To the uninitiated I may explain that No. 1 is the beginning of the spelling, and No. 2 is the beginning of word building. Hoary-headed men will spend hours discussing whether 'c-a-t' or 'ker-ar-te' are the best means of conveying the knowledge of how to read 'cat'. I must own an indifference to the point myself, and sympathise with teachers not allowed to settle it for themselves . . . 'Wake up, Johnny; it's not time to go to sleep yet. Be a good boy and watch teacher.'
>
> (Marshall, 1998: 115)

Most political education initiatives are introduced following claims that standards are falling, and the National Literacy Strategy was no exception. However, in spite of regular claims by the media, teachers, business people, politicians, etc., there was no evidence that standards of literacy had declined in England as Beard (1999) pointed out; something that Campbell (1997) also commented upon:

> On the current moral panic over the impact of the reforms on standards of attainment in literacy and numeracy, there are two things to say. First, no-one can be sure about standards in literacy and numeracy because of the failure – unquestioned failure – of the national agencies (NCC, SEAC and now SCAA) to establish an effective, credible and reliable mechanism for the national monitoring of standards over time since 1989.
>
> (Campbell, 1997: 22)

For nine years the National Literacy Strategy was imposed on primary schools in England. As we showed above, Brian Cox's edited book was very critical of the idea. In the first edition of our book (Wyse and Jones, 2001) we put forward a range of concerns. Wyse (2003) criticised the NLS Framework for its lack of evidence base. Have these concerns been shown to be valid following further research and evaluation?

The first annual report by the Ontario Institute for Studies in Education at the University of Toronto highlighted some key issues. Despite repeated claims by policy-makers that the NLS represents best practice, the report was much more circumspect in its conclusions:

> Clearly it would be naïve to conclude that the instructional and other practices included in NLNS were the sole causes of the gains being made. For example, as we have discussed in several other sections of this report:
>
> • There is, at best, uneven evidence that such practices can be counted on to 'produce' numeracy and literacy gains.
>
> (Earl et al., 2000: 36)

The second report affirmed this position with the claim that 'the strategies themselves are a unique blend of practices whose effects, to our knowledge, have never been carefully tested in real field settings' (Earl *et al.*, 2001: 81). It is unfortunate that the final annual review did not seek to explore these points further rather than restrict the focus to the observation that academic commentators have debated the research evidence and that 'we recognise . . . that both strategies have been contentious' (Earl *et al.*, 2003: 34).

Tymms' (2004) analysis of standards of literacy compared statutory test results with a range of other sources: he found that the gains shown in the statutory test results were not an accurate measure. More objective evidence found that standards rose modestly up to 2000 but then plateaued. Tymms suggests that even the modest gains in standards could have been a result of teachers getting better at preparing for the statutory tests. It is also reasonable to consider that embedding the Framework for Teaching might have taken at least two years, and once it was in place, standards stopped rising.

A series of research studies found in particular that the recommended pedagogy of the literacy hour were resulting in rather limited teacher–pupil interaction which was tending towards short initiation-response sequences and a consequent lack of extended discussion. Mroz *et al.* (2000) noted the limited opportunities for pupils to question or explore ideas. English *et al.* (2002) found that there was a reduction in extended teacher–pupil interactions. Skidmore *et al.* (2003) found that teachers were dominating the interaction.

In summary, it appears that the Framework for Teaching was not particularly effective. The government's intervention in the primary curriculum did not result in sufficient improvements in learning. The relentless focus on literacy and numeracy resulted in a narrowing of the curriculum (Boyle and Bragg, 2006). The control of teaching methods by politicians enforced by the ruthless approach of OfSTED had no justification. In the light of this, you would hope that lessons could have been learned and a more appropriate approach taken to future curriculum development.

The Primary National Strategy (PNS) Framework for Literacy, 2006 onwards

In October 2006, the new *PNS Framework for Literacy* was released. The first change from the NLS was that although paper copies of a reduced version of the framework were available, the full framework and guidance appeared on the PNS Frameworks website (http://www.standards.dfes.gov.uk/primaryframe-works/). Whereas with the NLS the names of those who developed the literacy framework were in the public domain, with the PNS Framework all the material is unattributed. It is important to know the authors of such materials because everyone brings their experience, beliefs and prejudices to this kind of curriculum development. For that reason knowing the author of a document can go some way to understanding why it is written in the way it is.

The writing of the second edition of this book has given us the opportunity to read most of the many documents that make up the PNS Framework online, and you will find we make reference to these and critically evaluate their relevance throughout the book. In general terms, there are some positive changes from the previous NLS Framework. The number of objectives has been drastically reduced. The tendency to encourage one-off lessons has been replaced with longer units of work. The division of objectives into word-level, sentence-level, and text-level has been abolished. The use of the internet to locate the framework is generally helpful although it will need careful and constant review to avoid conflicting messages and to ensure coherence.

There are also a number of aspects that are of concern. Let us begin with the illogical title, *Literacy* Framework. The objectives in the framework now include speaking and listening but of course these cannot be summarised under the title literacy (➡ Chapter 18 for our views on resolving this). As far as the sequence of learning is concerned, the attempt to have different objectives for each year of study has meant that the developmental sequence is unsatisfactory. Some objectives need to be addressed in more than one year, and in many cases, every year. In spite of the overall reduction in objectives, the framework as a whole, which includes many guidance documents and hyperlinks to other government resources, is unwieldy and too prescriptive. But our most serious criticism is the lack of choice for pupils and teachers. The type of books children will study is prescribed, the type of writing that they will carry out is prescribed. The way that this is to be taught has been specified in even more detail than the NLS. It appears that a dominant teaching model, rather than encouragement to use a range of approaches, is still being applied: (1) analyse a text; (2) teacher models the text; (3) children evaluate their work 'against agreed criteria'. There is nothing wrong with these teaching approaches *per se* but the problems are: (1) when they are used to the exclusion of other approaches that can achieve different outcomes; and (2) when they become a repetitive feature throughout children's lives at school.

The level of prescription is most marked in areas of the literacy curriculum that are of traditional, repetitive concern to politicians. The PNS objectives show a welcome reduction in the grammar objectives that were a feature of the NLS. However, as in most sections of the PNS Framework, a summary of NLS objectives is given for each section of planning to show that these are still being covered. There is also a continuing recommendation to use the *Grammar for Writing* resource which explicitly addresses the objectives from the NLS. Wyse's (2001) review of empirical evidence showed that traditional grammar teaching did not enhance children's writing, something that the systematic review by Andrews *et al.* (2004) confirmed, hence it seems questionable that this emphasis on grammar through reference to the old objectives is still encouraged.

The consultation process for the changes to the Literacy Framework as a whole seems to have become even less transparent than it was during the development of the NLS. There does not appear to be a report of the consultation process, its outcomes, number of contributors, distribution of views, etc. The consultation on specific changes to the programmes of study for reading in the Foundation Stage and in the National Curriculum at Key Stage 1 as a result of the Rose Report was similarly obscure but a report was at least published. The online consultation ran for only 12 weeks, from 8 May to 31 July 2006. It was claimed that a leaflet raising awareness of the consultation was sent to Key Stage 1 Schools, Foundation Stage settings, and other key partners and stakeholders. During a keynote speech that one of the authors of this book gave to a national early years conference, the audience was asked if anyone had seen the consultation leaflet. Not one of the delegates, a mixture of early years practitioners, local authority workers and academics, indicated that they had seen it.

However, the report of the consultation shows that there were 568 respondents, 372 of whom answered Question 1 about the National Curriculum, a question that required a yes or no response as to whether the following:

Reading strategies
1 To read with fluency, accuracy, understanding and enjoyment, pupils should be taught *to use a range of strategies to make sense of what they read.* (Department for Education and Employment (DfEE) and The Qualifications and Curriculum Authority (QCA), 1999: 46) [italics added]

should be replaced with this:

Reading Strategies
1. Pupils should be taught to read with fluency, accuracy, understanding and enjoyment. (Qualifications and Curriculum Authority (QCA), 2006a: 2)

Of the 372 respondents, 286 agreed with the change, which resulted in deletion from the National Curriculum of the explicit mention of use of a range of strategies to make sense of what is being read. Yet somewhat contradictorily, in the 'further comments' space on the consultation form, 'The most common comment, cited by a third (32%) of respondents, [was] that a variety of teaching/ learning methods needs to be used alongside phonics, including contextual understanding' (Qualifications and Curriculum Authority (QCA), 2006b: 13). In our opinion, the lack of publicity about the consultation and the very small number of respondents in favour of the change (only 286 out of the population of England) means that the statutory change to England's National Curriculum cannot be regarded as legitimate.

The curriculum for teaching reading in the early years and Key Stage 1 is the area that has been subject to the most political influence. This influence was originally made possible by the powers of control given to the secretary of State for Education as part of the Education Reform Act 1988. In 1997, the NLS Framework brought a new level of control of reading pedagogy. Finally, the Rose review in 2006 resulted in the requirement to use synthetic phonics to teach children younger than 5. This was swiftly followed by unelected politicians directly intervening in the curriculum of teacher education courses in universities to monitor their teaching as well. The details of the Rose Report and its implications are discussed fully in Chapter 3.

Practice points

- As a professional you should evaluate all educational initiatives critically to ensure that they reflect the needs of the children that you teach.
- You need to develop a knowledge of historical developments as a vital tool for understanding educational change.
- The PNS Framework will be subject to change. It is important that you take an active part in that process by: (1) fully understanding and evaluating the Framework; (2) communicating your opinions about its effectiveness.

Glossary

Dialects – regional variations of language shown by different words and grammar.
Etymology – the origins of words.
Line justification – ensuring that the beginnings and ends of lines of print are all lined up.
Loanwords – words adopted from other languages.
National Literacy Project – a three-year professional development project that was carried out with authorities and schools who wanted to raise their standards of literacy.
National Literacy Strategy – a national strategy for raising standards in literacy over a five- to ten-year period.

Phonological form – the sounds of the words that result from a particular pronunciation.

Progressive education – teaching approaches that rejected old-fashioned rote learning methods in favour of methods that put the child's interests and needs first.

Standard English – the formal language of written communication in particular. Many people call this 'correct' English.

Utilitarianism – the idea that education and learning can be reduced to crude skills and drills.

References

Andrews, R., Torgerson, C., Beverton, S., Locke, T., Low, G., Robinson, A., et al. (2004). 'The effect of grammar teaching (syntax) in English on 5 to 16 year olds' accuracy and quality in written composition', *Research Evidence in Education Library*. Retrieved February 5, 2007, from http://eppi.ioe.ac.uk/cms/

APU (Assessment of Performance Unit) (1988) *Language Performance in Schools: Review of APU Language Monitoring 1979–1983*. London: HMSO.

Barber, C. (1993) *The English Language: A Historical Introduction*. Cambridge: Cambridge University Press.

Beard, R. (1999) *National Literacy Strategy Review of Research and Other Related Evidence*. London: DfEE.

Board of Education (1921) *The Teaching of English in England (The Newbolt Report)*. London: HMSO.

Board of Education (1931) *The Primary School (The Second Hadow Report)*. London: HMSO.

Board of Education (1933) *Infant and Nursery Schools (The Third Hadow Report)*. London: HMSO.

Boyle, B. and Bragg, J. (2006) 'A curriculum without foundation', *British Educational Research Journal*, 32(4): 569–582.

Bryson, B. (1990) *Mother Tongue: The English Language*. London: Penguin.

Campbell, J. (1997) 'Towards curricular subsidiarity?' Paper presented at the School Curriculum and Assessment Authority conference 'Developing the Primary School Curriculum: the Next Steps', June.

Carter, R. (ed.) (1990) *Knowledge about Language and the Curriculum: The LINC Reader*. London: Hodder & Stoughton.

Cox, B. (1991) *Cox on Cox: An English Curriculum for the 1990s*. London: Hodder & Stoughton.

Cox, B. (1998) 'Foreword', in B. Cox (ed.) *Literacy Is Not Enough: Essays on the Importance of Reading*. Manchester: Manchester University Press and Book Trust.

Crystal, D. (1997) *The Cambridge Encyclopaedia of Language*, 2nd edn. Cambridge: Cambridge University Press.

Crystal, D. (2004) *The Stories of English*. London: Penguin/Allen Lane.

Department of Education and Science (DES) (1967) *Children and Their Primary Schools (The Plowden Report)*. London: HMSO.

Department of Education and Science (DES) (1975) *A Language for Life (The Bullock Report)*. London: HMSO.

Department of Education and Science (DES) (1988) *Report of the Committee of Inquiry into the Teaching of English Language (The Kingman Report)*. London: HMSO

Department of Education and Science and The Welsh Office (DES) (1987) *National Curriculum Task Group on Assessment and Testing (The TGAT Report)*. London: DES.

Department of Education and Science and The Welsh Office (DES) (1989) *English for Ages 5–16 (The Cox Report)*. York: National Curriculum Council.

Department of Education and Science and The Welsh Office (DES) (1990) *English in the National Curriculum*. London: HMSO.

Department for Education (DFE) (1995) *English in the National Curriculum*. London: HMSO.

Department for Education and Employment (DfEE) (1998) *The National Literacy Strategy Framework for Teaching*, London: DfEE.

Department for Education and Employment (DfEE) and The Qualifications and Curriculum Authority (QCA) (1999) *The National Curriculum: Handbook for Primary Teachers in England. Key Stages 1 and 2*. Norwich: Her Majesty's Stationery Office (HMSO).

Earl, L., Fullan, M., Leithwood, K., Watson, N. *et al.* (2000) *Watching and Learning: OISE/UT Evaluation of the Implementation of the National Literacy and Numerary Strategies*. Nottingham: DfES Publications.

Earl, L., Watson, N., Levin, B., Leithwood, K., Kullan, M., Torrance, N. *et al.* (2003) *Watching and Learning: OISE/UT Evaluation of the Implementation of the National Literacy and Numerary Strategies*. Nottingham: DfES Publications.

English, E., Hargreaves, L. and Hislam, J. (2002) 'Pedagogical dilemmas in the national literacy strategy: primary teachers' perceptions, reflections and classroom behaviour', *Cambridge Journal of Education*, 32(1): 9–26.

Gordon, P., Aldrich, R. and Dean, D. (1991) *Education and Policy in England in the Twentieth Century*. London: Woburn.

Greenbaum, S. (1986) 'Spelling variants in British English', *Journal of English Linguistics*, 19: 258–268.

Holmes, E. A. G. (1922) 'The confessions and hopes of an ex-Inspector of Schools', *Hibbert Journal*, vol. 20 (no further information in secondary source). Quoted in Gordon, P., Aldrich, R. and Dean, D. (1991) *Education and Policy in England in the Twentieth Century*. London: Woburn.

Lawson, J. and Silver, H. (1973) *A Social History of Education in England*. London: Methuen.

LINC (Language in the National Curriculum) (1991) *Materials for Professional Development*. No publication details.

Literacy Task Force (1997) *The Implementation of the National Literacy Strategy*. London: DfEE.

Marshall, B. (1998) 'English teachers and the third way', in B. Cox (ed.) *Literacy Is Not Enough: Essays on the Importance of Reading*. Manchester: Manchester University Press and Book Trust.

Meek, M. (1998) 'Important reading lessons', in B. Cox (ed.) *Literacy Is Not Enough: Essays on the Importance of Reading*. Manchester: Manchester University Press and Book Trust.

Mroz, M., Smith, F. and Hardman, F. (2000) 'The discourse of the literacy hour', *Cambridge Journal of Education*, 30(3): 380–390.

Office for Standards in Education (OfSTED) (1998) *The National Literacy Project: An HMI Evaluation*. London: OfSTED.

Office for Standards in Education (OfSTED) (1999) *The National Literacy Strategy: An Interim Evaluation*, London: OfSTED.

Protherough, R. and Atkinson, J. (1994) 'Shaping the image of an English teacher', in S. Brindley (ed.) *Teaching English*. London: Routledge.

Pyles, T. and Algeo, J. (1993) *The Origins and Development of the English Language*, 4th edn. London: Harcourt Brace Jovanovich.

Qualifications and Curriculum Authority (QCA) (2006a) Consultation: Implications of the Rose Review of early reading. Retrieved 1 June 2006, from http://www.qca.org.uk/232_16473.html

Qualifications and Curriculum Authority (QCA) (2006b) *Consultation on Proposed Changes to the Key Stage 1 English Programme for Reading and a Foundation Stage Early Learning Goal*. London: QCA.

Sainsbury, M., Schagen, I., Whetton, C. with Hagues, N. and Minnis, M. (1998) *Evaluation of the National Literacy Project Cohort 1, 1996–1998*. Slough: NFER.

Shayer, D. (1972) *The Teaching of English in Schools 1900–1970*. London: Routledge and Kegan Paul.

Skidmore, D., Perez-Parent, M. and Arnfield, D. (2003) 'Teacher-pupil dialogue in the guided reading session', *Reading Literacy and Language*, 37(2): 47–53.

Tymms, P. (2004) 'Are standards rising in English primary schools?' *British Educational Research Journal*, 30(4): 477–494.

Wells, G. (1992) 'The centrality of talk in education', in K. Norman (ed.) *Thinking Voices: The Work of the National Oracy Project*. London: Hodder & Stoughton.

Williamson, B. (1981) 'Contradictions of control: elementary education in a mining district 1870–1900', in L. Barton and S. Walker (eds) *Schools, Teachers and Teaching*. Lewes: Falmer Press.

Wyse, D. (2001) 'Grammar: for writing?: A critical review of empirical evidence', *British Journal of Educational Studies*, 49(4): 411–427.

Wyse, D. (2003) 'The National Literacy Strategy: A critical review of empirical evidence', *British Educational Research Journal*, 29(6): 903–916.

Annotated bibliography

Cox, B. (ed.) (1998) *Literacy Is Not Enough: Essays on the Importance of Reading*.
Manchester: Manchester University Press and Book Trust. This was a powerful rejection of the concept of the Literacy Strategy. Many of its criticisms can be levelled at the PNS Framework.
L2 **

Crystal, D. (2004) *The Stories of English*. London: Penguin/Allen Lane.
A tremendous achievement. One of the central concerns of this book is the narrow way that English is often perceived, particularly notions of Standard English. Relevance to the National Curriculum here.
L2 **

Department for Education and Skills (DfES) (2007) *Primary National Strategy: Primary Framework for Literacy and Mathematics*, retrieved 22 January, 2007, from http://www.standards.dfes.gov.uk/primaryframeworks/
The official Literacy Framework and all guidance materials.
L1 *

Hall, K. and Harding, A. (2003) 'A systematic review of effective literacy teaching in the 4 to 14 age range of mainstream schooling', *Research Evidence in Education Library*. Retrieved 5 February, 2007, from http://eppi.ioe.ac.uk/cms/
Concluded that effective teachers of literacy balance direct skills teaching with more holistic approaches and 'avoid the partisan adherence to any *one* sure-fire approach or method' (p. 3).
L3 ***

Myhill, D. and Fisher, R. (2005) *Informing Practice in English: A Review of Recent Research in Literacy and the Teaching of English*. London: Office for Standards in Education (OfSTED).
Useful overview of some recent thinking.
L3 **

National Literacy Trust (2007) Homepage. Retrieved February 5, 2007, from http://www.literacytrust.org.uk/
A very useful site to find out about new initiatives and stories in the press about literacy and the teaching of English.
L1 *

Shayer, D. (1972) *The Teaching of English in Schools 1900–1970*. London: Routledge and Kegan Paul.
A knowledge of history is vital to make sense of the present. This book makes very interesting reading particularly by showing how the debates about English have progressed and in some cases recurred again and again.
L3 **

Chapter 2

Theories of learning

The use of theories ☞ to guide practical action is a natural part of the human condition. One example of a theory is the idea that an objective-dominated education system is a good one. We address this idea in the chapter. We also critique what has become the fashionable idea of scaffolding. We conclude the chapter by outlining four linguistic theories that guide our thinking.

Some people might question the need for a chapter on theories at all. They could argue that becoming a teacher simply requires the learning of teaching techniques and that theory and research are not important, and all that needs to be learned can be learned through school practice. Of course it is not accurate to suggest that professional practice is only that, practice. Teachers' theories reveal themselves all the time, sometimes in turns of phrase: 'They've got no language, these kids' (deficit models); 'She's a bright girl' (nature more than nurture); 'Boys are always naughty' (gender and stereotypes); etc. A particularly well-known phrase is to call children 'able' or not. If you think about this a bit deeper, the idea suggests an innate level of intelligence that is not going to change. This is another deficit theory which can lead to low expectations of children. For this reason we prefer a phrase such as 'a high attaining child' or, if that is too much of a mouthful, to avoid the description able altogether and talk about the child's specific achievements.

Theories directly guide the practical decisions that you make all the time. They are particularly significant in guiding your decision-making in unfamiliar situations, which you will encounter throughout your career, because without direct practical experience of a situation then you have to rely on judgements which come from your theories. As you go through your teacher training course you should engage with these issues frequently. In particular you will take the ideas learned from your courses into schools to explore them in practice. Your lecturers will also be engaging with them by discussing teaching and learning with the practising teachers whom they work with.

Matters of theory and kinds of practice are part of all learning, not just education, and are rooted in a powerful historical tradition. Dunne's (1993) book showed the way that Aristotle established the concepts of *technē* and *phronésis* (or technical and practical reason). *Technē* is the kind of thinking required by the builder or the doctor when they make something or restore someone to good health. This is the thinking required for making things. *Phronesis* is a different kind of practical knowledge that emerges from conduct in a public space and is more personal and experiential. Practice, in a range of occupations, was seen by Aristotle 'as something nontechnical but not, however, nonrational' (ibid.: 10). Dunne argues for the modern relevance of the ideas of *technē* and *phronesis* by engaging in a written 'dialogue' with five modern philosophers.

In relating the book's complex philosophical exploration to practice, Dunne concludes overall that:

> In being initiated into the practice of teaching, student-teachers need not only experience in the classroom but also the right conditions for reflecting on this experience – so that reflectiveness (which we have all the time been clarifying under the name of 'phronesis') can become more and more an abiding attitude or disposition.

(ibid.: 369)

The early inspiration for the ideas in Dunne's book was a strong dissatisfaction with the technicist and rationalist theories of the behavourist objectives model reintroduced in the 1970s. Dunne perhaps couldn't have predicted that teaching dominated by objectives (and the associated testing and target-setting) would be one of the most powerful and enduring features of the English education system some 30 years later. Despite many modifications to elements of the curriculum, such as some details of the pedagogy of the PNS Framework, the idea that teaching should be dominated by objectives (as opposed to a wider range of teaching and learning intentions) has remained unchanged and largely unchallenged. For that reason it is important that we examine the rationale for this structural feature.

Kelly (2004) traces the idea of an objective-led model of the curriculum to the beginning of the twentieth century. The advances in science and technology at that time led to the idea that teaching and learning should be defined more scientifically. However, it wasn't until nearly two hundred years later that this idea began to be enforced. In the 1970s, pressure grew for the curriculum to be more clearly defined and more teachers were encouraged to use the objectives model. In 1997, the frameworks for literacy and numeracy were implemented. For the first time these listed the curriculum as a series of teaching objectives which pupils 'should be taught'. This prescriptive approach to the curriculum, coupled with the statutory assessment and target-setting system, has resulted in the strongest grip on the school curriculum by government in the history of the English education system.

Kelly (2004) identifies a number of theoretical problems with the objective model. First, it is a direct threat to the individual freedoms of pupils and teachers to make decisions about their curricula. He also argues that the model is particularly damaging to subjects such as those in the arts where good teaching encourages personal interpretation which should not be determined in advance by teaching objectives. As far as the teaching of English is concerned, Kelly says:

> In literature too the whole purpose of introducing pupils to great literary works is lost if it is done from the perspective of intended learning outcomes (Stenhouse, 1970). Again that purpose is to invite the pupil to respond in his or her own way to what he or she is introduced to. To approach a reading of *Hamlet*, for example, in any other way is either to reduce it to an instrumental role, designed to promote an understanding of words, poetic forms, even philosophy ☞, or to attempt to impose one's own moral and aesthetic values, one's own subjective interpretation of the play and response to it on one's pupils. If appreciation of literature or any of the arts means anything at all and has any place in education, it cannot be approached by way of prespecified objectives.
>
> (ibid.: 61)

Another way to address the issue of objective-led learning is ask whether there is research evidence to back up the claim that it is the most effective kind of teaching. Wyse (2003) examined this. The recent manifestation of the objective model was supported by claims that school effectiveness research provided evidence that objective-led lessons were the most effective. One of the significant publications was some work for OfSTED that Sammons *et al.* (1995) carried out. In a list of factors of effective schools Sammons *et al.* (1995: 16) cite three studies which they say show that 'effective learning occurs where teachers clearly explain the objectives of the lesson at the outset, and refer to these throughout the lesson to maintain focus'. Wyse (2003) examined each of these three studies and other publications that were cited to support the point about objective-led teaching. The evidence simply failed to back up the claim.

One of the better publications points out that the links between appropriate instructional behaviour and the teacher's objectives have rarely been studied directly; an 'assumption' is made about objectives based on opportunity to learn data. Brophy and Good (1986) also observe that objectives vary in their nature and that this necessitates a range of teaching approaches such as: problem-solving; decision-making; essay composition; preparation of research reports; or construction of some product. In other words some effective lessons may well be tightly focused around a short-term and clearly formulated lesson objective. Other lessons will be more effective if there is an overall goal, such as the publication of a class book, presentation or drama performance which guides the teaching and learning. The teacher knows that this process will lead to a range of valuable learning outcomes which do not need to be pre-specified because they will depend on the pupils' response to the task and to the teachers' interaction with them.

It is interesting to think about teaching and learning in the context of learning skills outside school. Learning to play a musical instrument, for example, involves the teaching of a skill. The teacher sets homework in the form of pieces of music to be practised and then responds to the students' playing during the lesson. The setting of pre-specified objectives would be completely counter-productive because it would not allow the teacher to respond to the specific needs of the students demonstrated by their playing of the music. Given that learning to play a musical instrument involves the learning of a complex set of skills, it is easy to see the parallels with learning to read and write. If pre-determined short-term objectives are normally inappropriate for the learning of a musical instrument, then perhaps they are not always appropriate when learning to read and write. The contexts of whole class teaching, small group teaching or individual teaching may well also change what is the most appropriate way to structure learning.

Given that there is a weak theoretical and empirical justification to the objective model which is so forcefully employed currently, it is difficult not to see this as a means of control over pupils, teachers and educationists exercised by politicians and policy-makers. In reviewing the changes to education over the period of the five editions of his influential book on the curriculum, Kelly (2004) shows that this level of political control has undoubtedly increased, has stifled democratic debate about the curriculum and is even beginning to look somewhat sinister.

We began this chapter on theory with a discussion of the place of theory at all. This led us to think about the influence of societal progress, through science and technology, and its impact on objective-led teaching. The question is, how do we proceed next? There are many competing areas of knowledge that have important theories of relevance to the teaching of English, language and literacy. For example, psychology remains a potent force in discussions about teaching and learning. Socio-cultural ideas are also central to many discussions about our subject; education as an academic subject has a distinct perspective on teaching and learning; and philosophy can reasonably claim to embrace all subjects.

One thing that philosophy shows us is the profound significance of the link between thinking and words. Words are of course the central concern of the subject English which is why it is the most important subject in the curriculum! The link was something that was famously explored in the book *Thought and Language* by Lev Vygotsky (1986). Vygotsky's work is located in psychology, but one of the interesting aspects of his contribution was the fact that he viewed psychology as a tool or method rather than as a subject of investigation. Vygotsky's subjects of investigation were culture and consciousness, as the editor's introduction explains:

Vygotsky argued that psychology cannot limit itself to direct evidence, be it observable behaviour or accounts of introspection. Psychological inquiry is *investigation*, and like the criminal investigator, the psychologist must take into account indirect evidence and circumstantial clues – which in practice means that works of art, philosophical arguments, and anthropological data are no less important for psychology than direct evidence.

(1986: xvi)

One of the reasons that Vygotsky's work has been so influential for education-ists is the fact that he applied his theories directly to schooling. In the course of the book Vygotsky develops some of the ideas of Jean Piaget who is perhaps one of the best-known theorists on child development. In the revised edition of Vygotsky's book the notes at the end include some of Piaget's responses to Vygotsky's reflections about Piaget's work. Part of their debate addresses the role of direct instruction and the learning of concepts. Piaget says:

All this raises at least two problems, which Vygotsky formulates, but in the solution of which we differ somewhat. The first concerns the 'interaction of spontaneous and nonspontaneous concepts.' This interaction is more complex than Vygotsky believes. In some cases, what is transmitted by instruction is well assimilated by the child because it represents in fact an extension of some spontaneous constructions of his own. In such cases, his development is accelerated. But in other cases, the gifts of instruction are presented too soon or too late, or in a manner that precludes assimilation because it does not fit in with the child's spontaneous constructions. Then the child's development is impeded, or even deflected into barrenness, as often happens in the teaching of the exact sciences. Therefore I do not believe, as Vygotsky seems to do, that new concepts, even at school level, are always acquired through adult didactic intervention. This may occur, but there is a much more productive form of instruction: the so-called 'active' schools endeavor to create situations that, while not 'spontaneous' in themselves, evoke spontaneous elaboration on the part of the child, if one manages both to spark his interest and to present the problem in such a way that it corresponds to the structures he had already formed himself.

(1986: 271)

Piaget and Vygotsky agreed that spontaneous learning is important. This is a side of their theories that needs to be re-evaluated in relation to modern educational practice. In particular by calling into question the over-emphasis on direct instruction and by reconsidering the role of spontaneous learning in the school curriculum.

One of Vygotsky's best-known ideas was the 'zone of proximal development'. He recognised that most psychological experiments assessed the level of mental development of children by asking them to solve problems in standardised tests.

He showed that a problem with this was that this testing only measured a summative aspect of development. In the course of his experiments Vygotsky discovered that a child who had a mental age of 8 as measured on a standardised test was able to solve a test for a 12-year-old child if they were given 'the first step in a solution, a leading question, or some other form of help' (Vygotsky, 1987: 187). He suggested that the difference between the child's level working alone and the child's level with some assistance should be called the zone of proximal development (ZPD). He found that those children who had the greater zone of proximal development did better at school.

There are a number of practical consequences to ZPD. Vygotsky's ideas point to the importance of appropriate interaction, collaboration and cooperation. He suggested that, given minimal support, the children scored much higher on the tests. All teachers must make decisions about the kind of interventions that they make. Although the tests showed the influence of appropriate support they also remind us that collaboration is an important way of learning and that in the right context there is much that children can do *without* direct instruction.

If we accept the idea of ZPD, it leaves a number of questions about how teacher interaction can best support pupils' learning within the ZPD. The term 'scaffolding' has become common in discussions about literacy teaching. For example, the idea that teachers should 'model' and scaffold aspects of writing. Unfortunately the didactic context for these recommendations is not the same as the original concept of scaffolding. David Wood coined the term scaffolding in his research on the teaching techniques that mothers used with their 3–4-year-old children. The mothers, who were able to help their children complete a task that could normally only be completed by children older than 7, scaffolded their children's learning in specific ways:

- They simplified problems that the child encountered; they removed potential distractions from the central task.
- They pointed things out that the child had missed.
- The less successful parent tutors showed the child how to do the task without letting them have a go themselves or they used verbal instructions too much.

Overall, Wood (1998) identified two particularly important aspects. When a child was struggling, immediate help was offered. Then, when help had been given they gradually removed support encouraging the child's independence. 'We termed this aspect of tutoring "contingent" instruction. Such contingent support helps to ensure that the child is never left alone when he is in difficulty, nor is he "held back" by teaching that is too directive and intrusive' (ibid.: 100).

The vital point here is that scaffolding happens in the context of meaningful interaction that is not inappropriately didactic. This idea of scaffolding is not typically what is happening when a teacher is demonstrating some aspect of the writing process. Although demonstration has a useful purpose, it should not be called scaffolding and given dubious theoretical authenticity by inaccurate reference to Vygotsky. Much more thought needs to be given to the encouragement of children's independence as part of the teaching of English.

Jerome Bruner built on some Vygotskian ideas and contributed a number of significant theories that have guided the teaching of language. One of these was the idea of a 'spiral curriculum' where 'an "intuitive" grasp of an idea precedes its more formal comprehension as part of a structured set of conceptual relationships' (Bruner, 1975: 25). The idea of a spiral curriculum is important in that it suggests that knowledge and concepts need to be revisited a number of times at increasingly higher levels of sophistication. It is also important because it calls into question the notion that learning is a simple sequence, where knowledge and concepts are only addressed on one occasion.

Bruner saw a close relationship between language and the spiral curriculum. He suggested that the spiral curriculum was supported by some essential elements in the learning process. Language learning occurs in the context of 'use and interaction – use implying an operation of the child upon objects' (ibid.: 25). In other words, it is important that children have first-hand experience of relevant 'objects' (including their local environment) to support their learning. In terms of English this suggests that the writing of texts should be supported by real purposes and that the reading of texts should first and foremost be about experiencing whole texts and, second, about analysis. There are many teaching strategies that encourage the direct use of objects and the environment to stimulate talking, reading and writing. Bruner argued that this kind of language learning was 'contextualised' and should be supported by people who were expert, like the teacher.

The more general theoretical exploration in this chapter leads us finally to a linguistic focus on four theories which we think underpin the teaching of English, language and literacy: (1) the communication of meaning is the driving force of language; (2) all language users seek to avoid ambiguity in their communication unless this is deliberately intended; (3) language is governed by conventions (rather than rigid rules) which are constantly changing; (4) the conventions of language are driven by what is the most efficient and quickest way to communicate meaning, therefore certain features become redundant if they do not support this.

Good teaching mirrors the significance of our first theory about communication by encouraging learners to engage in activities that require the construction of purposeful forms of language. The construction of whole texts is emphasised more than a concentration on fragments of text. A focus on unambiguous language use means that the clearest and most elegant kind of communication is learned and taught. Learners are also taught that the conventions of language are there to be seen in the real texts of life. Response to these texts and their conventions leads to much more accurate knowledge than the teaching of rules which are often based on historical precedence more than modern language use. Teachers recognise that non-standard forms of communication, such as electronic ones, are important because they are often very efficient at communicating meaning in novel ways. In time, some of these features add to the language and become 'standard' enhancing the richness of English as a language.

Practice points

- Be receptive to theories of learning and consciously use the ones that you think are important to inform your teaching.
- Remember that to help children learn you need to take account of social factors (like motivation) as well as cognitive ones.
- Develop the confidence to explore different approaches to teaching on the basis of theories.

Glossary

Theory – a principle or a set of principles that form the basis for action.

References

Brophy, J. and Good, T. (1986) 'Teacher behaviour and student achievement', in M. C. Wittrock (ed.) *Handbook of Research on Teaching*. New York: Macmillan.

Bruner, J. S. (1975) *Entry into Early Language: A Spiral Curriculum*. Swansea: University College of Swansea.

Dunne, J. (1993) *Back to the Rough Ground: Practical Judgement and the Lure of Technique*. Notre Dame, IN: University of Notre Dame Press.

Kelly, A. V. (2004) *The Curriculum: Theory and Practice*, 5th edn. London: Sage.

Sammons, P., Hillman, J. and Mortimore, P. (1995) *Key Characteristics of Effective Schools: A Review of School Effectiveness Research*. London: Office for Standards in Education (OfSTED) and Institute of Education, University of London.

Vygotsky, L. S. (1986) *Thought and Language*. Cambridge, MA: Harvard University Press.

Wood, D. (1988) *How Children Think and Learn*, 2nd edn. Oxford: Blackwell.

Wyse, D. (2003) 'The National Literacy Strategy: a critical review of empirical evidence', *British Educational Research Journal*, 29(6): 903–916.

Annotated bibliography

Lawton, D. and Gordon, P. (2002) *A History of Western Educational Ideas.* London: Woburn Press.
A useful introduction and overview of philosophical ideas.
L2 ***

Vygotsky, L. S. (1986) *Thought and Language.* Cambridge, MA: Harvard University Press.
Probably Vygotsky's best known book. Includes the description of the zone of proximal development.
L3 ***

Wood, D. (1998) *How Children Think and Learn*, 2nd edn. Oxford: Blackwell.
An excellent overview of the psychology of how children think and learn. Includes explanation of work on scaffolding learning.
L2 ***

Part II

Reading

Chapter 3

The development of reading

Helping children learn to read is one of the most important roles that primary teachers carry out. In order to support children effectively it is necessary to be aware of the ways children might develop. Detailed pictures of individual children's development are used to present stages of development in this chapter. These are followed by reflections on the impact that the Rose review had on the teaching of reading.

Descriptions of stages of development for reading and writing are an important feature of educational curricula. In England this feature is revealed in the National Curriculum levels of attainment. The PNS Literacy Framework attempts to do this through the sequencing of objectives and guidance papers on progression. It is reasonable to assume that reading and writing curricula should reflect research evidence on development but it is often unclear whether such evidence has been considered.

Tierney (1991: 180) observed that although there were a large number of longitudinal studies ☞ about children's encounters with print, too many of them focused narrowly on decoding skills. Tierney also argued that reading was represented in longitudinal work more than writing and that the writing research tended to be dominated by 'cross-sectional comparisons of students varying in age or ability rather than studies that have looked at the same children at different ages' (ibid.: 189). This kind of cross-sectional comparison can be seen in Loban's (1976) data on language development which was acquired mainly through sentence-level and word-level tests. The concluding chart of sequences and stages strongly emphasised grammatical development consistent with the kind of tests that were used.

Later work, such as that by Harste, Woodward and Burke (1984), convincingly portrayed the active and constructive nature of children's meaning-making. Wells (1986) confirmed such findings, and additionally concluded that listening to stories was more significantly correlated with children's literacy acquisition than looking at picture books and talking about them; drawing and colouring; or playing at writing. Ferreiro and Teberosky's influential semi-longitudinal study (1982: 263) concluded that by age 4 most children understand the main principle that 'writing is not just lines or marks but a substitute object representing something external to the graphics themselves'.

One feature of the research evidence focusing on the development of reading and writing has been the analysis of stages of development that are common to most children. Often these syntheses are derived from case-study data. For example, the Centre for Language in Primary Education (CLPE, 1989) developed reading scales through their work trialling the primary language record with teachers in London. Bearne (1998) worked closely with a group of 80 teachers to identify their expectations for children's development at the beginning and end of each school year.

Another important strand of case-study research, and longitudinal work, has been the use of individual child case studies; a methodology which, like Brooker (2002), we consider to be significant in the goal to better understand early childhood literacy. Seminal work ☞ in the field includes White (1954) and Butler (1975). The most important study of this kind, because of the richness of the data and its close link with other research evidence, is that by Bissex (1980) of her son Paul's development as a reader and writer between the ages of 5 and 11. Dyson (1983) cited the significance of the Bissex study arguing that it was unusual because it provided evidence of the purposes which writing serves in children's lives something that she argued many studies had neglected because of their narrow focus.

A common criticism of individual child case studies is that their findings cannot be reliably generalised because of such small sample sizes. However, the Bissex study has shown that generalisation is possible. Gentry (1982) carried out an analysis of the examples of Paul Bissex's spelling. Gentry identified five stages of spelling development which subsequently Ellis (1994: 156) confirmed: 'it is now generally agreed that children move through five distinct stages of spelling, viz: "precommunicative", "semiphonetic", "phonetic", "transitional", and "correct".'

The early 1980s saw a number of individual child case-studies from Australia, the USA and England which provided further data about children's development as readers and writers (those by Lass, 1982; Baghban, 1984; Kamler, 1984; Payton, 1984; Schmidt and Yates, 1985). In addition to the descriptions of developmental progression that these studies offered, a range of general conclusions was put forward. The most common themes of these conclusions were the need to alleviate the disjunction between home and school literacy learning, and the important part that appropriate social interaction played in literacy learning. However, one of the limitations of these studies was their lack of references to other similar case studies in order to build more reliable evidence about developmental progression. The lack of reference to other similar studies was something that continued in subsequent decades. Minns (1997) identified six key areas that the children in her study developed: (1) understanding that print carries a message; (2) the ability to predict key phrases and memorise chunks of book language; (3) familiarity with book handling and directionality; (4) understanding of and use of metalanguage; (5) understanding that there was a correspondence between letters and sounds; and (6) the ability to discriminate between letter shapes and recognise individual words. However, like Fadil and Zaragoza (1997), there was no reference to other case studies, not even to the seminal work of Bissex. Campbell (1999) concluded that children's learning is supported when they are actively involved and interested and that story reading and the opportunity to choose books are beneficial. Although Campbell did make reference to other case studies, it is not clear from his analysis how previous studies informed his reflections on developmental progression. Kress (2000) similarly did not explicitly build on previous developmental studies in his interesting thesis that pointed to the multiple meanings of children's spelling attempts.

The rich data that have been portrayed in case studies and syntheses provide useful insights into the development of reading and writing. The milestones presented in Tables 3.1, 3.2, and 3.3 were built from a synthesis of the case study data reviewed so far in this chapter and new data from Dominic's two children (see Appendix for methodology of the research and Wyse (2007) for examples from the data).

Knowledge about rich pictures of children's development is important because it can influence the way we teach our children. By knowing developmental milestones it is possible to anticipate these and provide teaching at the appropriate level. This influence means that our pedagogy ☞ is related to what we know about how children develop. However, none of the questions about reading development and reading teaching have simple answers and it is for this reason that reading pedagogy has attracted such fierce debate. In the remaining part of this chapter we look at the teaching of reading including the implications of the controversial Rose Report. Many of the issues that emerge from a consideration of the politics and research are ones that have recurred in previous manifestations of what have been called the *reading wars*.

The teaching of reading

The history of the debates about approaches to the teaching of reading has repeatedly hinged on fundamental disagreements related to models of learning to read. The seminal text in the debate of the modern era was Jean Chall's (1983) book *Learning to Read: The Great Debate* which was first published in the 1960s. In it she defines the differences between two models:

> The top-down models relate . . . to the meaning-emphasis approaches of beginning reading and stress the first importance of language and meaning for reading comprehension and also for word recognition . . . The reader

Table 3.1 Expectations for a child's reading at age 4

What you can expect	What you can do to help
Understands distinction between print and pictures	Talk about pictures and talk about print. Encourage children to point to print or point to pictures.
Can recognise and understand some words and signs in the environment	Encourage children to read food packets and to play 'shop'. Read signs, logos, and labels with them. Comment on text that appears on TV. Talk about greetings cards.
Understands that text has specific meaning	Read stories and other books with children. When reading a text that is at the child's level read all the words as written. Talk about what particular words and sentences mean.
Plays at reading	Make sure that children have easy access to a really good range of books. Encourage their playing with the books and their pretend reading. Encourage them to pretend to read to others or even to cuddly toys.
Uses words and phrases from written language when retelling stories	Respond to children's requests to hear favourite stories. Encourage children to predict what is coming next in a story. Suggest that they join in with repetitive phrases. Celebrate when they remember phrases from favourite stories.
Needs other people to help with reading aloud	Read aloud daily with children. Encourage discussion and always be looking to develop children's independence to read words.
Will choose favourite picture books to be read aloud	Encourage daily reading. Give easy access to books. Read children's favourites but intorduce them to new books as well.
Uses picture cues and memory of texts	Once children are familiar with a book encourage them to tell the story by looking at the pictures as prompts for their memory of the text.
Understands orientation of print and books	Talk about the front and back covers of books, where the print is, where the print starts on a page. Comment on books that play with these conventions.
Salient visual cues used to remember some familiar words like own name	Give frequent opportunities to read, write and play games with words such as names.

theoretically samples the text in order to confirm and modify initial hypotheses.

The bottom-up models – those that view the reading process as developing from perception of letters, spelling patterns, and words, to sentence and paragraph meaning, resemble the code-emphasis, beginning reading approaches.

(Chall, 1983: 28–29)

Table 3.2 Expectations for a child's reading at age 7

What you can expect	What you can do to help
Silent reading established	Provide time, space, opportunities and resources to encourage children to read regularly.
Can accurately read increasing number of unknown texts independently	Ensure that children have access to 'new' books on a regular basis.
Uses expression when reading aloud	Have fun with using expression when you are reading to children. Encourage children to read at a good speed and with expression when they share books with you. If children are involved in any kind of performance where they have to read out loud, such as a class assembly, help them with expression and clarity.
Uses a range of word-reading strategies appropriately	Help children to use semantic, phonological and orthographic knowledge to work out tricky words. Praise them for good guesses and supply the correct word if necessary but give them time to think.
Stronger individual preferences for particular texts	Encourage children to develop preferences for particular topics and types of texts. Talk to them about their preferences and those of the class.
Likes reading longer stories in addition to returning to picture books	Provide access to books with more text and fewer pictures.
Sight-word reading for rapidly increasing bank of familiar words	The more children read the more sight words they will acquire.
Phonological knowledge fully established. Growing awareness of irregularities of English spelling	Phonics teaching will have taken place. Help children to see that the one-letter-makes-one-sound idea is not accurate. Discuss the irregularities of English spelling.

The classic example of a top-down approach to reading would be the 'real book approach' or the 'whole language approach' and the contrasting bottom-up approach would be 'phonics'. Since Chall defined 'bottom-up' and 'top-down', new models have emerged that united the theory and practice of reading teaching. Wray suggested that proposals for 'interactive' and 'transactional' models of the reading process moved the field 'towards a synthesising theory' (1995: 58).

One of the main challenges for children learning to read in English is that it is the hardest language. The reason that it is easier to learn to read in some languages than others is to do with their linguistic complexity. As Goswami (2005) has shown, there are two key factors in this. The first is the way that consonants and vowels are linked together. Some languages, such as Italian, Spanish and Chinese are based on a simple consonant–vowel syllable structure (like *panini* [pa-ni-ni] in Italian or *tapa* [ta-pa] in Spanish). This makes them

Table 3.3 Expectations for a child's reading at age 11

What you can expect	What you can do to help
Reflective reader with strong preferences	Discuss texts that children are reading and seek to extend their understanding of the issues raised.
Uses different reading styles for different texts	Encourage children to become involved with things like map-reading or locating information on the internet through cross-curricular work.
Can follow instructional texts	Do some cooking together which requires use of a recipe book. Involve children in following instructions to assemble things including instructions that their peers have written.
Can sort and classify evidence	Encourage reading and writing of a range of formats for summarising information.
Varies pace, pitch and expression when reading aloud and varies for performance purposes	Discuss occasions when children have to perform. Encourage involvement in dramatic activities at home and at school.
Can adopt alternative viewpoints	The starting point for this might be the ability to empathise with others. Encourage consideration of evidence from different sides of an argument.
Recognises language devices used for particular effects	Enjoy the imagination of authors who like to play with text effects. Re-read texts like poetry to discover effects.
Can discuss different author styles	Encourage children to read a series of books by the authors that they like and to think about their style.
Enjoys selecting and reading appropriate adult texts	Encourage access to newspapers and magazines.

less complex than English. English has very few consonant-vowel syllables. Words such as 'baby' and 'cocoa' are examples that do exist (see Table 3.4). The most frequent syllable type in English is consonant–vowel–consonant, as in words like 'dog' and 'cat'.

The second key factor is the consistency of how the written symbols represent sounds. In some languages, such as English and Dutch, one letter or one cluster of letters can have many different pronunciations. In other languages, such as Greek, Italian and Spanish, the letters and clusters are always pronounced in the same way no matter which word they appear in, which is simpler

Table 3.4 Examples of words in English with consonant/vowel syllables

Word	Syllable	Consonant	Vowel(s)	Syllable	Consonant	Vowel(s)
baby	ba	b	a	by	b	y
cocoa	co	c	o	coa	c	oa

Table 3.5 Data (% correct) from the large-scale study of reading skills at the end of grade 1 in 14 European languages

Language	Familiar real words	Pseudo-words
Greek	98	92
Finnish	98	95
German	98	94
Austrian German	97	92
Italian	95	89
Spanish	95	89
Swedish	95	88
Dutch	95	82
Icelandic	94	86
Norwegian	92	91
French	79	85
Portuguese	73	77
Danish	71	54
Scottish English	34	29

Source: Goswami (2005: 275)

to learn. A large study of 14 European languages clearly showed the dramatic differences by measuring the reading of real words and made-up words in different languages, with English right at the bottom of the list (see Table 3.5).

Reading models

In order to recognise words visually, children rely on representations of words at three levels: meaning (*semantic*); sounds (*phonology*) and spelling (*orthography*) (Reimer, 2006). If you take the semantic representation of words, then the prompt, 'Does that make sense?' after a sentence, phrase or word that has been attempted can be helpful. Encouraging children to read to the end of a sentence and then return to a problem word can help them use the meaning of the sentence to recognise a particular word. If they substitute a different word from the one printed in the text, then asking, 'Is that right?' encourages them to think about the meaning of what they have been reading and to confirm whether the guess they made is accurate.

Awareness of orthographic representations is helped by looking at chunks of words. For example, you can help the child to see words broken down into syllables so that they can read one syllable, then another. Prefixes ☞ and suffixes ☞ are a useful part of this. If you take the word 'play' and add 'ed', you get 'played'. 'ed' can, of course, be added to most verbs (poured; danced; acted; planted; painted) although this suffix will sound different, depending on the word: either /ed/ or /d/; act-/ed/ as opposed to play-/d/. If you add 're' to the beginning of play, you get 'replay'. The prefix 're' can also be added to many words (repair; react; reward; reply).

Using the phonological representation of words is particularly important from age 5 onwards. This is the point at which phonics teaching is particularly important (➡ Chapter 7). At the most basic level, the question, 'Can you sound it out?' encourages the child to attempt to work out what phonemes the letters of a problem word make. Many children struggle with identifying phonemes at first.

Between 1997 and 2006 the teaching of reading in the NLS Framework was underpinned by the searchlights model (Department for Education and Employment, 1998). But by 2007 it had been replaced by the *simple view of reading* (Figure 3.1).

Morag Stuart and Rhona Stainthorp were invited to develop this model as part of the Rose review of the teaching of reading (which we address in the next section of this chapter). Officially endorsed models of this kind tend to have a more lasting impression than the finer detail of reports because they summarise the main thrust of changes to teaching. For that reason it is important that they are informed by the widest possible research base. The Rose review could have invited reading specialists with expertise in reading models and theories to reach some basic agreements on appropriate models for reading. However, the decision was taken to invite Stuart and Stainthorp. The question that has to be asked is why these two people and not others? One of the answers to this is that their work, including their contributions to official meetings which preceded the Rose review, had already demonstrated an interest in and commitment to synthetic phonics.

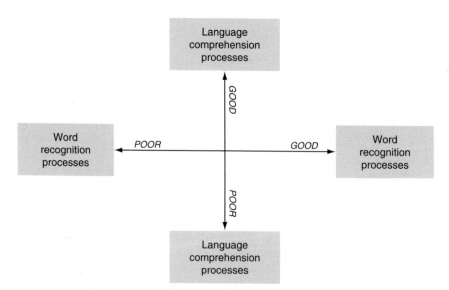

Figure 3.1 The simple view of reading.

The simple view of reading accompanied an immediate and quite dramatic change in policy and practice. Because of its likely impact for many years to come, the model needs to be subject to extensive critical evaluation so that we can be sure that its influence is justified. The following issues will need to be addressed:

- Is there agreement that the simple view of reading is the most appropriate model?
- Does the simple view appropriately reflect the evidence that is used to justify it?
- Does the simple view reflect research on the teaching of reading?

The Rose Report

In the period from 1997 onwards, there were many criticisms of the NLS Framework for Teaching, one strand of which questioned the lack of research evidence in support of its pedagogy (Wyse, 2003). An opposing line of criticism came from those who advocated synthetic phonics. From 2004, research into a synthetic phonics approach carried out in Clackmannanshire, a small authority in Scotland, was promoted strongly by the media. This resulted in a recommendation by England's Education Select Committee (a parliamentary committee charged with overseeing educational matters) that there should be a governmental inquiry into the teaching of reading (House of Commons Education and Skills Committee, 2005). In June 2005, the government duly announced a review of the teaching of early reading, to be headed by the ex-inspector and education consultant, Jim Rose. The interim report was released in December 2005, and the final report was published at the end of March 2006 (Rose, 2006).

The final report (hereafter the Rose Report) addressed five concerns:

1   What best practice should be expected in the teaching of early reading and synthetic phonics (ibid.: p. 7);
2   how this relates to the development of the birth to five framework and the development and renewal of the National Literacy Strategy *Framework for Teaching* (ibid.: 7);
3   the needs of children with significant literacy difficulties;
4   the implications for school leadership and management;
5   the value for money of proposed changes.

The Rose Report started by stressing the importance of including *systematic* phonics instruction in early reading programmes, a position that is supported by international research. But, in recommending that early reading instruction must comprise *synthetic* phonics, it moved to a position that is not supported by research evidence.

The potential impact of the Rose Report on the early years and primary curriculum spreads beyond England. While other Anglophone countries had imposed systematic phonics on their education systems (National Institute of Child Health and Human Development, 2000; Australian Government, Department of Education, Science and Training, 2005), England was the first to impose *synthetic* phonics on all early years settings, including schools.

One of the key paragraphs in the Rose Report was this:

> 51. Having considered a wide range of evidence, the review has concluded that the case for systematic phonic work is overwhelming and much strengthened by a synthetic approach.
>
> (Rose, 2006: 20)

Before we address the research base for the Rose Report, it is interesting to make the following comparison. In 1990, a report by HMI (Her Majesty's Inspectorate, the predecessor of OfSTED) on the teaching of reading was published, to very little press or government interest. It drew on evidence from visits to 120 primary schools. 'The teaching and learning of reading were observed in 470 classes and over 2,000 children read aloud to HMI . . . particular attention was paid to the children's ability to read fluently, accurately and with understanding' (Her Majesty's Inspectorate (HMI), 1990: 1). It was concluded that: 'phonic skills were taught almost universally and usually to beneficial effect' (ibid.: 2) and that 'Successful teachers of reading and the majority of schools used a mix of methods each reinforcing the other as the children's reading developed' (ibid.: 15). Indeed, in the UK, phonics has always been widely regarded as a necessary skill for learning to read, write and spell, but not necessarily the prime skill or the one that must be acquired 'first and fast'. As Dombey (2006: 6) accurately observed:

> The most successful schools and teachers focus both on phonics and on the process of making sense of text. Best practice brings these two key components together, in teaching that gives children a sense of the pleasures reading can bring, supports them in making personal sense of the texts they encounter and also shows them how to lift the words off the page.

In contrast, as part of the Rose review, HMI only visited 10 schools using synthetic phonics (in addition to 10 schools following the less favoured NLS approach). The synthetic phonics schools were recommended by 'experienced advocates' (Rose, 2006: 66) of the approaches that they used. These school visits were deemed sufficient to provide an evidence base for quite dramatic changes in reading pedagogy.

Research evidence and systematic phonics

One of the most significant contributions to debates about research evidence and the teaching of reading was the report of the US National Reading Panel (NRP) on reading instruction, carried out by the National Institute of Child Health and Human Development (National Institute of Child Health and Human Development, 2000). This extensive meta-analysis addressed a number of questions including: 'Does systematic phonics instruction help children learn to read more effectively than non-systematic phonics instruction or instruction teaching no phonics?' (Chapter 1, p. 3). As far as differences between analytic and synthetic phonics are concerned, the NRP concluded that 'specific systematic phonics programs are all significantly more effective than non-phonics programs; however, they do not appear to differ significantly from each other in their effectiveness although more evidence is needed to verify the reliability of effect sizes for each program' (ibid., Chapter 2, p. 93). The point about systematic phonics, as opposed to synthetic phonics, is contrary to the Rose Report's conclusion that the case for systematic phonics is much strengthened by a synthetic phonics approach.

In 2006, the UK Department for Education and Skills (DfES) commissioned a systematic review of approaches to the teaching of reading. The methodology of the NRP was refined to produce a meta-analysis that included only Randomised Controlled Trials (RCTs) ☞. On the basis of their work, Torgerson *et al.* conclude, once again in direct contrast to the Rose Report, that 'There is currently no strong RCT evidence that any one form of systematic phonics is more effective than any other' (2006: 49). This finding supports their pedagogical recommendation that 'Since there is evidence that systematic phonics teaching benefits children's reading accuracy, it should be part of every literacy teacher's repertoire and a routine part of literacy teaching, *in a judicious balance with other elements*' (ibid.: 49, italics added). One of the difficulties of forming policy recommendations for reading pedagogy is that this judicious balance can easily be disrupted by policy thrusts that lack a sufficient evidence base.

This work in the USA and the UK was complemented by an Australian government report recommending that:

> teachers [should] provide systematic, direct and explicit phonics instruction so that children master the essential alphabetic code-breaking skills required for foundational reading proficiency. Equally, that teachers [should] provide an integrated approach to reading that supports the development of oral language, vocabulary, grammar, reading fluency, comprehension and the literacies of new technologies.
>
> (Australian Government, Department of Education,
> Science and Training, 2005: 14)

The Australian report also appropriately cautioned that:

> While the evidence indicates that some teaching strategies are more effect-
> ive than others, no one approach of itself can address the complex nature
> of reading difficulties. An integrated approach requires that teachers have a
> thorough understanding of a range of effective strategies, as well as know-
> ing when and why to apply them.
>
> (ibid.: 14)

The Rose Report claimed that

> there is ample evidence to support the recommendation of the interim
> report that, for *most* children, it is highly worthwhile and appropriate
> to *begin* a systematic programme of phonic work by the age of five,
> if not before for some children, the way having been paved by related
> activities designed, for example, to build phonological awareness.
>
> (2006: 29, italics as in original, underlining added)

Early years educators have been particularly concerned about the dangers of
an inappropriate curriculum being imposed on young children. The research
evidence on this matter was quite clear and once again contradicted the report.
The majority of evidence in favour of systematic phonics teaching referred
to children age 6 and older. Some 20 out of the 43 studies covered in the
Torgerson *et al.* (2006) and NRP reviews were carried out with children
aged 6–7. Only nine studies were carried out with children aged 5–6. No studies
were carried out with 4-year-olds. The idea that children younger than 5 will
benefit from a synthetic phonics is not supported by evidence and is arguably
one of the most controversial recommendations of the Rose Report.

The importance of an appropriate reading context

The extent to which reading teaching should contextualise the material to be
taught has been at the heart of arguments about reading pedagogy. There is
continuing disagreement about the best ways to balance work on whole texts
with sub-word-level work. Although the Rose Report said that phonics teaching
should be 'securely embedded within a broad and language-rich curriculum'
(2006: 16), its advocacy of synthetic phonics contradicted this aim. The report
adopted Torgerson *et al.*'s (2006: 15) definition of synthetic phonics as 'an
approach to the teaching of reading in which the phonemes associated with
particular graphemes are pronounced in *isolation* and blended together (syn-
thesized)' [italics added]. As far as teaching synthetic phonics is concerned, it
was argued that, 'From work considered by this review, the balance of advantage favours teaching it *discretely* as the prime approach to establishing word
recognition' (Rose Report, 2006: 20, italics added). Therefore, 'In practice, this

means teaching relatively short, *discrete* daily sessions, designed to progress from simple elements to the more complex aspects of phonic knowledge, skills and understanding' (ibid.: 16, italics added). Whereas the Rose Report provided considerable detail about the ways phonics was to be taught, there was very little detail about other important aspects of reading teaching such as how reading comprehension could be enhanced and what the report meant by a 'language-rich curriculum'.

Yet the 43 studies in the NRP and Torgerson *et al.* (2006) reviews reported gains where phonics instruction was integrated with text-level learning, often as part of the classroom literacy or language arts curriculum. At the time of the Rose review, the study by Berninger was one of the most up-to-date. The Berninger *et al.* study is particularly important because it directly addressed the question of contextualisation of phonics instruction. It was indicative of the majority of studies covered by the reviews in its conclusions about the importance of careful contextualisation of phonics teaching. In this study, second-grade teachers in eight schools serving diverse student populations were asked to refer their 'poorest readers'. These children were then tested by project staff to check whether children met the inclusion criteria. Forty-eight pairs of children were randomly assigned to four teaching conditions: (1) explicit and reflective word recognition; (2) explicit and reflective reading comprehension; (3) combined explicit word recognition and explicit reading comprehension, or (4) a control group, given practice in reading skills without any instruction. The most effective condition featured phonics teaching carefully integrated with reading comprehension training:

> It is intriguing to consider why explicit comprehension instruction might facilitate learning to decode written words – the skill on which at-risk readers have the most difficulty. One explanation for the transfer from comprehension training to phonological decoding may be that explicit instruction in reading comprehension develops broad-based metalinguistic awareness (Mattingly, 1972) that may generalize across levels of language in the functional reading system.
>
> (Berninger *et al.*, 2003: 112)

In contrast to the recommendations of the Rose Report, the reading instruction studies included in the two reviews showed the particular benefits of *different* types of phonics instruction when carefully integrated with whole text work making use of a range of teaching strategies.

The Rose Report resulted in unprecedented level of direct political involvement in the work of teachers and teacher trainers. Its conclusions about synthetic phonics did not adequately reflect the evidence that was available. It missed an opportunity to take forward the debate about reading in a constructive way opting instead for its more controversial approach and findings. This meant that the reading wars were once again ignited. It may well take another ten years of fighting to ensure that the reading curriculum is returned to one that is more balanced. This will require all involved in education, including parents, to work for a more democratic approach to the early years and primary curriculum and its reform.

Practice points

- A truly objective and balanced approach to the teaching of reading is vital.
- Work on your observation skills and extend your understanding of children's reading development.
- Phonics teaching should be regular, brief and as enjoyable as possible.

Glossary

Longitudinal studies – research that looks at development over several years rather than a year or less.
Pedagogy – approaches to teaching and learning.
Prefix – an addition to the beginning of a root word that modifies its meaning, e.g. *in*-finite.
Randomised Controlled Trials – a particular kind of research which analyses the effect of an intervention on experimental groups and a control group to which the participants have been randomly allocated.
Seminal work – classic (often old) academic work that continues to be referenced by large numbers of writers.
Suffix – an addition to the end of a root word that modifies its meaning, e.g. infinite-*ly*.

References

Australian Government, Department of Education, Science and Training (2005) *Teaching Reading. Report and Recommendations: National Enquiry into the Teaching of Literacy*. Barton, Australia: Department of Education, Science and Training.

Baghban, M. (1984) *Our Daughter Learns to Read and Write: A Case Study from Birth to Three*. Newark, DE: International Reading Association.

Bearne, E. (1998) *Making Progress in English*. London: Routledge.

Berninger, V. W., Vermeulen, K., Abott, R. D., McCutchen, D., Cotton, S., Cude, J., et al. (2003) 'Comparison of three approaches to supplementary reading instruction for low-achieving second-grade readers', *Language, Speech, and Hearing Services in Schools*, 34: 101–116.

Bissex, G. L. (1980) *GNYS AT WRK: A Child Learns to Write and Read*. Cambridge, MA: Harvard University Press.

Brooker, L. (2002) 'Five on the first of December!: What can we learn from case studies of early childhood literacy?' *Journal of Early Childhood Literacy*, 2(3): 291–313.

Butler, D. (1975) *Cushla and Her Books*. Auckland: Hodder & Stoughton.

Campbell, R. (1999) *Literacy from Home to School: Reading with Alice*. Stoke-on-Trent: Trentham Books.

Centre for Language in Primary Education (CLPE)/Inner London Education Authority (ILEA) (1989) *The Primary Language Record Handbook for Teachers*. London: Centre for Language in Primary Education.

Chall, J. S. (1983) *Learning to Read: The Great Debate* (updated edition). New York: McGraw-Hill.

Department for Education and Employment (DfEE) (1998) *The National Literacy Strategy Framework for Teaching*. Sudbury: DfEE Publications.

Department for Education and Employment (DfEE) and The Qualifications and Curriculum Authority (QCA) (1999) *The National Curriculum: Handbook for Primary Teachers in England. Key Stages 1 and 2*. Norwich: Her Majesty's Stationery Office (HMSO).

Dombey, H. (2006) 'How should we teach children to read?' *Books for Keeps*, 156: 6–7.

Dyson, A. H. (1983) 'Individual differences in emerging writing' in M. Farr (ed.) *Advances in Writing Research*, Vol. 1: *Children's Early Writing Development*. Norwood, NJ: Ablex.

Ellis, N. C. (1994) 'Longitudinal studies of spelling development', in G. D. A. Brown and N. C. Ellis (eds) *Handbook of Spelling: Theory, Process and Intervention*. Chichester: John Wiley and Sons, Ltd.

Fadil, C. and Zaragoza, N. (1997) 'Revisiting the emergence of young children's literacy: one child tells her story', *Reading*, 31(1): 29–34.

Ferreiro, E. and Teberosky, A. (1982) *Literacy Before Schooling*. Portsmouth, NH: Heinemann.

Gentry, J. R. (1982) 'An analysis of developmental spelling in *GNYS AT WRK*', *The Reading Teacher*, 36: 192–200.

Goswami, U. (2005) 'Synthetic phonics and learning to read: a cross-language perspective', *Educational Psychology in Practice*, 21(4): 273–282.

Harste, J. C., Woodward, V. A. and Burke, C. L. (1984) *Language Stories and Literacy Lessons*. Portsmouth, NH: Heinemann Educational Books.

Her Majesty's Inspectorate (HMI) (1990) *The Teaching and Learning of Reading in Primary Schools*. London: Department of Education and Science (DES).

House of Commons Education and Skills Committee (2005) *Teaching Children to Read: Eighth Report of Session 2004–2005. Report, together with Formal Minutes, Oral and Written Evidence*. London: The Stationery Office.

Kamler, B. (1984) 'Ponch writes again: a child at play', *Australian Journal of Reading*, 7(2): 61–70.

Kress, G. (2000) *Early Spelling: Between Convention and Creativity*. London: Routledge.

Lass, B. (1982) 'Portrait of my son as an early reader,' *The Reading Teacher*, 36(1): 20–28.

Loban, W. (1976) *The Development of Language Abilities, K-12*. Urbana, IL: National Council for Teachers of English.

Minns, H. (1997) *Read It to Me Now! Learning at Home and at School*, 2nd edn. Buckingham: Open University Press.

National Institute of Child Health and Human Development (2000) *Report of the National Reading Panel. Teaching Children to Read: An Evidence-Based Assessment of the Scientific Research Literature on Reading and its Implications for Reading Instruction: Reports of the Subgroups* (NIH Publication no. 00–4754). Washington, DC: US Government Printing Office.

Payton, S. (1984) *Developing Awareness of Print: A Young Child's First Steps Towards Literacy*. Birmingham: University of Birmingham, Educational Review.

Reimer, J. (2006) 'Developmental changes in the allocation of semantic feedback during visual word recognition', *Journal of Research in Reading*, 29(2): 194–212.

Rose, J. (2006) *Independent Review of the Teaching of Early Reading*. Nottingham: DfES Publications.

Schmidt, E. and Yates, C. (1985) 'Benji learns to read naturally! Naturally Benji learns to read', *Australian Journal of Reading*, 8(3): 121–134.

Tierney, R. J. (1991) 'Studies of reading and writing growth: longitudinal research on literacy development', in J. Flood, J. M. Jenson, D. Lapp and J. R. Squire (eds) *Handbook of Research on Teaching the English Language Arts*. New York: Macmillan.

Torgerson, C. J., Brooks, G. and Hall, J. (2006) *A Systematic Review of the Research Literature on the Use of Phonics in the Teaching of Reading and Spelling*. London: Department for Education and Skills (DfES).

Wells, G. (1986) *The Meaning Makers: Children Learning Language and Using Language to Learn*. Sevenoaks: Hodder & Stoughton.

White, D. (1954) *Books Before Five*. Auckland: New Zealand Council for Educational Research.

Wray, D. (1995) 'Reviewing the reading debate', in D. Wray and J. Medwell (eds) *Teaching Primary English: The State of the Art*. London: Routledge.

Wyse, D. (2003) 'The National Literacy Strategy: a critical review of empirical evidence', *British Educational Research Journal*, 29(6): 903–916.

Wyse, D. (2007) *How to Help Your Child Read and Write*. London: Pearson/BBC Active.

Annotated bibliography

Rose, J. (2006) *Independent Review of the Teaching of Early Reading*. Nottingham: DfES Publications.

The Rose Report. Controversially concluded that synthetic phonics should be the preferred phonics approach. Includes the rationale for the simple model of reading.
L2 **

TACTYC (2007) 'Reflecting on early years issues', retrieved 4 February, 2007, from http://www.tactyc.org.uk/reflections_papers.asp
Part of the TACTYC early years organisation site which has short opinion pieces about a range of issues including early reading.
L1 *

Torgerson, C. J., Brooks, G. and Hall, J. (2006) *A Systematic Review of the Research Literature on the Use of Phonics in the Teaching of Reading and Spelling*. London: Department for Education and Skills (DfES).
This review restricts its focus to randomised controlled trials arguing, somewhat severely that these are the only kind of studies that should be considered when thinking about which approaches are more effective. In spite of the narrow focus, a significant document.
L3 ***

Weaver, C. (1994) *Reading Process and Practice from Socio-psycholinguistics to Whole Language*, 2nd edn. Portsmouth, NH: Heinemann.
The classic account of whole language teaching from the perspective of research, theory and practice.
L3 ***

Chapter 4

Children's literature

Texts are the lifeblood of the teaching of English, language and literacy. We explore some of the issues related to the selection and use of texts in the classroom. Picture fiction and longer fiction are followed by a look at the use of non-fiction.

> Willy didn't seem to be any good at anything. He liked to read . . . and listen to music . . . and walk in the park with his friend, Millie.
>
> (Brown, 1985: 1–3)

Margaret Meek argued forcefully and logically that the specific texts that children experience are one of the most important ingredients in their learning to read. If this is the case, it follows that all teachers must be knowledgeable about texts and the particular ways that different texts support reading.

Fiction

The quality of the best picture books ☞ continues to be extremely high. There are now a number of well-established classics ☞ that have been available for more than 30 years. In addition, the quality of the images and text of the best new picture books is breathtaking. The issue of quality is an important and contentious one. People who work with children clearly want them to get the maximum benefit from the texts that they are exposed to. But how do we define high quality? For teachers, one of the main criteria has to be about the learning that is likely to arise from the reading of the book. Another way to determine high quality might be through children's preferences for and enjoyment of particular texts: this is certainly one important measure of quality. However, there are a number of dilemmas that exist when solely using children's judgements. Sometimes their judgements can be incomplete if they have not had the opportunity to read a wide range of texts and actively discuss their quality. The same is true of teachers: if you have not read widely and analytically, it is impossible to have informed judgements about the quality of texts.

The following list suggests things that you could be thinking about when selecting picture books for your classroom/setting:

- Will the book support the children's learning?
- Is the subject of the book one that will interest the children?
- Does the book link with the children's experience in a meaningful way and/ or offer new perspectives?
- Is the narrative strong?
- Does the book involve playfulness, e.g. intriguing plot lines, games, twists, riddles?
- Are the pictures artistically original and memorable? Does the link with the text go beyond the literal?
- Are the amount and level of text appropriate for the age of the children (this will include some books which really stretch the children's capabilities)?
- What kind of knowledge might children acquire by reading the book?
- Is the structure of the book effective and satisfying?
- Is repetitive and realistic language used naturally? Is the voice of the author distinctive?

Picture books offer children a unique opportunity to connect with the author's imaginary world. This can be a particularly intense experience. The features of books that generate such experiences include a stimulating text and arresting illustrations. The best picture books have illustrations which them-selves often contain a number of sub-plots ☞. For example, when Lily (in *Lily Takes a Walk*: Kitamura, 1987) takes a seemingly peaceful walk her dog is subjected to a range of nightmare visions conjured by ordinary features of the urban landscape. Arizpe and Styles carried out some research to investigate how children respond to the pictures in this and some other classic picture books. When asked what they expected the book to be about by looking at the front cover, the children said things like: 'You think, "What's the dog scared of?" So you, like, turn the page and then look and then just carry on reading and there's some more monsters and you just want to see the rest of it' (2003: 57). The book has the words 'A Spooky Surprise Book' as part of the front cover, but the car-toon-like illustrations and facial expressions hint at something funny. This is why the children's views varied between expecting a funny book or a scary book. This ambiguity is a deliberate device created by the author to foster children's thinking. The researchers also asked the children about the dual plot of the book:

Researcher: Do you think the pictures are telling the same story as the words?
Selma: Yes, plus a bit more . . . [the pictures] seem to bring out the story.

In conclusion, the researchers found that children aged 4–11 in their study responded in sophisticated ways to the pictures in the books. The children 'read colours, borders, body language, framing devices, covers, endpapers, visual metaphors and visual jokes', and 'most children were keen to discuss the moral, spiritual and environmental issues [the pictures] raised'.

High-quality texts operate on a number of semantic levels ☞. First and foremost, the texts should appeal directly and powerfully to children, but adults should also find aspects that engage their curiosity and analytic skills. Such books are usually characterised by the different layers of meaning they contain that only reveal themselves through rereading and analysis. Books like this also stand the test of time and become classics. *The Very Hungry Caterpillar* is a wonderful example that has been 'translated into over 25 languages, and has sold 15 million copies. "So much from so little, as one of my friends once put it!" says [the author Eric] Carle merrily' (Carey, 1999: 13).

Authors of children's fiction find a variety of ways of rooting their work in children's culture. Janet and Allan Ahlberg's important contribution is in the ways that they weave children's stories and nursery rhymes within one text (sometimes called 'intertextuality'), a good example of this is *Each Peach Pear Plum*. The text is structured in rhyming couplets with each double page having one couplet and an accompanying illustration. The rhythm and rhyme appeal to young children and aid their memory of the text. The book also draws on the game 'I spy' as each couplet includes the words from the game, for example, 'Baby Bunting fast asleep/I spy Bo-Peep'. As you have probably guessed a whole range of nursery rhyme characters populate the story culminating in a picnic which includes plum pie:

> Three Bears still hunting
> THEY spy Baby Bunting
> Baby Bunting safe and dry
> I spy Plum Pie
> Plum Pie in the sun
> I spy . . .
> . . . EVERYONE!
> (Ahlberg and Ahlberg, 1978: 24–31)

Anthony Browne's work is notable because of the way that his books often focus on important issues while maintaining genuinely interesting narratives. Examples of such issues include: sexism – *Piggybook*; self-esteem and bullying – *Willy the Champ*; one-parent families – *Gorilla*; class – *A Walk in the Park*; gender and sibling rivalry – *The Tunnel*. All his books are accompanied by mesmeric illustrations that seem to derive from surrealist ☞ art.

Trish Cooke's book *So Much* was a multiple prizewinner when it was published in 1996. Although prizes don't always identify the best books, on this occasion the awards of the Smarties Book Prize, the Kurt Maschler Award and the *She*/WH Smith awards were justified. Indeed, Anthony Browne is quoted on the back of the book: 'It is always a delight to see an established artist taking risks, breaking new ground and succeeding brilliantly.' *So Much* explores an aspect of Black British children's culture and like many children's books has a naturally repetitive structure:

> They weren't doing anything
> Mum and the baby
> nothing really . . .
> Then,
> DING DONG!
> 'Oooooooh!'
> Mum looked at the door,
> the baby looked at Mum.
> It was . . .
> (Cooke, 1994: 7)

As can be seen from the extract, the text encourages children to predict what will happen next; this helps to develop an important reading strategy and recognises their enthusiasm for guessing and problem solving. The illustrations show accurate and positive images of a British Afro-Caribbean extended family and as each character arrives at the house they first want to do something with the baby, such as squeeze him (Auntie Bibba), kiss him (Uncle Didi), eat him (Nanny and Gran-Gran), or fight him (Cousin Kay Kay and Big Cousin Ross):

> And they wrestle
> and they wrestle.
> He push the baby first,
> the baby hit him back.
> He gave the baby pinch,
> the baby gave him slap.
> And then they laugh
> and laugh and laugh.
> 'Huh huh huh!'
> (ibid.: 28)

The language of the book brilliantly uses some of the rhythms and repetitions of African English which links it with other writers such as the Guyanese poet John Agard. Once again, one of the core features of the book reflected in the title is based on a common childhood experience; the adult and child game: 'How big's baby?' or 'How much do we love you?'

Two books which continue this tradition of high-quality picture fiction are *Billy's Bucket* (Gray and Parsons, 2003) and *Traction Man is Here* (Grey, 2005).

Billy's Bucket describes a boy who wants a bucket for his birthday. Once filled with water he imagines all the amazing things that could be swimming around in it. The use of a humorous twist in the story revealed on the final page is reminiscent of Tony Ross's *I'm Coming to Get You*. *Traction Man* uses comic-strip features for its wonderfully evocative depiction of a boy's imagination inspired by his Action Man figure that he gets for Christmas.

Longer fiction

One of the challenges for teachers of Key Stage 2 children is developing knowledge of texts that are much longer than picture books. You will need to read novels for children in order to assess their usefulness for the classroom. The 'class reader', a book that you read to the whole class daily over an extended period, gives the opportunity to extend your own knowledge and the knowledge of the children about such texts. A good strategy for locating books is to use guides: *The Ultimate Book Guide* (Hahn *et al.*, 2004), covering books for children aged 8–12 is a very good example. The internet has a huge range of information about books, not least from publishers who are finding increasingly imaginative ways to market their books.

In Chapter 5 we recommend two longer novels and show you ways of working with them. One of these is from a modern English author and the other is an established English classic. There is also some outstanding children's literature coming from the USA, in particular, the stunning book called *Holes* by Louis Sachar (2000). The precise control of language shown through the author's voice and the clever use of plot are unlike any other book of recent years.

The phenomenon of crossover texts which appeal to adults and children alike was most powerfully demonstrated by the Harry Potter books by J. K. Rowling. *The Curious Incident of the Dog in the Night* by Mark Hadden has also been described as a crossover text but its themes of adultery and killing place it in a very different position to Harry Potter. The Alex Rider books, which are particularly popular with boys, were marketed as James Bond for children: the way that they draw on the adult film franchise is related to this concept of crossover.

Published schemes

In the past there has been much debate about the merits of reading scheme books (or *basal* readers as they say in the USA) versus 'real' books. The typical reading provision for most schools consisted of one or more reading schemes arranged into levels of difficulty. Usually this consisted of a core scheme of the school's choice supplemented by examples from other reading schemes and selections of real books. Children worked through the scheme individually and had to read all the books in the sequence until they were allowed to choose their own reading books. Unfortunately in some schools this practice continued as far as Year 5 or even Year 6 with children having little opportunity to choose their own books and develop preferences and interests. Here is an example of a text from one of the most popular reading schemes (GINN 360):

Help!
Where is Dad?
Dad, can you help?
I can help.
Here it is.
Dad, come here.
Can you help?
Yes, I can help.
Come in here.
Look, here it is.
No, stop!
Not in here.
Help! Where is Dad?
        (Oakley, 1988)

Many people have commented on the disjointed flow that such books have because of the controlled vocabulary that they use. You may also have noticed that there are no speech marks; presumably it is felt that young children will be confused by such things. Although you will be able to find some shocking and sometimes amusing examples of old-fashioned reading scheme texts, in recent years the publishers have brought out newer reading schemes that address some of the early problems. For example, Collins Pathways offered children choice within a graded band of books. Real authors, as opposed to consultants, wrote the books and the language was very close to that of real books:

Leon was given six chocolate dinosaurs for his birthday.
They were wrapped in silver paper.
Leon stood the dinosaurs in a long line in his bedroom.
'One, two, three, four, five, six!'
Just then his mum called him.
He ran downstairs to the kitchen, and while he was away who should spot the dinosaurs but Davina.
She was Leon's little sister.
        (Magee, 1994: 2–7)

Each time modifications are made to the Framework for Teaching, publishers work on new schemes and resources for teachers. In the period between 1997 and 2005 one of the biggest problems with these resources was their choice of texts. Frequently short extracts were used, often taken from texts no longer under copyright because this doesn't require the payments of permission fees. One of the guiding principles for our approach to teaching English is that complete, real texts should be used whenever possible in order to inspire children and as the basis for a range of analyses. We argue that uncritical use of schemes is poor practice. Here are some of the other limitations of some schemes:

1 They are not flexible enough to reflect the changing needs of your particular class.
2 They are written by consultants who often work under short time-scales which can result in poor materials.
3 They tend to be individualised and neglect collaborative learning.
4 The objectives are set by the scheme not by the teacher and this can result in lack of clear learning focus in your classroom.
5 They minimise the importance of talk because they tend to require individual work.
6 They tend to involve passive learning based on photocopied worksheets.

Non-fiction

Non-fiction texts for children have shown some dramatic improvements in the past 20 years. With the advent of the internet there was expectation that such improvements would be multiplied but this has not been as straightforward as expected (➡ Chapter 25 for examples of the benefits and limitations of internet sites). Before the developments in the internet, the publisher Dorling Kindersley extended the range and quality of information books for children. In particular, it set new standards through the visual images and presentation of its books. Some of its best texts were aimed at young children who in the past had very little choice as far as non-fiction was concerned.

Another publisher who changed the face of non-fiction texts for young children and who continue to do so is Moonlight Publishing who have produced a stunning set of non-fiction books for children that use innovative physical features to enhance their appeal. One of the early books from the series is called *Fruit* (Valat *et al.*, 1990). It doesn't sound particularly promising, does it? The first page shows a striking picture of red apple which makes your mouth water. It realistically includes the stalk, with leaf attached, and a small imperfection in the skin. The text?: 'Do you like eating apples?' So simple yet something that could open a stream of thoughts for the young child. The language of the book as a whole brilliantly mixes crystal-clear explanations with new vocabulary such as 'Boskoop; Starking; Russet and Cox'. This elegant simplicity is all the more surprising when you realise that it has been translated from French. Perhaps the book's *pièce de résistance* is its use of acetate overlay pages which literally add layers of meaning. So when you turn the first page the reverse of the red apple shows its inside, complete with pips. The question which previously had been viewed through the clear bottom of the acetate is still visible but six different apples' names with pictures are displayed along with a simple caption. The books procedes to take us through cutting apples; growing from a pip; trees in different seasons; fruits from around the world; a safety warning about which fruits in the countryside you can eat; and a final image of a French fruit *tarte* – yum!

For older children, *A Street Through Time* (Millard and Noon, 1998) is a large format book which shows the way that a street looks through several hundred years of history. The changes are fascinating, particularly what happens after the Romans leave. Talking of Romans, our final recommendation is the *Horrible Histories* series. The information in these is densely packed, at a level suitable for Key Stages 2 and 3, historically accurate and complete with cautions about history being interpretative, but the success lies in the humorous and varied way that the subjects are presented.

Practice points

- Your knowledge of *all* the texts that you use with children needs to constantly improve throughout your teaching career.
- Use published schemes with caution and read them carefully before you use them.
- Enjoy the ever increasing range of texts that are available including those on the internet.

Glossary

Classics – books that remain of interest to significant numbers of people long after their initial publication date. They are also regarded to be of special significance.

Picture books – books for children where the pictures are equally as important as the text. Larger than A5 children's novels with full-colour artistic illustrations.

Semantic levels – the different meanings or interpretations that are possible: from basic to complex.

Sub-plots – story lines that are additional to the main one.

Surrealist – art particularly linked with the work of Salvador Dali. The paintings contain bizarre dreamlike images such as melting clocks drooped over tree branches.

References

Ahlberg, A. and Ahlberg, J. (1978) *Each Peach Pear Plum*. London: Penguin.

Arizpe, E. and Styles, M. (2003) *Children Reading Pictures: Interpreting Visual Texts*. London: RoutledgeFalmer.

Browne, A. (1977) *A Walk in the Park*. London: Macmillan.

Browne, A. (1983) *Gorilla*. London: Random Century.

Browne, A. (1985) *Willy the Champ*. London: Little Mammoth.

Browne, A. (1989) *Piggybook*. London: Reed Consumer Books.

Browne, A. (1992) *The Tunnel*. London: Walker Books.

Carey, J. (1999) 'The very busy author', *Guardian*, November 23.

Carle, E. (1970) *The Very Hungry Caterpillar*. London: Penguin Books.

Cooke, T. (1994) *So Much!* London: Walker Books.

Gray, K. and Parsons, G. (2003) *Billy's Bucket*. London: Red Fox.

Grey, M. (2005). *Traction Man is Here*. London: Jonathan Cape.

Hahn, D., Flynn, L. and Reuben, S. (eds) (2004) *The Ultimate Book Guide*. London: A & C Black.

Kitamura, S. (1987) *Lily Takes a Walk*. London: Picture Corgi.

Magee, W. (1994) *Davina and the Dinosaurs*. London: Collins Educational.

Millard, A. and Noon, S. (1998) *A Street through Time*. London: Dorling Kindersley.

Oakley, H. (1988) *On My Bike*. Aylesbury: Ginn.

Sachar, L. (2000) *Holes*. London: Bloomsbury.

Valat, P. M., Jeunesse, G. and de Bourgoing, P. (1990) *Fruit*. London: Moonlight Publishing.

Acknowledgements

Extract from *So Much!* reproduced by permission of the publisher, Walker Books Ltd, London. Text © 1994 Trishe Cooke, illustrated by Helen Oxenbury.

Annotated bibliography

Hahn, D., Flynn, L. and Reuben, S. (eds) (2004) *The Ultimate Book Guide*. London: A & C Black.
  Excellent selection of books with some illustrations accompanied by thoughtful comments.
  L1 *

Hunt, P. (ed.) (2004) *International Companion Encyclopedia of Children's Literature*, 2nd edn., vol. 1. London: Routledge.
  A comprehensive account of recent work in the children's literature field. A tremendous achievement.
  L3 ***

Meek, M. (1988) *How Texts Teach What Readers Learn*. Stroud: The Thimble Press.
  Argues strongly for the importance of specific high-quality texts as one of the main things that will help children learn to read.
  L2 **

Wray, D. and Lewis, M. (1997) *Extending Literacy: Children Reading and Writing Non-fiction*. London: Routledge.

This book is based on the Exeter University Extending Literacy Project which has been influential. Practical examples are given that show how children can be encouraged to engage with non-fiction texts.
L2 **

Chapter 5

Working with texts

We consider two main kinds of texts in this chapter: picture books and longer stories. Having selected some favourite texts of our own we show the kinds of points that can inform your interaction and the kinds of activities that might take place inspired by the texts.

During the busy work of thinking about teaching objectives from the literacy framework it is possible to forget that your most important job is to inspire children to read for themselves. As we showed in Chapter 4, having read widely, you will have identified some favourite books that you want to share with the children in your class. The first time you read the text aloud to the class is vital: it is a time for your story-telling skills. How do you start? Sometimes it will be as simple as ensuring that the children are settled and then launching into a dramatic telling. At other times, particularly on subsequent readings, you will want to engage the children in discussion at various points during the reading. Having gained the children's interest, the main activities of the session will develop the children's understanding of the text and their reading more generally. It is important to remember that the analysis of texts should not be at the expense of enjoyment and personal response. Many readers cite occasions when they felt they could have enjoyed a particular book but it was 'done to death' at school. Some people can despise this kind of process so much that it can be difficult for them to recover a love of reading.

One of the main principles of working with texts is that the children should experience whole texts, rather than extracts, wherever possible. This is because the meaning of an extract can only be fully understood in relation to the text as a whole. Another principle is that these texts should be real texts not poor imitations designed to address teaching objectives rather than for a real purpose and readership. The analysis of the features of real texts leads to a more accurate knowledge and a more rewarding experience. Although there are naturally short texts such as some poems, working with complete texts necessitates longer periods of work. For example, the whole class needs to read a novel in order to engage in activities that you set although on some occasions the work can usefully proceed chapter by chapter.

Picture books

A useful strategy for developing children's understanding of texts in the early years is the use of props to engage children's play. *Story sacks* contain things such as puppets for the characters, key objects from the story, non-fiction books related to the topic of the story, extracts of text-only or pictures-only for matching, games to play, etc. Sometimes the story sacks remain in the setting, at other times they are borrowed by families to enhance the reading experience with their child. A particularly worthwhile activity can be to involve children (and parents) in the making of story sacks which become a valuable resource during the year and which the child gets to keep once they finish the year. Bromley (2000) advocates the making of games related to books in order to extend children's understanding.

As children get older the need for physical resources lessens (although puppets, for example, have value throughout the primary school). The exploration is more abstract although close attention to the texts themselves routes the work in a productive context. Anthony Browne's book *Voices in the Park* can be used in Key Stage 1 or Key Stage 2. It is one of few picture books that addresses the issue of social class. At a straightforward level the book is about different children and their parents going to the park. As usual, Brown's surreal illustrations are a source of endless fascination for children. The narrative (☞) is organised into four *voices*. Each voice represents a different social background. The nuances of text and illustration that characterise the voices even stretch to different fonts. The following list is based on Merchant and Thomas's (1999) ideas about how this text might be used:

The whole text

- Group of four children. Each reads a different voice. Discuss what the narrator for each section is like, what they think about things and how they feel.
- Make notes in four columns about the nature of the different voices.
- Discuss how the illustrations and other visual things change for the different voices? How do the illustrations reflect the feelings of the characters? Make a list of the events that happen to different characters.
- Choose one point (such as when the son is called to go home) and compare across the different voices.
- Encourage the children to imagine that they were a fifth voice/character and write their account.

Sentences and words

- Compare the descriptive phrases that are used. For example, 'a very rough looking child' described by the mother is called 'quite nice' by the boy.
- Use speech bubbles to write the different things that the voices might say about: a roller coaster; a lost kitten; a television.
- Choose some adjectives that best describe the different voices.

Cross-curricular themes

- Work with a partner. Describe in writing an event that both children have experienced. Compare the different perspectives.
- Make a drawing of an object from at least two different visual perspectives and think about how this is similar to the idea of perspectives in the book.
- Think about historical events or media stories described from different perspectives.

Links to other texts

Voices in the Park is a reworking of *A Walk in the Park* also by Browne. Try reworking another Anthony Browne text.

Longer stories

A wonderful book written for this age-range in recent years is *Skellig*, by David Almond. The plot focuses on something that a boy called Michael finds at the back of the dilapidated garage that's part of the house he has just moved into. The other plot line concerns the health of Michael's baby sister who has a heart problem. Throughout the book, Almond portrays Michael's uncertainties and worries about his sister in the most authentic and touching way. Towards the end of the book, his sister recovers from an operation, and mum and the baby return home:

> 'Welcome home, Mum,' I whispered, using the words I'd practised. She smiled at how nervous I was. She took my hand and led me back into the house, into the kitchen. She sat me on a chair and put the baby in my arms. 'Look how beautiful your sister is,' she said. 'Look how strong she is.' I lifted the baby higher. She arched her back as if she was about to dance or fly. She reached out, and scratched with her tiny nails at the skin on my face. She tugged at my lips and touched my tongue. She tasted of milk and salt and of something mysterious, sweet and sour all at once. She whimpered and gurgled. I held her closer and her dark eyes looked right into me, right into the place where all my dreams were, and she smiled.

'She'll have to keep going for check-ups,' Mum said. 'But they're sure the danger's gone, Michael. Your sister is really going to be all right.'

We laid the baby on the table and sat around her. We didn't know what to say. Mum drank her tea. Dad let me have swigs of his beer. We just sat there looking at each other and touching each other and we laughed and laughed and we cried and cried.

(p. 168)

The use of language in this passage is exquisite. The human senses of sight, touch, smell and taste overwhelm us. The image of the view through the eyes to 'the place where all my dreams were' is striking. The profound relief about the baby's escape from death is made more poignant by the seemingly mundane language of 'swigs' of beer.

Skellig is good for children of 9 or 10 onwards because it's a gripping story. But like all the best children's literature it also encourages a greater depth of thought in its readers through its recurring themes. Its main theme is a celebration of life, but this is contrasted with exploration about what happens to things when they die. Another theme concerns learning and education. Michael meets a new friend called Mina. One of their discussions is about owls and Almond uses the opportunity to present factual information about owls in the guise of the children's curiosity. During another one of their conversations, we hear Mina's description of her learning. This section perhaps reveals some of Almond's beliefs:

'My mother educates me,' she said. 'We believe that schools inhibit the natural curiosity, creativity and intelligence of children. The mind needs to be opened out into the world, not shuttered down inside a gloomy classroom.'

(p. 15)

The kinds of questions that might follow a reading of this passage start with some straightforward ones to check understanding and proceed to much more searching ones that require inference ☞

- What happens in the passage?
- Have you ever been worried about a brother or sister?
- Which sentences describe the use of the senses?
- Why did they laugh *and* cry?
- Where is the place, 'where all my dreams were'? Why is this such a striking metaphor?
- What does 'swigs' mean? Why does Almond use this word here?

These kinds of questions could address the objective: 'Infer writers' perspectives from what is written and from what is implied' in particular. The objective 'Use knowledge of word derivations and word structure, e.g. affixes, acronyms, and letter omission, to construct the meaning of words in context' is more difficult to address meaningfully with this extract although discussion about 'swigs' would involve thinking about derivation in terms of dialect.

Having engaged the children in discussion about the text, the lesson turns to main activities. Let's change our focus to another excellent text, this time a classic: *Goodnight Mr Tom*. The use of drama, sometimes for its own sake and sometimes leading to writing, can be a very good way to explore texts. Using the first chapter of *Goodnight Mr Tom* we might do the following:

- *Mime*: Children identify a character and portray their body language in the scene.
- *Freeze frame*: Children work in small groups to create opening scene then freeze the position.
- *Speaking thoughts*: Select children from the groups to voice the thoughts of their character.
- *Conscience alley*: Divide the class into two large groups. One half of the class should think about reasons why Mr Tom *should* take the child, the other half argue why he shouldn't. After the preparation time, 'Mr Tom' walks down the 'alley' formed by the two groups facing each other. He approaches and/or indicates children to 'voice their conscience' about the issue when Mr Tom passes them.
- *Acting in pairs*: Tom and Willie – the tour or Tom's house or the first meal.
- *Storying*: Three large groups representing the Billeting Officer(s), the evac-uees, and the hosts. Each of the sets discusses experiences with others in similar position. Individuals from the groups are encouraged to share their experiences, in role.
- *Hot seating*: Three children to play Tom, Willie, and the Billeting Officer. Others in class to come up with questions for each character.
- *Moving to film:* Draw a picture to show what the first three scenes will look like. Make a list of sounds/music that will be heard in the first scene.
- *Compare with the film*: Show opening and analyse the differences the text and film.

(I am grateful to Ainé Sharkey for the origins of some of these ideas.)

Another way to think about texts is through structure. One of the most commonly cited ideas about story structure is that they have a beginning, middle and end (or as Philip Larkin mischievously suggested a beginning, *muddle* and end). Martin *et al.* (1987) developed this simple idea about struc-ture and suggested further categories: Abstract; Orientation; Complication; Evaluation; Resolution; and Coda as stages in stories. Wray and Medwell (1997) modify the structure and relate it to *Little Red Riding Hood* as shown in Box 5.1.

This structure gives you the opportunity to explore the ways in which other stories may fit the model. At text level, structures like this are one way that

Box 5.1 *Story structure*		
Martin et al. (1987)	*Wray and Medwell (1997)*	
Abstract	Title of the story and introductory ideas	*Little Red Riding Hood*
Orientation	Setting of the story including characters	A forest and the two cottages
Complication	The main event	Red Riding Hood meets the wolf dressed as her grandmother
Evaluation	The impact of the main event on the characters	She runs away and finds the woodcutter
Resolution	The final implications of the main event	The woodcutter kills the wolf
Coda	Ending the story	The moral

writing maintains cohesion ☞. Each stage requires the one before it if the text is to make sense. Of course one of the interesting things about any kind of model like this is the way that so many texts do not simply conform. Traditional tales such as *Little Red Riding Hood* are often used as illustrations to show how such structures work. However, narrative is a wildly diverse form which resists simple classification. How well would this structure apply to some of the following: the script of the film *Pulp Fiction*, which contains three linked stories; multi-author internet texts; choose your own adventure texts; or *Bridget Jones's Diary*? You will also be familiar with narrative devices such as flashbacks (e.g. *Carrie's War*: Bawden, 1973) and traditional stories told from different points of view (e.g. *The True Story of the Three Little Pigs*: Scieszka, 1989) which make this kind of classification difficult.

The other thing to remember about this kind of structural analysis is that it is only one way of analysing texts. For example, we might choose to analyse the text by exploring the idea that *Little Red Riding Hood* is overtly about the dangers of child abuse. At first sight this might seem a bit extreme or that we are reading *too much* into the text (can one read too much?). However, a useful website provides us with a translation of Perrault's original written version:

> The wolfe seeing her come in, said to her, hiding himself under the clothes. Put the custard, and the little pot of butter upon the stool, and come into bed with me. The Little Red Riding-Hood undressed her self, and went to

bed, where she was very much astonished to see how her grandmother looked in her night-cloaths . . .

THE MORAL . . .

With luring tongues, and language wondrous sweet,
Follow young ladies as they walk the street,
Ev'n to their very houses and bedside,
And though their true designs they artful hide,
Yet ah! these simpring Wolves, who does not see
Most dang'rous of all Wolves in fact to be?

(Salda, 2000)

Our analysis here has been historical as we decided to locate one of the original versions – although like other traditional stories these started their lives as oral tales. The analysis also took a social dimension by hypothesising about the link with abuse. The 'moral' of the tale, written in rhyming couplets, once again leads us to question whether the narrative structure that we illustrated above can be universally applied.

Practice points

- Encourage children to think about texts in a variety of ways: some structured by you, and others taken from their own ideas.
- Develop your critical appreciation of texts including a strong understanding of inference and bias.
- Keep a balance between analysis and straightforward enjoyment.

Glossary

Cohesion – the way that different parts of a text work together to convey meaning.

Inference – the knowledge of textual meanings beyond the literal or 'obvious'.

Narrative – a text which retells events often in chronological sequence.

References

Bawden, N. (1973) *Carrie's War*. London: Victor Gollancz.

Bromley, H. (2000) *Book-based Reading Games*. London: Centre for Language in Primary Education.

Martin, J. R., Christie, F. and Rothery, J. (1987) 'Social processes in education: a reply to Sawyer and Watson (and others)', in I. Reid (ed.) *The Place of Genre in Learning*. Victoria: Deakin University.

Merchant, G. and Thomas, H. (eds) (1999) *Picture Books for the Literacy Hour*. London: David Fulton.

Salda, M. N. (2000) *The Little Red Riding Hood Project.* University of Southern Mississippi. Version 1.0, December 1995. Drawn from the 'de Grummond Children's Literature Research Collection. [online – cited 23 Jan. 2000] http://www.dept.usm.edu/~engdept/lrrh/lrrhhome.htm

Scieszka, J. (1989) *The True Story of the Three Little Pigs!* London: Penguin.

Annotated bibliography

Arizpe, E. and Styles, M. (2003) *Children Reading Pictures: Interpreting Visual Texts.* London: RoutledgeFalmer.
Wonderful exploration of children's responses to pictures coupled with interviews of picture book authors.
L3 **

Barrs, M. and Cork, V. (2001) *The Reader in the Writer.* London: Centre for Language in Primary Education (CLPE).
A detailed look at how teachers use texts to stimulate writing and the impact such texts had on children.
L2 **

Hayhoe, M. and Parker, S. (1990) *Reading and Response.* Buckingham: Open University Press.
A useful link between education and studies of English literature. Tackles the idea that texts are never one-dimensional and that readers apply all kinds of different interpretations and analyses to the texts that they read.
L3 ***

Sarland, C. (1991) *Young People Reading: Culture and Response.* Milton Keynes: Open University Press.
Sarland raises the question of popular versus classical texts. He found that children's views about popular films such as *Rambo* were worthy of interest by teachers.
L3 ***

Chapter 6

Listening to children read

Listening to children read is a key area of understanding for teachers. The chapter addresses this in the context of shared and paired reading. It concludes with thoughts about the kinds of conversations that take place with more experienced readers.

The advent of the National Literacy Strategy brought with it an abrupt move away from an emphasis on reading with individual children to an emphasis on whole class and small group reading (➡ Chapter 8, 'Routines for reading'). Literacy in the Primary National Strategy maintains the emphasis on shared and guided reading and adds more discrete teaching of reading through phonics. The lack of attention to one-to-one reading perhaps needs further thought. The teacher's ability to interact with a small group, or a whole class can be greatly enhanced if they understand the subtleties of reading with an individual child. In the early years in particular, the supportive, personal context of one-to-one reading is very important. The strategy can provide a natural link with the kinds of reading that many children experience at home with parents and other family members. In addition, if teachers are to advise parents on effective ways of working with their children, then they need to be knowledgeable and effective at one-to-one reading themselves. One-to-one reading is also important because of its significant value to struggling readers. Teachers who work with struggling readers themselves or who delegate this responsibility to teaching assistants need to fully understand the possibilities of one-to-one reading.

Shared reading

The term *shared reading* or *shared read* is now associated with a whole class objective-led lesson which features a text that a whole class can access, either one that is enlarged electronically or a *big book* ☞. It is used throughout the primary phase (➡ Chapter 8). However, this was not the original idea of shared reading.

Don Holdaway developed a system called 'shared book experience' in 1979. Although he was one of the first to recommend the use of big books, because they enabled the group of children to see the print clearly, his approach had other aspects that are not part of the PNS version of shared reading. Holdaway's approach was cross-curricular, for example, involving the children in the making of enlarged versions of favourite picture books with an emphasis on the artwork required for the pictures. Phonics teaching was included as part of the shared book experience rather than as a separate session. Holdaway's developmental approach recognised and built upon children's prior experiences. For example, acknowledging the importance of the 'pre-school bedtime story learning cycle':

1   The parent introduces a new story. The child is curious so they ask questions and predict the things that are likely to happen next.
2   If the child likes the story, they ask for it to be re-read immediately and/or later on. They participate more each time they hear the story. The number of questions they ask increases.
3   If the book is stored somewhere accessible, they use it later to play at reading and to re-enact the story independently which gives them additional satisfaction.
4   Further re-readings result in the child becoming more familiar with the book.
5   Play-reading and re-enactment become closer to the language of the text.
6   The concepts, language and attributes of the story are extended into play.
7   The book may become an 'old favourite' and/or attention turns to the beginning of the cycle with a new book.

The practice of shared reading in England prior to the NLS was defined by Campbell (1995: 132): 'Shared reading involves a child and a teacher (or other adult) reading together, in a one-to-one interaction, from a book.' The following example from Campbell (1990) is indicative. The extract is from a shared reading session that took place over a period of approximately five minutes which ended with the teacher and the child discussing the story for a few minutes more and the child telling of her own pet's adventures.

Five-year-old Kirsty was sharing a new book with her teacher. First, the teacher read the story while Kirsty looked at the pictures. Then they read through the story again with the teacher asking Kirsty questions that drew her into conversation about different incidents in the story. Then, when the teacher felt Kirsty was ready, she asked her to read aloud:

Teacher: Your turn to read it, All right, let's see.
Kirsty: The dog sees a box.

Teacher:	Mmmh.
Kirsty:	He sniffs in the box.
Teacher:	He sniffs it, doesn't he?
Kirsty:	He kicks the box. He climbs in the box.
Teacher:	Oh, now what happens?
Kirsty:	He falls down the stairs. The dog falls out the box. The (hesitates)
Teacher:	The (pauses)
Kirsty:	The dog falls over.
Teacher:	He does, doesn't he?
	Then what does he try to do?

Original text:

> The dog sees the box.
> The dog sniffs the box.
> The dog kicks the box.
> The dog gets in the box.
> The dog gets out of the box.
> The dog falls over.
>   (Campbell 1990: 29–30)

Although Kirsty was not reading every word accurately, the meaning of the text had largely been retained, so the teacher did not correct the child, although she did make several interjections to support and encourage Kirsty's reading. When the child hesitated, the teacher simply restarted the sentence, then paused, prompting Kirsty to respond appropriately. Such one-to-one interactions can effectively take place with all levels and ages of children learning to read in the primary school. The level of text may change, but the principles of encouragement, support, discussion, instruction and enjoyment will not.

Paired reading

Hearing reading on a one-to-one basis is the natural way that parents work with their children. Early years settings and primary schools have encouraged parents to read with their children by sending home books along with reading diaries (➡ Chapter 24). However, there are some who believe that parents should use more structured approaches than simply sharing books with their children. Leach and Siddall (1990) favoured an approach called *Direct Instruction*. This approach includes materials which are sequentially arranged in pre-planned lessons. The lessons are scripted to include the specific language to be used and explanations about how to guide children's responses and how to correct errors. Another structured method that has documented its success through research outcomes is paired reading. Keith Topping developed the paired reading approach. Although the approach is structured, it is not too technical; a pragmatic consideration that has to be taken into account with any method for parents. Paired reading involves the following stages:

1   Ideally, the child chooses the book or text to be read.
2   The book should be briefly discussed before reading aloud commences.
3   The adult and the child begin by reading the text aloud together.
4   The child may follow the text with a finger.
5   When the child wants to read alone they indicate this by tapping the table or arm of the adult.
6   The adult ceases reading immediately and praises the child for signalling.
7   The child continues alone.
8   When a child makes a miscue, the adult supplies the word.
9   The child then repeats the word.
10 Praise is given for the correct reading of difficult words and for self-corrections ☞.
11 If a child is unable to read a word or correct an error in about 5 seconds, the adult and child return to reading in unison.
12 The child makes the signal when they feel confident enough to resume reading alone.
13 Further praise and encouragement are given at the end of the session.

One important feature of paired reading is that the adult provides a model of appropriate reading behaviour for the child alongside the child's own attempts at reading satisfactorily.

Reading with more experienced readers

As children's reading becomes more fluent, the priorities for one-to-one reading change. For the majority of children, efficient use of teachers' time can be made by gradually moving towards more emphasis on group reading. Overall there is less of a need for one-to-one sessions for fluent readers, however, this does not mean that they should be completely abandoned. One of the most important things that can be discovered by talking to a child about their reading in the one-to-one session is their motivation for reading. Do they read for pleasure? If so, what kinds of texts are they interested in? A motivated reader is surely one who is likely to progress further in their understanding of English than one who is not motivated. The one-to-one session also allows for a more in-depth exploration of children's understanding of and response to particular texts.

Another thing that one-to-one sessions can help with is the identification of struggling readers. Although small group reading is supposed to enable the teacher to work with individuals there is some risk that children with reading difficulties might not be identified during a small group read. A one-to-one session is an ideal opportunity to assess a child's understanding of a text, their ability to decode the words, and any problems in these areas. If the teacher aims to read individually with every child in their class at the beginning and towards the end of the year, this can provide a very useful addition to their assessment of the child's learning.

Practice points

- Make time for extended one-to-one reading with individual children at least twice per year.
- Constantly work at refining your skills of interaction when supporting children's reading aloud.
- Think carefully about the way that children read texts aloud: in particular, assess their comprehension and the strategies they use when attempting any problem words.

Glossary

Big book – enlarged version of children's book designed to aid group reading.
Self-correction – the ability to recognise miscues during reading and to correct them yourself. An important facet of reading skills.

References

Campbell, R. (1990) *Reading Together*. Buckingham: Open University Press.
Campbell, R. (1995) *Reading in the Early Years Handbook*. Buckingham: Open University Press.
Durkin, D. (1966). *Children who Read Early*. New York: Teachers College Press.
Leach, D. and Siddall, S. (1990) 'Parental involvement in the teaching of reading: a comparison of hearing reading, paired reading, pause, prompt, praise, and direct instruction methods', *British Journal of Educational Psychology*, 60: 349–355.

Annotated bibliography

Campbell, R. (1995) *Reading in the Early Years Handbook*. Buckingham: Open University Press.
Sixty different topics relating to reading are presented alphabetically and succinctly. Each of these is followed by suggestions for further reading in the very useful form of annotated bibliographies. A number of interesting classroom examples are included to focus on specific concerns.
L2 **
Hall, K. (2003) *Listening to Stephen Read: Multiple Perspectives On Literacy*. Buckingham: Open University Press.
A wonderful example of different perspectives on a child's reading.
L2 **

Singleton, C. (2005) 'Dyslexia and oral reading errors', *Journal of Research in Reading*, 28(1): 4–14.
  Makes the case that the study of oral reading is still of value to the teacher and researcher alike.
  L3 ***
Topping, K. (2006) 'Thinking reading writing', retrieved October 24, 2006, from http://www.dundee.ac.uk/fedsoc/research/projects/trw/
  This website includes an extensive analysis of paired reading studies.
  L1 ** **and L3** ***

Chapter 7

Phonics

Phonics teaching is one of the key aspects of early reading. This chapter introduces some of the main ideas that you need to be aware of as you start teaching reading. We discuss examples from the PNS advice and from commercial phonics teaching schemes.

Phonics is commonly known as a method of teaching children to read. One of the most recent manifestations of what is a very long-running debate was the arguments about whether synthetic or analytic phonics is more effective. The American National Reading Panel (National Institute of Child Health and Human Development, 2000) described *synthetic phonics* programmes as those that emphasise teaching students to convert letters (graphemes) ☞ into sounds (phonemes) ☞ and then to blend the sounds to form recognisable words. *Analytic phonics*, on the other hand, is taken to refer to larger-unit phonics programmes, which introduce children to whole words before teaching them to analyse these into their component parts, and emphasise the larger subparts of words (i.e. onsets, rimes, phonograms, spelling patterns) as well as phonemes. However, at the heart of all phonics teaching is the idea that you can and should teach children about 'phonemes'. Many children develop some general knowledge of sounds – i.e. they develop some 'phonological awareness' ☞ – before they enter school.

One of the ideas that has emerged from the research on phonics is the significance of onsets ☞ and rimes ☞, the beginnings and ends of syllables. An understandable mistake is to confuse 'rime' and 'rhyme': the following poem helps to illustrate this:

Spellbound

I have a spelling chequer
It came with my PC
It plainly marks four my revue
Miss takes I cannot sea.

I've run this poem threw it
I'm shore your pleased too no;
It's letter perfect in it's weigh
My chequer tolled me sew.
(Vandal, 1996: 14)

The *rhymes* in lines 2 and 4, and 6 and 8, are present because the 'rime' of the words 'C' (letter names are also words, in this case spelled 'cee') and 'sea', and 'no' and 'sew' are the same. This poem nicely illustrates the problems that we can have when representing phonemes with letters.

Using the concept of onset and rime, Goswami (1995: 139) emphasised the importance of reading by analogy: 'Analogies in reading involve using the spelling-sound pattern of one word, such as *beak*, as a basis for working out the spelling-sound correspondence of a new word, such as *peak*.' Children's development of phonological understanding tends to proceed from the ability to identify syllables, then onsets and rimes, and finally the ability to segment phonemes. The use of analogies draws on children's early recognition of onsets and rimes.

In order to see further potential for analogies, it is necessary to briefly look at the irregularity of English. It has often been pointed out that the links between sound and symbol in the English language are notoriously irregular and Frank Smith (1978) raised this in his controversial chapter 'The fallacy of phonics'. For example, what is the sound of the vowel phoneme in the following word: 'read'? You may have assumed that it was /ee/. However, if we explained that the sentence context is 'Yesterday I read a good book', then it is clear that not just the meaning of the word but the meaning of the sentence as a whole has an impact on the particular vowel phoneme. This perhaps reached the height of irregularity in the name of the university department, 'The Centre for Reading in Reading'. Also, consider the way that the /sh/ phoneme is represented in the following words: appreciate, ocean, machine, moustache, stanchion, fuchsia, schist, conscious, extension, pressure, admission, sure, initiate, attention, and luxury.

A short anecdote helps us to explore further the irregularities of sounds and symbols. A child in one of the classes we were teaching was writing a book with the following joke:

Saima: Will you remember me tomorrow?
Dominic: Yes.
S: Will you remember me in a week?
D: Yes.
S: Will you remember me in a month?
D: Yes.
S: Will you remember me in a year?
D: Yes.

S: Knock, knock.
D: Who's there?
S: You've forgotten me already!

Saima was stuck on the spelling for 'remember' and I was about to suggest that she sound out the word, when it struck me that each time the letter 'e' is used in 'remember' it represents a different phoneme.

One of the important aspects of onset and rime is that when young children learn nursery rhymes and simple songs, their awareness of sounds is raised and it is often their attention to the rime of the words that is strong. Because this is the case, it has been argued that teaching which emphasises onset and rime can be beneficial particularly if it is linked to the different ways that onsets and rimes can be written down. Children's understanding of rime seems to be part of a normal developmental process whereas the ability to segment phonemes does not come so naturally.

Teaching phonemes

The English language has 26 letters which are used to represent the 44 phonemes. All the words in the English language are spoken using combinations of the 44 phonemes. All the words in the English language are written using combinations of the 26 letters. Table 7.1 was taken from the first version of the government's *Playing with Sounds* (DfES and PNS, 2004) resource that was designed to support the teaching of reading in the early years. Table 7.1 shows all 44 phonemes and gives examples of phonemes in the context of words. It is organised into consonant phonemes and vowel phonemes.

An important concept is the way that different groups of letters represent the same sound. For example, if you look at the vowel phoneme /ie/ which is the long I sound, you can see that the examples of words given are 'tried, light, my, shine, mind'. The idea that the letters 'igh' represent the /ie/ sound can be counter-intuitive for some people. The old-fashioned way would be to say that these letters sound as /i/ /g/ /h/. But if we said this, it would mean that we would pronounce the word 'light' as 'liguhut' which of course would be ridiculous (although this can be one useful strategy to remember spellings)! So, it is quite accurate to say that the /ie/ sound in the spoken word can be represented in the written word by the letters 'ie' or 'igh' or 'y' or 'ine'.

Following the Rose Report (➡ Chapter 1), the government introduced a strict sequence of teaching for phonics.

Introducing grapheme–phoneme correspondences
Children should be taught the 26 letters of the alphabet and a sound for each letter. They should be taught to write each letter, forming it correctly. Once correspondences have been taught, they should be frequently revised and practised so that responses are automatic. Sounds should be produced

Table 7.1 Phonemes and representative words

Consonant phonemes and their more usual graphemes

consonant phonemes	International Phonetic Alphabet	representative words	consonant phonemes	International Phonetic Alphabet	representative words
/b/	b	baby	/r/	r	rabbit, wrong
/d/	d	dog	/s/	s	sun, mouse, city, science
/f/	f	field, photo	/t/	t	tap
/g/	g	game	/v/	v	van
/h/	h	hat	/w/	w	was
/j/	d₃	judge, giant, barge	/y/	i	yes
/k/	k	cook, quick, mix, Chris	/z/	z	zebra, please, is
/l/	l	lamb	/th/	ð	then
/m/	m	monkey, comb	/th/	θ	thin
/n/	n	nut, knife, gnat	/ch/	ʃ	chip, watch
/ng/	ŋ	ring, sink	/sh/	ʃ	ship, mission, chef
/p/	p	paper	zh/	₃	treasure

Vowel phonemes and their more usual graphemes

vowels	International Phonetic Alphabet	representative words	vowels	International Phonetic Alphabet	representative words
/a/	æ	cat	/oo/	u	look, would, put
/e/	e	peg, bread	/ar/	a:	cart, fast (*regional*)
/i/	ɒ	pig, wanted	/ur/	₃:	burn, first, term, heard, work
/o/	ɒ	log, want	/au/	œ	torn, door, warn, haul, law, call
/u/	ʌ	plug, love	/er/	ə	wooden, circus, sister
/ae/	eɪ	pain, day, gate, station	/ow/	au	down, shout
/ee/	i:	sweet, heat, thief, these	/oi/	ɔɪ	coin, boy
/ie/	aɪ	tried, light, my, shine, mind	/air/	ɛə	stairs, bear, hare
/oe/	ou	road, blow, bone, cold	/ear/	ɪə	fear, beer, here
/ue/	u:	moon, blue, grew, tune	/ure/	ʊ0	pure, tourist

phonemes are shown between slashes //

quickly in response to letters, and letters should be pointed to or written quickly in response to sounds. Blending and segmenting need to be taught explicitly.

Reading and spelling simple regular words

The skills of blending and segmenting CVC words are easily adapted to words containing consecutive consonants in CCVC and CVCC words (such as 'spit' and 'mint') and then to more complex words (such as 'split' or 'crust'). This is an important phase for widening the words available to children for reading.

Introducing sounds that are represented by more than one letter

Sounds that can be represented only by letter-groups (mostly digraphs, at this stage) should be taught: 'sh', 'ch', 'th' (these can represent two sounds, one 'voiced' and one 'unvoiced', as in 'thin' and 'then'), 'ng' ('sing'), 'ee', 'ay', 'ie' ('pie'), 'oa' ('boat'), 'oo' (two sounds, as in 'moon' and 'book'), 'or' ('port'), 'ar' ('car'), 'er' ('fern'), 'ow' ('town'), 'oy' ('boy'), 'air', 'ear'.

Introducing alternative grapheme–phoneme correspondences

Alternative sounds for spellings already covered should be taught. Such examples include the /s/ sound of 'c' ('city'), the /j/ sound of 'g' ('gem') and the /o/ sound of 'a'. This can often be covered during the teaching of high frequency words: for example, 'was' and 'want' illustrate the /o/ sound which 'a' tends to have after a /w/ sound.

Alternative spellings for the sounds already covered should also be taught. Examples would include 'ea' for the already-taught /ee/ sound, 'oe' for the already-taught /oa/ sound and 'igh' for the already-taught /ie111/ sound.

Introducing 'tricky' words

Once children are starting to blend CVC words, high frequency words that do not follow the letter-sound correspondences taught can be introduced. This may be done at the rate of two or three per week but the professional judgement of the pace must lie with the teacher or practitioner.

(Primary National Strategy, 2006: 7)

In the light of this sequence you need to decide how it will be taught. Schools can decide to develop their own programmes, just as individual teachers can. Or they could adopt a published scheme. One of the recurring issues in relation to teaching methods is the extent to which you as a professional have the autonomy to make decisions about the methods that you think will work best for your class. In 2007, this autonomy was further challenged with the plans to establish a panel to 'vet' commercial phonics programmes. The programmes that meet the government criteria are officially endorsed. Schools are then at liberty to select from these either a commercial programme or *Letters and Sounds*, the programme developed by the Primary National Strategy which replaced Playing with Sounds and *Progression in Phonics*.

One of the most popular commercial schemes is Jolly Phonics. The example from this series shown in Figure 7.1 is from *The Phonics Handbook* which provides photocopiable worksheets with each sheet covering one phoneme. Like some other programmes multi-sensory (☞) approaches are used so that each sheet is accompanied by an action that the children have to carry out. The phonemes are linked to a storyline to help the children remember them.

There are a number of more questionable ideas. The sheets include a picture related to the suggested storyline which is left blank for children to colour in; something that is not particularly educationally valuable. Additionally, a handwriting exercise is offered which encourages the children to write two letters that represent the phoneme. The problem here is a confusion of learning objectives (handwriting and learning phonemes) and the fact that most phonemes can be represented by a range of letter combinations, not just the ones that are offered.

One of the most controversial ideas of synthetic phonics programmes is the recommendation that books are withheld. In Jolly Phonics:

> During the first 8–9 weeks the aim is to prepare the children for reading books. Stories and poems are read to them, but the children are not expected to try and read books for themselves . . . Teachers and parents may find it difficult not to give children books to read in the first few weeks.
>
> (Lloyd, 1998: 25–26)

An example of another synthetic phonics teaching programme that was praised by the Rose Report also denies children books during the programme: 'This is a very accelerated form of phonics that does not begin by establishing an initial sight vocabulary. With this approach, before children are introduced to books, they are taught letter sounds' (House of Commons Education and Skills Committee, 2005: Ev 61).

There is a wealth of evidence pointing to the fact that pre-school children acquire a range of sophisticated understandings. Many 2-year-old children, for example, enjoy choosing books from their book shelves in the home and flicking through the pages or sharing the books with siblings or parents. The idea that when children come to school this opportunity to read books should be denied for 8–9 weeks seems extraordinary and does not fit with the recommendations of the PNS Framework.

th th
voiced and unvoiced th

ACTION

Child pretends to be a little rude by sticking out tongue a little and saying *th* (as in them), and very rude by sticking tongue further out and saying *th* (as in thumb).

that   **thin**

then   thumb

this   thick

feather thunder

with   moth

th

Figure 7.1 A page from the 'Jolly Phonics' scheme.

Practice points

- Phonics teaching should be carefully contextualised in real texts, sentences and words.
- Make a clear distinction between sounds and letters names. Help children to understand that various letter combinations can produce the same sound.
- Remember that learning to read is a complex process that requires a broad range of teaching strategies, of which phonics is one important part.

Glossary

Grapheme – written representation of a sound, e.g. a letter of the alphabet.

Multi-sensory – approaches that use sight, sound and touch to reinforce language learning.

Onset – any consonant sounds that come before the vowel, in a syllable.

Phoneme – the smallest unit of sound in a word.

Phonological awareness – understanding of the links between sounds and symbols.

Rime – the vowel and any consonants that follow the onset in a syllable.

References

Department for Education and Skills (DfES) and Primary National Strategy (PNS) (2004) *Playing with Sounds: A Supplement to Progression in Phonics*. London: DfES Publications.

Goswami, U. (1995) 'Phonological development and reading: what is analogy, and what is not?', *Journal of Research in Reading*, 18(2): 139–145.

House of Commons Education and Skills Committee (2005) *Teaching Children to Read: Eighth Report of Session 2004–2005. Report, Together with Formal Minutes, Oral and Written Evidence*: London: The Stationery Office.

Lloyd, S. (1998) *The Phonics Handbook*. Chigwell: Jolly Learning.

National Institute of Child Health and Human Development (2000) *Report of the National Reading Panel: Teaching Children to Read: An Evidence-based Assessment of the Scientific Research Literature on Reading and its Implications for Reading Instruction. Reports of the Subgroups* (NIH publication no. 00-4754). Washington, DC: US Government Printing Office.

Primary National Strategy (2006) 'Phonics and early reading: an overview for headteachers, literacy leaders and teachers in schools, and managers and practitioners in early years settings', *Guidance Papers*. Retrieved 2 February, 2006, from http://www.standards.dfes.gov.uk/primaryframeworks/literacy/Papers/

Smith, F. (1978) *Reading*. Cambridge: Cambridge University Press.

Vandal, N. (1996) 'Spellbound', in J. Foster (compiler) *Crack Another Yolk and Other Word Play Poems*. Oxford: Oxford University Press.

Annotated bibliography

Dombey, H., Moustafa, M. and the staff of the Centre for Language in Primary Education (CLPE) (1998) *Whole to Part Phonics: How Children Learn to Read and Spell*. London: CLPE.
A practical alternative to standard phonics approaches. This book shows how phonological understanding can be successfully developed in the context of whole texts first and foremost.
L1 **

Lewis, M. and Ellis, S. (eds) (2006) *Phonics: Practice Research and Policy*. London: Paul Chapman Publishing.
A very strong contribution to the debate on phonics teaching. This book clearly shows the complexities of phonics teaching and in the process reveals the inadequacies of a one-size-fits-all model.
L2 **

Torgerson, C. J., Brooks, G. and Hall, J. (2006) *A Systematic Review of the Research Literature on the Use of Phonics in the Teaching of Reading and Spelling*. London: Department for Education and Skills (DfES).
This review is restricted to research studies which were randomised controlled trials which the authors claim are most important kinds of studies for judging teaching effectiveness.
L3 ***

Chapter 8

Routines for reading

The aim of reading teaching is to develop enthusiastic and independent readers. This chapter illustrates some of the practical techniques that teachers need to adopt to support this aim. Thoughts on classroom organisation are followed by outlines of two significant strategies: shared and guided reading.

In Chapter 4 we underlined the importance of you reading widely in order to choose texts to inspire the children in your class. Your knowledge of texts for children influences many of the decisions you make about the teaching of literacy. It will enable you to select a class reader ☞ (or readers) which you will read daily and which will motivate and interest the children. Your reading and interaction with the children provide a powerful model of the reading process and show why books are fascinating. For this reason you should know the texts well and be willing to offer a dramatic telling, even if in performance terms this may be quite modest. The aim of reading teaching is to develop enthusiastic and independent readers.

One of the most straightforward influences that your wide reading will have is over your choice of texts for the areas in your classroom where books are stored, displayed and promoted. An initial consideration in any teacher's classroom is how space is utilised to the best possible effect. There are many advantages to a comfortable and attractive carpeted area which allows the class to sit together and share ideas. It has to be acknowledged, however, that the size of many classrooms makes this difficult to achieve. Whether there is a carpeted area or not, the classroom organisation needs to accommodate a range of teaching including discussion, shared reading, and word work, such as phonics. In the early years and at Key Stage 1, designated areas that support language and literacy work are useful. These include a reading area with comfortable seating such as cushions; listening points with CD players/computers and headphones; display areas such as 'author of the week'; message boards; and role-play areas. These areas are, arguably, very valuable at Key Stage 2 as well although role-play areas tend to be equated with early years and infant practice.

Whether you have a carpeted reading area or not, the display and storage of books are important considerations. As a teacher you need to know about the books in your reading area, you need to display them in a way that will entice children, and you need to think about how often books will need to be changed. There should be a wide range of fiction ☞, non-fiction ☞ and poetry, including books made by the class. Magazines and newspapers are often overlooked. This is partly because of the value that we put on books above other media and partly the fact that newspapers and magazines are not as durable as books. However, many children read these at home, particularly those who show reluctance to read fiction at school. For that reason we would recommend a regular occasion, perhaps one day per week, where children are encouraged to bring any reading materials at all to school. This can serve a number of purposes: it motivates many children; as the teacher you get an insight into their reading interests; and the children share their interests with their peers who may read more as a consequence. This approach shows that you value a wider range of reading materials and offers examples of different genres which may be used during teaching. Multiple copies of reference books such as atlases, dictionaries and thesauri should also be clearly labelled and accessible.

A whole class session when each child in the class reads a book of their choice used to be called *quiet reading*. This has attracted a number of acronyms over the years, e.g. ERIC Everyone Reads in Class; USSR Uninterrupted Silent Sustained Reading. It used to be one of the main strategies for the teaching of reading and was characterised by the teacher reading with individual children while the rest of the class read independently. The main advantage of this approach is that children can make *choices* over the texts that they read, something that has been unreasonably restricted in recent years. We would argue that this kind of reading time should be a frequent part of the routines of the classroom.

Shared reading in the Primary National Strategy

As we mentioned in Chapter 6, 'Listening to children read', shared reading in the literacy hour is considerably different from its original practice. Shared reading helps to form a bridge between the teacher reading to the pupils and independent reading by children. Its main feature is that the teacher and pupils read a single text together as a whole class. The key features of shared reading are as follows:

- a text pitched at or above average attainment level;
- a shared text, such as a *big book* or other enlarged text, or multiple copies of the text in normal size;
- high quality teacher–pupil interaction;

- discussions about the text focusing on meanings and on words and sentences;
- the modelling of reading processes;
- teaching which is informed by lesson objectives;
- preparation for main activities.

Books that you choose for shared reading can be a little above the attainment level of the class because you are reading the text for them. This is an opportunity to extend their thinking and knowledge. If it is the first time that you have shared the book, then it is normal for you to read it without comment from the children. This gives them the opportunity to hear the text as a whole. If the text is a story or poem, it gives you the opportunity to offer a dramatic reading to highlight the memorable features and to motivate the class. On subsequent readings, which may or may not happen on the same day, you will engage the children in discussion about a range of things that are of interest in the text.

An enlarged text, which could be a big book, is particularly helpful to discuss features of the text and the subtleties of the illustrations. However, just because it is a big book does not mean that it is a good book. It is far better that you share a normal size version of a really good text than an enlarged version of a poor text. Some of the so-called 'interactive' texts available on the internet which are convenient to use on whiteboards are examples of very poor texts. As with any teaching resource you need to critically evaluate them to assess their value in supporting learning.

Research into literacy teaching has shown that teacher–pupil interaction during whole class work such as shared reading is frequently rather limited. Teachers tend to do most of the talking, resulting in pupil responses that are short and low level. In part, this reflects the limitations of whole class teaching when is driven by short-term teaching objectives, but it can reflect a lack of thought by the teacher. Our advice is to keep shared reading sessions relatively brief. Fifteen minutes should be ample time to engage the children in a text. Younger children in particular have spent far too much time in the relatively passive aspects of whole class teaching at the expense of more active hands-on activities to develop their learning. It is also important that you remember to elicit the children's responses to texts, not just require them to answer the questions that you have planned in relation to your lesson objectives.

One of the outcomes of the Rose review was that the separation between phonics work and comprehension work was further emphasised, and this had an impact on shared and guided reading.

Part 1 of this overview explained that schools and settings should put in place a systematic, discrete programme as the key means for teaching high-quality phonic work. Shared and guided reading sessions should not be used to replace discrete phonics teaching but they can provide opportunities to reinforce children's developing phonic knowledge and skills, in the context of achieving the ultimate goal of the sessions, which is the development of comprehension.

(Primary National Strategy, 2006: 9)

Guidance papers from the PNS explained that although shared reading could be used to consolidate the learning of decoding skills this was not its main purpose:

> Shared reading has a number of specific functions in the teaching of early reading:
>
> • inducting children into the world of literature, meaning and response
> • providing rich opportunities for increasing children's stock of words and teaching early reading behaviours
> • serving as a vehicle for extending children's understanding of what is being read, that is their language comprehension
> • providing opportunities to apply acquired decoding skills in context, reinforcing children's developing phonic knowledge and skills gained from discrete, daily phonic sessions.
>
> (ibid.: 9)

Evidence as to whether this separation is the most appropriate way to teach children reading will emerge over the coming years.

The other feature of the shared read is that it can be used to introduce a main lesson activity. It is our view that this works best if the activity involves further active engagement with the text, exploration of the issues that it raises, and active practical work to extend understanding (➡ Chapter 5, 'Working with texts' for examples of such work).

Guided reading

Effective teaching of reading requires work with individual children (➡ Chapter 6), small groups of children and the whole class. Small group reading in the PNS is called *guided reading*. The main features of guided reading are as follows:

• Multiple copies of texts are used, one for each pupil in the small group.
• Books are matched to the achievement levels of the group.
• It involves introduction to a new text or reflections on a known text, or section of text, read previously.
• Following discussion, the teacher supports the children as they read independently.
• The other groups of the class are engaged in independent group work.
• At Key Stage 1 the emphasis is on helping children learn to read (➡ Chapter 6, 'Listening to children read', for examples of interaction strategies).

- At Key Stage 2 the objectives are to analyse and discuss the text although some children will still require help in learning to read.
- The teacher works with a different group on each day of the week.

One of the positive features of small group work is that children often find it easier to contribute to discussions in that context as opposed to the whole class. So it is disappointing that research on guided reading has found that the dialogue between pupils and teacher has shown some familiar problems. Skidmore *et al.* (2003) recorded examples of discussions in guided reading sessions in four primary schools. They concluded that the teacher:

- rarely asked authentic questions, i.e. ones where they did not have the correct answer in their head;
- normally controlled turn-taking by nominating the next speaker;
- kept a tight grip on the topic of conversation;
- did most of the talking.

This finding is perhaps not surprising when lesson content is so closely prescribed by the objectives (➡ Chapter 2) of the PNS Literacy Framework which the teacher is supposed to use to focus all aspects of the lesson. Skidmore *et al.* say that

> it may be timely to reexamine the conduct of discussions in the Literacy Hour, which government guidance advises should be teacher-led. There may be a case for relaxing the teacher's directing influence over the talk for part of the session, and allocating time for pupils to formulate and explore their own understandings of what they have read, in their own words.
>
> (ibid.: 53)

Practice points

- Selection of texts of the highest quality is a vital first step in your reading teaching.
- Constantly work to improve your skills interacting with individual children and use these during guided reading in particular.
- Give plenty of opportunities for independent reading including choice over reading materials.

Glossary

Class reader – a text, usually fiction, which the teacher reads aloud to the class. This is normally carried out as a regular session outside of the main English teaching.

Fiction – text which is invented and in the main is not factual; novels are described as fiction.

Non-fiction – texts which are factual. Information books are non-fiction.

References

Primary National Strategy (PNS) (2006) 'Phonics and early reading: an overview for headteachers, literacy leaders and teachers in schools, and managers and practitioners in early years settings', retrieved 23 November, 2006, from http://www.standards.dfes.gov.uk/primaryframeworks/literacy/Papers/phonicsoverview/

Skidmore, D., Perez-Parent, M. and Arnfield, D. (2003) 'Teacher-pupil dialogue in the guided reading session', *Reading Literacy and Language*, 37(2): 47–53.

Annotated bibliography

Centre for Language in Primary Education (CLPE) Barrs, M. and Thomas, A. (eds) (1991) *The Reading Book*. London: CLPE.
An important practical guide based on close work with London teachers. Introduces the idea of a 'core' selection of high-quality books to support reading. Equal opportunities is a strong strand to the work.
L1 *

Graham, J. and Kelly, A. (2007) *Reading Under Control: Teaching Reading in the Primary School*. 3rd edn. London: David Fulton.
A very useful account with a particularly strong section on 'Reading Routines' which develops a number of the points about reading that we touch on in this book.
L1 **

Hobsbaum, A., Gamble, N. and Reedy, D. (2006) *Guided Reading: A Handbook for Teaching Guided Reading at Key Stage 2*, 2nd edn. London: The Institute of Education.
An excellent resource which includes an overview of guided reading and recommended texts for different year groups.
L2 *

Skidmore, D., Perez-Parent, M. and Arnfield, D. (2003) 'Teacher-pupil dialogue in the guided reading session', *Reading Literacy and Language*, 37(2): 47–53.
Important research evidence about how teacher–pupil dialogue can help or hinder during guided reading.
L2 ***

Chapter 9

Reading recovery

The work of Marie Clay in the field of struggling readers has been outstanding. Her work is central to this chapter because she mixed down-to-earth practice with rigorous research. Descriptions of the practice she recommends are given, following some general considerations. Research on reading recovery is reviewed.

One of the main concerns for many primary school teachers is what to do with children who struggle with their reading. The ability to read gives access to so many areas of learning. For some children their difficulties may not be recognised early enough and this can make the job of catching up even more difficult. First and foremost it is important to remember that the reasons for struggling with reading are many and complex. Some people would suggest that the quality of teaching is the main reason why children struggle. However, factors such as confidence, self-esteem, motivation can all be part of the picture. Whatever the nature of the child's needs, it should be remembered that collaboration with parents is a vital aspect of supporting children with reading difficulties. It is also important to remember that for a small number of children there may be problems with eyesight and/or hearing that contribute. Such children will be supported through the code of practice for special educational needs. In the course of assessing children's needs it may be decided that they are dyslexic. The nature of dyslexia (☞) is a complex and hotly debated area to which we could not do justice in this chapter.

Multi-sensory approaches have been recommended as a way of supporting children with reading difficulties. The basic underlying idea is that the combination of touch, sight, hearing, and speaking can enhance the development of language. Specific examples of multi-sensory techniques include: the way that handwriting movement can support spelling memory; the forming of letter shapes in a range of media such as sand and paint; using actions to reinforce memory of letter sounds and shapes; hearing and seeing onsets and rimes; and so on.

To illustrate aspects such as the importance of building relationships with children, their confidence, their motivation, and collaboration with parents, consider this comment offered by an experienced teacher who was also the special needs coordinator:

> Darren had struggled with his reading throughout the school. I asked if I could read with him one day. It was an uncomfortable experience. His intonation and expression were very low. He stopped and stared when he didn't know a word. If he was stuck on a word he would sound out every letter. The result of this often didn't give him enough of a clue to the word because he wasn't using the other cueing strategies to support his reading. When I asked him about sections that he had read he would only offer minimal information. The class teacher felt that I should give him more phonics practice and that perhaps we should try earlier books in the reading scheme. My heart sank because I knew that the boy had had phonics and reading schemes throughout the school. It was clear to me that he already had enough phonic knowledge. Knowing that my daughter had learnt to read at the age of three simply by sharing and discussing books and other texts I wondered whether a variation on this would work with Darren.
>
> The following academic year he joined my own class having progressed very little. I decided that the first thing I had to tackle was his motivation. I collected ten picture books that I thought he might be interested in which I labelled with green stickers. These books were kept for him alone. The next thing I knew I had to do was to start talking to him about why he didn't like reading. At the time I was in contact with his mum who was quite sceptical that this would work after so many years. I followed these two main ideas of talking to the child and trying to find texts that would motivate him for the best part of the year. When it came to his next assessment the educational psychologist gave Darren a standardised reading test and was astonished.
>
> I wondered if some extra tuition that he had at home had contributed but his father said that until his motivation changed Darren wasn't prepared to work with a tutor. That child had gone through repeated systematic phonics programmes in the past and they had simply not worked.

The kinds of intervention necessary to prevent and alleviate literacy difficulties are seen by government in three waves:

Wave 1: The effective inclusion of all children in a daily and high-quality literacy hour.

Wave 2: Additional small-group intervention for children who can be expected to catch up with their peers as a result of the intervention.

Wave 3: Specific targeted approaches for children identified as requiring SEN support (on School Action, School Action Plus or with a Statement of special educational needs).

Wave 1 requires schools to ensure that literacy teaching for all children is of a high standard. The other two waves are based on the recognition that in spite of high standards there may well be children who require extra support. Wave 2 interventions include early literacy support, additional literacy support, and further literacy support which are small-group interventions developed by government. Reading recovery is a good example of a wave 3 intervention.

The work of Marie Clay

The reading recovery (☞) initiative was introduced throughout the UK in 1992 and funding was withdrawn in 1995. According to the Literacy Task Force report, their evidence suggested that reading recovery had been shown to be effective by national and international evaluations and the report recommended that it be 'kept under review' (Literacy Task Force, 1997: 31). It was also argued that it was expensive: certainly the training and employment of specialist reading recovery teachers, who worked on a one-to-one basis with children, did cost a significant amount of money.

'Reading recovery' is a term that was coined by Marie Clay and it sums up a necessarily complex view of the strategies that are necessary to support struggling readers. Clay maintains that selected teachers should undergo a training programme in order to become experts in reading recovery techniques. This happened in the UK when money was available, and schools had individual teachers who supported children with reading difficulties on a one-to-one basis outside their ordinary lessons. However, many of Clay's ideas can be used to underpin class teachers' thinking about how to help children who are struggling.

One of the most important features of reading recovery is the idea that children who are struggling should be identified by the time they have been at school for one year. In order to do this, systematic observation is required. Clay outlines a diagnostic survey that includes a range of assessments. One of these is the 'running record': it is important to remember that running record is a specific strategy for recording children's ability to decode (➡ Chapter 10, 'Assessing reading').

Reading recovery is an early intervention programme for children with reading difficulties and it is important to point out that: 'Most children (80–90%) do not require these detailed, meticulous and special reading recovery procedures or any modification of them. They will learn to read more pleasurably without them' (Clay, 1979: 47). The teaching procedures for reading recovery include a range of ideas for enhancing children's reading. As far as the use of text is concerned, although Clay is critical of the controlled vocabulary of reading schemes (she emphasises the importance of natural language), she does not particularly emphasise the significance of the particular texts that children read.

Clay's procedures include: learning about direction of text and pages; 'locating responses' that support one-to-one correspondence (☞) (e.g. locating words and spaces by pointing or indicating); spatial layout; writing stories; hearing the sounds in words; cut-up stories (i.e. cutting up texts and reassembling them); reading books; learning to look at print; linking sound sequences with letter sequences; word analysis; phrasing and fluency; sequencing; avoiding overuse of one strategy; memory; and helping children who are hard to accelerate.

Another procedure that Clay emphasised is the importance of 'teaching for operations or strategies' (ibid.: 71). Within this, is the idea that readers need to be able to monitor their own reading and solve their own problems. It is suggested that teachers should encourage children to explain how they monitor their own reading. The process of explanation helps to consolidate the skills. Clay offers useful examples of language that teachers might use:

Teacher: What was the new word you read?
Child: Bicycle.
Teacher: How did you know it was bicycle?
Child: It was a bike (semantics)
Teacher: What did you expect to see?
Child: A 'b'.
Teacher: What else?
Child: A little word, but it wasn't.
Teacher: So what did you do?
Child: I thought of bicycle.

Teacher: (reinforcing the checking) Good, I liked the way you worked at that all by yourself.
Teacher: You almost got that page right. There was something wrong with this line. See if you can find what was wrong.
Child: (child silently rereads, checking) I said Lizard but it's Lizard's.
Teacher: How did you know?
Child: 'Cause it's got an 's'.
Teacher: Is there any other way we could know? (search further)
Child: (child reruns in a whisper) It's funny to say 'Lizard dinner'! It has to be Lizard's dinner like Peter's dinner, doesn't it?
Teacher: (reinforcing the searching) Yes, that was good. You found two ways to check on that tricky new word.

(Clay, 1979: 73–74)

Evaluations of reading recovery

As we said at the beginning of this chapter, reading recovery is an internationally recognised approach for supporting children with reading difficulties. It was pioneered in New Zealand, and because of this questions were asked about whether it was possible to adopt such a programme in the UK. This is a matter that is a serious consideration when thinking about any initiatives that have been developed in another country because the varying cultural and historical backgrounds of countries do make a difference. A number of research projects have tried to discover how effective reading recovery is.

Surrey Education Authority was the first authority in England to introduce reading recovery in 1990. Wright (1992) carried out an evaluation to compare the success of reading recovery in the UK with the New Zealand experience. She found that on average, children took about two weeks longer before they could finish the reading recovery tuition. She also found that 'only three of the 82 children taken into the programme in the two years did not achieve average levels for their classes after 20 weeks of teaching' (ibid.). Achievements in the SATs were also improved and overall Wright concluded that reading recovery could be successfully implemented in the UK. Her positive views about reading recovery are supported by Clay's own research carried out over a number of years where she found that 'as a result of accelerated progress the children typically leave the programme with average levels of performance in three to six months' (1979: 105).

Other research has compared reading recovery with a particular phonological training (☞) intervention, and control groups. Immediately after the interventions were completed the research found that the effects of the reading recovery were large: 'approximately an 8 month reading age advantage over the control children' compared with the phonological training where there was 'no measurable effect on reading' (QCA, 1998: 20). An advantage for reading recovery was maintained in the second follow-up. The third follow-up had a more complex picture. Reading recovery had been particularly successful for those children who 'started as complete non-readers' but the phonological intervention was more successful for those children 'who had a slightly better grasp of reading before they were given the intervention' (ibid.: 26). D'Agostino and Murphy's (2004) meta-analysis of 36 studies that have evaluated reading recovery found that there were positive effects for children on the programme and for children who had discontinued the programme, for whom the effects were greatest.

Practice points

- Identify children who are struggling as early as possible.
- Decisions should be made in terms of time and resources for extra support including the use of classroom assistants.
- Improve the relationship with the child and try to understand and empathise with their particular problems.

Glossary

Dyslexia – a formally recognised condition that results in specific difficulties with reading and writing.
One-to-one correspondence – the understanding that one word on the page corresponds with one spoken word. Evidence comes from finger pointing at words and numbers.
Phonological training – teaching children to understand sound/symbol links.
Reading recovery – a set of techniques developed by Marie Clay designed to eradicate children's reading problems.

References

Clay, M. M. (1979) *The Early Detection of Reading Difficulties*, (3rd edn.). Auckland: Heinemann.
D'Agostino, J. and Murphy, J. (2004) 'A meta-analysis of reading recovery in United States schools'. *Educational Evaluation and Policy Analysis*, 26(1): 23–38.
Literacy Task Force (1997) *The Implementation of the National Literacy Strategy*. London: DfEE.
Qualifications and Curriculum Authority (QCA) (1998) *The Long-term Effects of Two Interventions for Children with Reading Difficulties*. London: QCA.
Wright, A. (1992) 'Evaluation of the First British Reading Recovery Programme'. *British Educational Research Journal*, 18(4): 351–368.

Annotated bibliography

Burroughs-Lange, S. (2006) 'Evaluation of reading recovery in London schools: every child a reader 2005–2006', retrieved 12 December, 2006, from http://ioewebserver.ioe.ac.uk/ioe/cms/get.asp?cid=9263&9263_0=9261
Useful study of impact of reading recovery. Includes helpful review of literature. Part of the Institute for Education Reading Recovery site.
L3 **
Clay, M. M. (1979) *The Early Detection of Reading Difficulties*, 3rd edn. Auckland: Heinemann.
This gives a full account of how to implement the reading recovery approach. One of the many useful aspects includes information on what a typical tutoring session looks like.
L2 **
D'Agostino, J. and Murphy, J. (2004) 'A meta-analysis of reading recovery in United States schools'. *Educational Evaluation and Policy Analysis*, 26(1): 23–38.
In-depth analysis of the impact of reading recovery. Carries out statistical analysis of effects of a large number of relevant studies.
L3 ***

Qualifications and Curriculum Authority (QCA) (1998) *The Long-term Effects of Two Interventions for Children with Reading Difficulties.* London: QCA.
A detailed research report which is useful because it does not hide the complexities of helping children with reading.
L3 ***

Chapter 10

Assessing reading

Assessment of children's reading is built on an understanding of reading development. This chapter emphasises the importance of one-to-one inter-action in assessing reading. It evaluates the importance of understanding children's reading errors (or miscues) and the continuing influence of Good-man's theories. The chapter concludes with some reflections on statutory and standardised tests.

The perceptive assessment of children's reading is built on a strong knowledge of children's likely development (➡ Chapter 3) and the ability to observe care-fully and interact appropriately. Although children's reading can be assessed during whole class and small group work, the most accurate assessment comes through one-to-one interaction. The simplest, yet arguably one of the most powerful, forms of reading assessment is a notebook of observations of child-ren's reading which is completed during one-to-one reading sessions and when noteworthy things occur at other times. These notebooks are sometimes called *reading diaries*.

The reading diary is one of the most flexible and open-ended forms for recording reading development. Teachers usually write brief observational jot-tings, appropriately dated, noting significant features of the child's reading as they occur, e.g. 'Leanne knows several words by sight and uses both phonics and picture clues to help her' or 'James can appreciate nuances in text with support – he understood the idea of "puns" when explained to him'. Over time, patterns of development and areas for further support become evident.

Reading diaries are also frequently sent home to support work that parents do to help their children's reading. If parents are able to write comments, then the diary can offer an even richer picture of the child's development. Children too can contribute or keep their own reading diaries (sometimes called 'reading journals' or 'logs'). Periodically teachers and other adults may participate in a written dialogue with the child about their reading, the books they like to read in and out of school and even problems they are having with their reading. Some of the comments by children taken from actual diaries read like this: 'I enjoyed this book because it was in English as well as Gujerati'; 'I found the story quite difficult because there were some very long words and lots of names that were a bit hard'; and 'I wish I could read like you, Miss. I enjoy it when you read to us because it makes the stories even better'.

Analysing miscues

An important part of assessing children's reading is how we respond to their mistakes, or miscues ☞. This will be affected by our understanding of the reading process and our understanding of models of how children read. In a seminal paper Ken Goodman argued that children's reading errors should 'be called miscues, rather than errors, in order to avoid the negative connotation of errors (all miscues are not bad) and to avoid the implication that good reading does not include miscues' (Goodman, 1969: 12). In the paper he put forward a 28-item taxonomy of the kinds of miscues that children frequently made when reading aloud. He also suggested that the reader uses three basic kinds of information: *graphophonic*, *syntactic* and *semantic* ☞. These three basic kinds of information have in some ways overshadowed the taxonomy of cues and miscues that were the more important aspect of Goodman's paper.

Subsequently other researchers combined Goodman's taxonomy with different ways of assessing children's miscues such as the *Neale Analysis of Reading Ability* which is still used today as a standardised reading test. Goodman's theory that children's miscues can tell us useful things about their reading is accepted by many people, however, some of his other theory has been more heavily criticised. The most serious of the criticisms is about his assumption that skilled readers are more likely to be influenced by context than less skilled readers. Research has now shown that the reverse is true. *Less skilled readers are more likely to be influenced by context.* This is probably because their knowledge of the links between letters and phonemes is underdeveloped. A further complication about the assumption Goodman made about miscues is that 'just because an oral reading error is contextually acceptable it cannot be assumed that the reader is necessarily making use of context' (Singleton, 2005: 8).

The three basic kinds of information that Goodman identified, graphophonic, syntactic and semantic, are subject to another problem. It is very difficult to identify a clear distinction between the influence of syntactic information and semantic information, and contextual information more generally. It seems to us that appropriate use of contextual information when reading requires use of both syntax, or grammar, *and* meaning. For that reason we prefer Reimer's (2006) three-level model (Figure 10.1).

To read effectively children need to use semantic information (meaning *and*

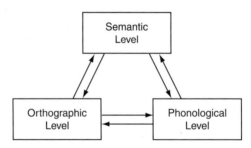

Figure 10.1 A partial model of visual word recognition based on the general interactive-activation framework.

grammar), orthographic information ☞ (spelling) and phonological information ☞ (sounds). 'In such models, word recognition is a highly interactive process whereby the bidirectional flow of activation helps ensure the selection of the most appropriate representation at each level . . . For example, activation is not only allowed to spread from the orthographic and phonological levels to the semantic level, but can spread from the semantic level back to the phonological and orthographic levels as well' (Reimer, 2006: 195).

The running record

The running record represents a relatively easy way of recording and assessing the oral reading of the child. As the child reads aloud from a book or other text, the teacher encodes the reading onto a photocopy of the text using a specified coding system such as the following one:

✓   word read accurately

T   word told by teacher

'is'   substituted word written down

O   omission of word

SC   self-correction of word by child

For example, Helen, age 7, read the following text 'There was soup for dinner. Chicken soup for all the children' as: 'There is soup for dinner. Children . . . Chicken soup for all the children.' The teacher duly coded this as ✓ 'is' ✓ ✓ ✓ SC ✓ ✓ ✓ ✓ ✓ indicating that the child read the piece accurately apart from substituting the word 'is' for 'was'. Also, when she substituted 'children' for 'chicken' she immediately corrected herself when she realised that 'children soup' was very unlikely.

Once a child has finished reading for the running record, the teacher might discuss with them some of the miscues made, particularly the substitutions ☞, to determine which cueing strategies the child is currently employing and how they might be taken forward in their reading development

The great advantage with a running record is that it is immediate, in the sense that special materials are unnecessary – just a pen and a photocopy of the text. Provided you have memorised the codings, you can complete one or more records during one-to-one reading, or at any other suitable times of the day. There are limitations, however. Instant coding by the teacher is likely to be inaccurate from time to time, because some utterances by children need greater reflection or, at least, need to be listened to more than once or twice. The running record is one of the techniques used for teacher assessment at Key Stage 1 for determining children's National Curriculum levels for reading.

Statutory tests

The statutory tests (known as SATs) have become an increasingly dominant feature of the curriculum in England. Although they are carried out in Years 2 and 6, their influence stretches far beyond these years because of the target-setting that is required throughout schooling. It is not surprising (although undesirable in relation to the narrowing of the curriculum) that teachers of all years in the primary school have focused more and more on key areas that are required by the tests. For these reasons we include a short analysis of a recent reading test. The Key Stage 2 reading test consists of a booklet that children have to read and a series of questions they have to answer. In 2006, the booklet was called *Heart Beat* and was an information text about drumming that included a short introduction; a short biography about Evelyn Glennie, the world-famous percussionist; some information about drumming around the world; and a section on skills needed to become a drummer. The booklet was in full colour, including photos of drums, other percussion and a variety of performers from around the world. As a text, not bad at all, and something that could interest many children. There will, of course, always be some children who are not in the slightest bit interested in the chosen topic. In this case, despite the picture of a young person playing kit drums on the front cover, the main information was all about the classical percussionist Evelyn Glennie, a topic less likely to appeal to the majority of children than information focusing, say, on pop music. This highlights a big problem with a national testing system as opposed to a system based on teacher assessment. In the national tests *one* text has to be chosen for all children, whereas children could be assessed reading and responding to a text of their choice if the teacher was doing the assessment. The nature of children's reading differs according to the text they are reading.

Having read the text in the booklet, pupils then have to write answers to questions. The answers have four different formats: short answers of a word or phrase (these include ticking a box as part of multiple choice); several line answers; longer answers which require a more detailed explanation of the pupil's opinion; and other answers which have different requirements. A very worrying aspect of this test is that nearly all the answers are of the kind which require a short answer, based on low-level comprehension of the text. Only three of the questions, out of 30, attracted three marks for a correct longer answer. And even one of these required the completion of missing cells in a table of summary information.

Question 13 was a question which did require inference and a higher level of thought. The booklet explaining the marking criteria includes examples of answers from pupils who trialled the tests. The quote below is taken from the guidance. You will see that it starts with the test question followed by the assessment focus that is linked to the question. Examples are then given of answers to the question that would attract different marks.

13. Why do you think many people admire Evelyn Glennie?

up to 3 marks

Assessment focus 3: deduce, infer or interpret information, events or ideas from texts (complex inference).
    Possible points might refer to Evelyn's:

- musical ability
- sensory ability
- determination/perseverance
- professional success
- inspiration to others

Award **3 marks** for answers which provide substantial coverage of at least two points, e.g.:

- *I think many people admire her because she is such a talented person and she can sense the notes through her body and it is very interesting, almost as if she is psychic. Also many people may just learn from her example* (sensory ability and inspiration)

Award **2 marks** for answers which **either** explore one of the points above in more detail / with textual support **or** explore two of the points super-ficially, e.g.:

- *because she is a great musician and also because she can't hear but she still performs and plays successfully* (musical ability and determination)

Award **1 mark** for answers which are **either** very general **or** refer to a very specific detail relating to one of the points above, e.g.:

- *she gives around 110 concerts a year* (success)

In the light of the bias towards short-answer questions, the obvious advice to help your pupils succeed in the reading test would be: ask them lots of short, specific comprehension questions about texts that they read. The problem with this advice is that it would result in less exploratory talk (see Chapter 18) about texts. It's also very limited and might actually detract from the deeper thinking about text of the kinds we explored in Chapter 5.

A note on standardised reading tests

At times it is important to know how well the children in your class read in comparison to others of the same age. Although in theory the statutory assessments should be able to do this, the fact that they change from year to year makes this difficult. Reading tests are standardised by trialling them with large samples of children (typically thousands from a range of backgrounds) in order to identify the typical score that a child of a particular age will score. This enables teachers to compare the children in their class with other children of the same age. Once standardised, the tests remain the same for a number of years. Let's look at a popular one: the NFER-NELSON Group Reading Test II. It is called a group reading test because it can be administered to a whole class or groups of smaller sizes. The sentence completion test consists of 48 items which require the child to fill in the gap in a sentence:

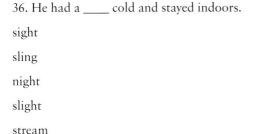

36. He had a _____ cold and stayed indoors.

sight

sling

night

slight

stream

The child has to shade in a small rectangular box next to the word suitable for reading by an optical mark reader. The context comprehension test features a passage of text written in paragraphs, once again with words missing from the sentences (the numbers in the quote below are question numbers):

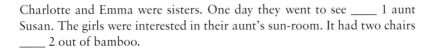

Charlotte and Emma were sisters. One day they went to see _____ 1 aunt Susan. The girls were interested in their aunt's sun-room. It had two chairs _____ 2 out of bamboo.

There have been many criticisms of reading tests over the years. Some criticisms have resulted in continuing improvements of reading tests. However, most of the problems with standardised tests can be avoided if you bear in mind that there are acknowledged limitations to their use. Standardised tests offer a summative judgement about a child's reading. They are rarely diagnostic in character. One thing that they *can* help with is in assessing whether a particular approach to the teaching of reading has been successful, particularly if the test information is collected over a period of years.

Practice points

- Carry out reading observations of all the children in your class very early in the year in order to identify those who need help. Talk to the previous class teacher to confirm your judgements.
- Decide the kinds of assessment strategies you will use throughout the year and plan for when they will happen.
- Adjust your planning regularly based on frequent analysis of the results of your assessments.

Glossary

Miscues – examples of mistakes where children's reading differs from the words in the printed text.

Orthographic information – information about the spelling system which is used to help decode words.

Phonological information – information about the links between phonemes (sounds) and letters which is used to help decode words.

Semantic, syntactic and graphophonic reading cues – mental strategies that people use to read texts. Most commonly described as semantic (using meaning), syntactic (using grammar) and graphophonic (using sound and symbol correspondences).

Substitutions – words guessed in place of unknown printed words.

References

Goodman, K. (1969) 'Analysis of oral reading miscues: applied psycho-linguistics', *Reading Research Quarterly*, 1(3): 9–30.

Reimer, J. (2006) 'Developmental changes in the allocation of semantic feedback during visual word recognition', *Journal of Research in Reading*, 29(2): 194–212.

Singleton, C. (2005) 'Dyslexia and oral reading errors', *Journal of Research in Reading*, 28(1): 4–14.

Annotated bibliography

Clay, M. M. (1979) *The Early Detection of Reading Difficulties*, 3rd edn. Auckland: Heinemann.

Marie Clay created the running record and she shows how its use can feed directly into teaching decisions.

L2 **

Coles, M. and Jenkins, R. (eds) (1998) *Assessing Reading 2: Changing Practice in Classrooms: International Perspectives on Reading Assessment.* London: Routledge.

One of two substantial books that look at the theory and practice of assessment. This book uses case studies to focus on practice and serves as a reminder that assessment is a complex process.

L3 **

Department for Education and Skills (DfES), and Primary National Strategy (PNS) (2007) *Guidance Papers: Learning and Teaching.* Retrieved 6 February, 2007, from http://www.standards.dfes.gov.uk/primaryframeworks/literacy/Papers/learningandteaching/

At the bottom of the list of guidance papers there is a pupil tracking sheet. Further assessment information is available in other areas on the site including a focus on assessment for learning.

L1 *

Singleton, C. (2005) 'Dyslexia and oral reading errors', *Journal of Research in Reading*, 28(1): 4–14.

Explores the significance of Goodman's theories about miscue analysis and links this with reflections on one of the first published papers to address oral reading errors.

L3 ***

Part III

Writing

Chapter 11

The development of writing

Historically, the teaching of writing has been much less of a focus than the teaching of reading. However, just as we illustrated for reading, in order to teach writing effectively it is necessary to be aware of how children learn. We return to the evidence from case-studies of children (➡ Chapter 3, 'The development of reading') in order to look at writing development. This picture of development is followed by a large section on the teaching of writing and the different views that have been expressed in relation to the importance of creativity, expression and choice.

It is important to understand the typical stages of development that children pass through in their writing. This knowledge helps you to pitch your planning and interaction at an appropriate level for the children you are teaching. People who have already experienced such development as teachers and parents are in an advantageous position. However, teachers who are inexperienced need to grasp the fundamental aspects of such development. One of the reasons for this is that it heightens your awareness of what to look for when you have the opportunity to interact with young writers.

As we showed in Chapter 3, there are a number of in-depth case studies of individual children that can help in acquiring knowledge about children's development. Studies of individual children do not act as a blueprint for all children: one of the important things that such case studies show us is that children's experiences vary greatly. However, if we focus on certain key concepts and significant milestones, these can be applied to larger groups of children. These milestones are likely to happen at roughly the same age for many children but there will be significant numbers of children whose development is different. Once again the stages of development are based on our analysis of case studies of children's writing development which more frequently feature young children's development than older children.

Tables 11.1 to 11.3 illustrate the development of children's writing through the primary school.

Table 11.1 Expectations for a child's writing at age 4

What you can expect	What you can do to help
Understands distinction between print and pictures	Talk about the differences between pictures and print. Show what you do when you write and tell children that you are writing.
Plays at writing	Provide a range of accessible resources. Encourage the use of writing as part of role play.
Assigns meaning to own mark-making	Ask children about their writing and discuss its meaning with them. Set them challenges to write things for you like little notes.
Often chooses to write names and lists	Help children to write their name properly. Encourage them to sign their name on greetings cards.
Uses invented spelling	Encourage children to have a go at writing and spelling in their own way. Once they have this confidence help them move towards conventional spellings.
Has knowledge of letter shapes particularly those in child's name	Teach children how to form the letters properly. Teach them how to write their name.
Recognises some punctuation marks	Help them to recognise the difference between letters and punctuations marks.
Knows about direction and orientation of print	Talk to children about left and right, top and bottom. Use your finger to point as you read from time to time. Ask questions to encourage children to show you their knowledge about orientation of print.

The teaching of writing

In Chapter 3 on the development of reading we described how the pedagogy (☞) of reading teaching had been dominated by the 'reading wars'. As far as writing is concerned, it is much more difficult to identify a central theme to the discussions about teaching. In part, this reflects the fact that writing continues to attract less attention than reading: less research is devoted to writing and there are fewer publications on the subject. Writing also seems to attract less attention in the media although standards of spelling and grammar recurrently hit the news. However, overall the disagreements in relation to the teaching of writing have tended to centre on the amount of creativity and self-expression that is desirable and how these should be balanced with acquiring the necessary writing skills. As we work through a number of key moments in the history of writing pedagogy you will see that this central point about creativity and skills will recur.

The first national curriculum for primary schools was the elementary code of 1862 (Table 11.4). Children were tested by inspectors, and this had a direct impact on the pay that teachers would receive. It was a system called *payment*

Table 11.2 Expectations for a child's writing at age 7

What you can expect	What you can do to help
Occasional interest in copying known texts	Encourage this provided it does not become the main form of writing over time. Use the opportunity to help with letter formation and whole word memory.
Range of genres of chosen writing more limited reflecting specific interests and motivation	Encourage children to explore the things that they are interested in and to write about those topics.
Able to write longer texts such as stories	Children's stamina for writing improves as the conventions like handwriting and spelling get a little easier. They will still need help with structuring their texts as they try to control these longer forms.
Understands the need to make changes to writing	Help children to see how redrafting writing can help them to get better outcomes.
Understands that writing is constructed in sentences	Explain that a sentence is something that makes complete sense on its own.
Word segmentation secure and all phonemes represented in invented spellings	Help children by engaging them with the visual aspects of words. Word games, word chunks, etc. should be the focus to help them understand English spelling.
Use of punctuation for meaning. Full stops used conventionally	Help children to organise their writing in sentences and to remember to check for capital letters and full stops.
Handwritten print of lower and upper case letter shapes secure	Keep an eye on letter formation and remind children from time to time if they are not forming letters conventionally.

by results. You can see that writing teaching at that time began with copying, in the early years, and progressed to writing from dictation.

Shayer points out that:

> 'Imitation' was not simply an isolated classroom exercise, but a whole way of thinking that was taken for granted by a great many teachers, if not by the vast majority, certainly until 1920 and even beyond. Briefly, the pupil (elementary or secondary) is always expected to imitate, copy, or reproduce.
>
> (1972: 10)

He goes on to give some examples from Nelson's *Picture Essays*, 1907, of typical activities of the time:

> 'Describe a cow; general appearance. Horns … teeth … hoofs … tail. Food. Breeds. Uses.'

Table 11.3 Expectations for a child's writing at age 11

What you can expect	What you can do to help
Using information sources and writing to learn	Support the skills of note-taking and/or tabulating information, etc.
Will redraft composition as well as transcription elements	Help children to see the value of redrafting to improve the final product. Support their proof-reading skills.
Able to successfully control a range of text forms and have developed expertise in favourites	Encourage experimentation to find types of writing that they enjoy.
Length of writing increasing	Help children to control the larger structural elements such as headings and paragraphs.
Growing understanding of levels of formality in writing	Discuss differences between things like emails to friends and family as opposed to formal letters.
Standard spelling most of the time. Efficient use of dictionaries and spell checking	Help children to enjoy the wealth of information contained in dictionaries. Show them how to use standard adult dictionaries.
Basic punctuation secure. Aware of a range of other marks	Encourage use of full range of punctuation. Enjoy spotting things like the 'grocer's apostrophe', e.g. apple's and pears
Presentation and fluency of handwriting differentiated for purpose	Support handwriting with good quality pens and other implements. Encourage proper typing when using computer keyboard.

'Write on "Our Town" as follows: 1. *Introduction* – Name; Meaning; Situation; Population. 2. *Appearance* – General appearance, chief streets, buildings, parks, etc. 3. *General Remarks* – Principal trades and industries. Any historical facts, etc.'

(1972: 10)

The Story of a Shilling
Hints
    Where and when was it born?
    What did it look like?
    Who was its first owner?
    What did he do with it?
    Invent some adventures for it, and tell what became of it in the end.
        (J. H. Fowler, *A First Course in Essay-Writing*, 1902)

In the describe a cow activity we see a simple three-part structure offered. For the story of a shilling the stimulus is offered through a series of questions. Although this early history of writing is fascinating, our main historical interest in this chapter begins with the 1960s.

Table 11.4 The curriculum specified by the Revised Code of 1862

	Standard I	Standard II	Standard III	Standard IV	Standard V	Standard VI
Reading	Narrative in monosyllables.	One of the Narratives next in order after monosyllables in an elementary reading book used in the school.	A short paragraph from an elementary reading book used in the school.	A short paragraph from a more advanced reading book used in the school.	A few lines of poetry from a reading book used in the first class of the school.	A short ordinary paragraph in a newspaper, or other modern narrative.
Writing	Form on black-board, from dictation, letters, capital and small, manuscript.	Copy in manuscript character a line of print.	A sentence from the same paragraph, slowly read once, and then dictated in single words.	A sentence slowly dictated once by a few words at a time, from the same book, but not from the paragraph read.	A sentence slowly dictated once, by a few words at a time, from a reading book used in the first class of the school.	Another short ordinary paragraph in a newspaper, or other modern narrative, slowly dictated once by a few words at a time.
Arithmetic	Form on black-board, from dictation, figures up to 20; name at sight figures up to 20; add and subtract figures up to 10; orally from examples on the blackboard.	A sum in simple addition or subtraction, and the multiplication table.	A sum in any simple rule as far as short division (inclusive).	A sum in compound rules (money).	A sum in compound rules (common weights and measures).	A sum in practice or bills of parcels.

Creative writing

As a reaction against rather formal approaches, 'creative writing' flourished in the 1960s. One of the most famous texts from this time is Alex Clegg's book *The Excitement of Writing*. Clegg recognised the extensive use – and potentially damaging effect – of published English schemes. As an alternative he showed examples of children's writing

> taken from schools which are deliberately encouraging each child to draw sensitively on his own store of words and to delight in setting down his own ideas in a way which is personal to him and stimulating to those who read what he has written.
>
> (1964: 4)

Protherough (1978) provided a very useful summary of the impact of creative writing and his paper also signalled some of the criticisms that were emerging. Overall he felt that the creative writing movement was an important one and that 'the emphasis on personal, imaginative writing [needed] to be maintained and extended' (1978: 18). But he felt the model had some weaknesses. One of these weaknesses was the restriction on the forms of writing that were used. The teacher provided a stimulus (such as a piece of music or visual art) which was followed by an immediate response, and this implied brief personal forms of writing such as a short descriptive sketch or a brief poem. The model did not encourage the writing of other forms such as argument, plays, or even short stories. Protheroe recommended that

> the stimulated writing is to be seen *not* as the end-product, but as a stage in a process. Pupils need to be helped to develop their work, and to learn from each other as well as from the teacher.
>
> (ibid.: 18)

As you will see later, the process approach took these ideas forward.

By the end of the 1970s, concerns were growing about the emphasis on 'feeling' in writing teaching and the fact that much of the creative stimuli required an immediate response which did not allow for suitable reworking or redrafting. Allen (1980) pointed out that too much focus on expressive writing could lead to a lack of emphasis on more 'abstract modes'. At this time it was suggested that the teaching of writing required tighter structures that were deemed to be missing from the creative writing ideas.

One of the influential thinkers of the period, James Britton, proposed that writing could be categorised into several key forms (Figure 11.1). Britton offers a scientific report as one example of transactional writing (☞). He argued that this kind of writing 'may elicit the statement of other views, of counter-arguments or corroborations or modifications, and is thus part of a chain of

Transactional/ ◄————/Expressive/ ————►/Poetic/
1   2   3   4   5

Figure 11.1 Britton's categorisation of forms of writing.

Source: Reproduced from *Language and Learning*. Harmondsworth: Allen Lane The Penguin Press, 1970, second edition 1972. Copyright © James Britton, 1970, 1972.

interactions between people' (1970: 175). He contrasts this with poetic writing where the reader is invited to share a particular verbal construct (☞). The sharing of the writer's thoughts in poetic writing does not 'elicit interaction' in the same way that transactional writing does.

Britton suggested that most of children's writing produced in the primary school is expressive writing. But it develops, through Britton's transitional categories (2 and 4), towards transactional and poetic forms as they gain greater experience and control over their writing. Britton argued that children's expressive writing needs to adapt to the more public writing of transactional and poetic forms. Transactional writing needs to be more explicit, for the unknown reader. Poetic writing on the other hand emphasises implicit meanings in order to create 'sounds, words, images, ideas, events, feelings' (1979: 177). At this time there was a feeling that expressive writing could and should be a foundation for other more abstract forms. However, overall, Allen maintains that the mid- to late 1970s were characterised by uncertainty and lack of consensus on approaches to the teaching of writing.

Developmental writing

The creative writing movement can be seen as linked with philosophies such as those of Rousseau who advocated that children's free expression was vital. But there was a lack of research evidence to support claims about children's 'natural' development. One of the reasons that in-depth case studies of individual children became important was that they documented children's natural development as language users. This kind of data was also collected from larger groups of children. Harste *et al.* (1984) were able to extend our knowledge of children's writing by looking at 3- and 4-year-olds. Their conclusions signalled concern about the lack of 'uninterrupted' writing in most early years settings. One of the striking features of their work was the researchers' ability to focus on the positive features of early writing rather than the deficits: an extract from 'Lessons from Latrice' – a chapter from their book – is shown in Figure 11.2.

The researchers initially confessed to being more unsure about Latrice's writing than any of the other children they studied: she was developmentally the least experienced child that they encountered. The researchers asked Latrice to write her name and anything else that she could write; she was then asked to draw a picture of herself. By positively and actively searching for evidence of

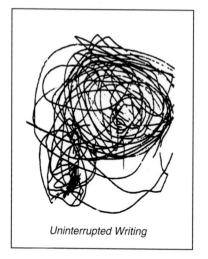
Uninterrupted Writing

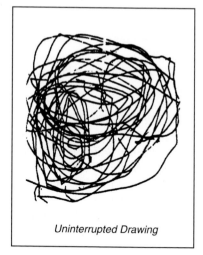
Uninterrupted Drawing

Name

Figure 11.2 Samples of Latrice's writing.

Source: Reproduced from Harste *et al.* (1984) *Language Stories and Literary Lessons*, Oxford: Heinemann. Used with permission.

Latrice's achievements they were able to understand her writing in great depth. The following is a list of some of the knowledge that Latrice had already acquired:

- Latrice was aware of how to use writing implements and paper.
- She understood and demonstrated the difference between writing and pictures.
- She switched between writing and drawing as a strategy to maintain the flow of her writing.
- Each new mark represented a new or different concept.

- She had developed some knowledge of the importance of space in relation to text.
- She was aware of the permanence of meaning in relation to written language.

Another important point that Harste *et al.* made is that judgements about children's writing based on the final product do not give us enough information about their writing achievements. It is only by analysing the process of writing, in addition to the product, that valid information can be gathered.

The research evidence on children's natural literacy development led to new theories on writing pedagogy. It was argued that as children seemed to develop to a large extent by using their own natural curiosity and ability, perhaps formal teaching should take account of this reality. The theories of 'emergent literacy' developed alongside approaches such as 'developmental writing'. The use of the term 'emergent literacy' in education was popularised by Hall (1987) in his book *The Emergence of Literacy*. The basis of the philosophy is the notion of the child as an active and motivated learner who experiments with a wide range of written forms out of a sense of curiosity and a desire to learn. Hall described emergent literacy as follows:

> It implies that development takes place from within the child . . . 'emergence' is a gradual process. For something to emerge there has to be something there in the first place. Where emergent literacy is concerned this means the fundamental abilities children have, and use, to make sense of the world . . . things usually only emerge if the conditions are right. Where emergent literacy is concerned that means in contexts which support, facilitate enquiry, respect performance and provide opportunities for engagement in real literacy acts.
>
> (1987: 9)

The theory of emergent literacy was very closely linked with the practice of developmental writing. The following list identifies some of the key features of developmental writing and was influenced by Browne's (1996: 21) points that characterise such writing:

1 Builds on children's literacy experience prior to coming to school.
2 Encourages independent writing from day one of the nursery.
3 Modelling is provided by physical resources and the actions of the teacher.
4 Transcription errors are dealt with after the meaning has been established. A smaller number of errors are corrected but each one in more detail.
5 Learning to write developmentally can be slow but the benefits in future motivation for writing are the result.
6 Writing tasks emphasise purpose and real reasons.

7   Children have time to develop pieces of writing in depth.
8   The confidence to take risks is encouraged.

Developmental writing differs from the creative writing of the 1960s and 1970s in two main ways. Both approaches share the recognition that children must be given opportunities to carry out uninterrupted writing which uses their previous knowledge and experience. However, with developmental writing there is a stronger expectation that the teacher will interact, particularly with individual children, in order to take learning forward. The second difference relates to the first in that the teacher's interaction during developmental writing is based on a high level of knowledge about common developmental patterns in the children's writing and this informs the focus of their interaction. With these clearer pictures of development came different and more realistic expectations of children's learning.

The freedom of developmental writing was replaced in the early 1980s by a continuing recognition of the importance of children's self-expression, but with the realisation that routines to support the process of writing were helpful.

The process approach to writing

The uncertainty of the 1970s was finally transformed by the process writing of the 1980s. The work of the New Zealander Donald Graves became very influential, culminating in international recognition for his work and great demand for him as a keynote speaker. Czerniewska (1992: 85) described Graves as 'one of the most seductive writers in the history of writing pedagogy'. Graves's approach to writing became known as the 'process approach' and had a significant influence on the teaching of writing in the UK. It is difficult to assess exactly how many schools and teachers took up the approach in the UK but, for example, the National Writing Project and the Language in the National Curriculum Project both involved many schools in the UK, and it is clear from their reports of practice that the process approach was influential. Frank Smith was also very popular at the time and although his theories on reading have attracted some severe criticism, his theories on writing, particularly the separation between composition and transcription, have remained better intact.

> It has been argued that writing is learned by writing, by reading, and by perceiving oneself as a writer. The practice of writing develops interest and with the help of a more able collaborator provides opportunity for discovering conventions relevant to what is being written . . . None of this can be taught. But also none of this implies that there is no role for a teacher. Teachers must play a central part if children are to become writers, ensuring that they are exposed to informative and stimulating demonstrations and helping and encouraging them to read and to write. Teachers are

influential, as models as well as guides, as children explore and discover the worlds of writing – or decide that writing is something they will never voluntarily do inside school or out.

(Smith, 1982: 201)

Smith expresses some of the key ideas of the process approach and particularly the notion of children being regarded as writers from the start. However, the idea of the teacher as primarily a demonstrator, as role model, and as an 'encourager' has received repeated criticism because of the perception that this does not involve direct instruction. Graves's work (which fitted with Smith's ideas) developed classroom routines which turned such theories into a practical reality for many teachers.

One of the fundamental principles of Graves's process approach was down-played in the UK. He was quite clear that children needed to be offered choices in their writing.

Children who are fed topics, story starters, lead sentences, even opening paragraphs as a steady diet for three or four years, rightfully panic when topics have to come from them . . . Writers who do not learn to choose topics wisely lose out on the strong link between voice and subject . . . The data show that writers who learn to choose topics well make the most significant growth in both information and skills at the point of best topic. With best topic the child exercises strongest control, establishes ownership, and with ownership, pride in the piece.

(Graves, 1983: 21)

This choice was not the restricted kind offered when a teacher has decided the form of writing. Graves advocated that children should select the topic and form of the writing. Graves's most popular work *Writing: Teachers and Children at Work* is frequently cited as an account of the process approach. But as Wyse (1998) showed in *Primary Writing*, teachers in England used the process approach in quite different ways to those characterised by Graves.

The genre theorists

In the late 1980s the popularity and optimism of the process approach began to be attacked by a group of Australian academics called the 'genre theorists'. The tide began to turn away from the importance of self-expression towards greater emphasis on skills and direct instruction. The three authors who perhaps have been referred to most in relation to genre theory are J. R. Martin, Frances Christie and Joan Rothery. One of the key texts from 1987 was *The Place of Genre in Learning* where these three authors put forward some of their ideas as a response to other authors in the book. They also offered some criticisms of the process approach.

In a section of Martin *et al.*'s chapter they examine the notion of 'freedom' during the process approach. They ask a series of important questions:

> What is freedom? Is a progressive process writing classroom really free? Does allowing children to choose their own topics, biting one's tongue in conferences and encouraging ownership, actually encourage the development of children's writing abilities?
>
> (Martin *et al.*, 1987: 77)

To answer these questions the authors report on a school in the Australian Northern Territory with a large population of Aboriginal children. They claimed that over the course of the year the children had only written about one of four topics: '(a) visiting friends and relatives; (b) going hunting for bush tucker; (c) sporting events; (d) movies or TV shows they have seen' (ibid.: 77). This example is used to cast doubts on the effectiveness of the process approach claiming that the range of forms that children choose is limited. However, as Wyse (1998) showed, the process approach can have the opposite effect. The following is a snapshot of children's writing carried out during a writing workshop. It also gives a contextual background pointing to the origin of the idea and indication of the nature of teacher support given during a writing conference:

Computer Games and How to Cheat.
The two pupils came up with the idea. The teacher suggested a survey of other children in the school who might be able to offer ways of getting through the levels on computer games. The teacher also suggested a format which would serve as a framework for the writing about each game.

A Book of Patterns
Self-generated idea with the teacher offering guidance on the amount of text that would be required and the nature of that text.

Tools Mania
A flair for practical design technology projects resulted in one of the pair of pupils choosing this topic which involved writing a manual for the use of tools. Both pupils found the necessary expository writing a challenge.

The New Girl
The girl herself was new to the school and this title may have provided her with a means of exploring some of her own feeling when she first arrived.

Manchester United Fanzine
This was a particularly welcome project as it involved three girls work-

ing on an interest they had in football. It was an opportunity to challenge the stereotypes connected with football. The teacher set a strict deadline as the project seemed to be growing too big and also suggested the girls send the finished magazine to the football club to see what they thought.

Football Story
The pupil worked unaided only requesting the teacher's support to check transcription.

A Book of Children's Games
Using a book from home the pupil chose her favourite games and transcribed them in her own words.

Secret Messages
Various secret messages were included in the book which the reader had to work out. This was aimed at the younger children and involved a series of descriptions of unknown objects which the reader had to find around the school.

Kitten for Nicole
This was an advanced piece of narrative; the teacher made minor suggestions for improving the ending. Unfortunately the child decided she didn't like the text and started on a new one without publishing this.

Book for Young Children
The two boys used pop-art style cartoons for the illustrations as a means of appealing to the younger children. The teacher gave some input on the kinds of material that were likely to appeal to the younger children. One of the pair tended to let the other do most of the work and the teacher encouraged the sharing out of tasks.

Football Magazine
There had been an epidemic of football magazines and the teacher made a decision that this was to be the last one for a time in order to ensure a balance of forms. The two boys used ideas from various professional magazines combining photographs with their own text.

Information about Trains
Great interest in one of the school's information books which included impressive pull-out sections was the stimulus for this text. At the time the work in progress consisted of a large drawing of a train. The teacher had concerns that concentration on the drawing could become a strategy for avoiding writing.

The Magic Coat
An expertly presented dual language story which had been written with help from the child's mother for the Urdu script. The home computer had also been used to create borders and titles. The teacher's role simply involved taking an interest in the progress.

Catchphrase
Pupil's doodling had given the teacher an idea for an activity which involved devising catchphrases based on the television programme. This pupil decided to compile a book of her own catchphrases.

Chinwag
Originally two pupils had been encouraged to devise and sell a school magazine. This included market research around the school, design, word processing, editing other children's contributions, selling, accounting, etc. This was a large-scale project and the original editors felt they would like to delegate the responsibility for the second issue to someone else, so two new editors took over.

Newspaper
The idea came from the two pupils but coincided fortuitously with a competition organised by the local paper encouraging students to design their own paper. The children asked various people around the school to offer stories. Layout became an important issue. The children brought in their own camera and took pictures to illustrate their text. BBC and Acorn computers were both used, necessitating understanding of two different word processors.

Modern Fairy Tale
The two pupils were struggling for an idea so the teacher suggested they contact another school to find out the kinds of books they liked with a view to writing one for them. The school was in a deprived area and had many more bilingual children than the two pupils were used to. They realised that their initial questionnaire would need modification if it was to be used again. The children at the other school expressed a preference for traditional stories so the two pupils decided to write a modern fairy tale. They were encouraged by the teacher to ask the opinion of bilingual peers on suitable subject matter and some information about India.

Joke Book
The two pupils surveyed the children in the school for good jokes. This was a popular title and had been done before in the course of the year.

The Primary National Strategy Framework

In spite of a number of serious criticisms (Barrs, 1991; Cairney, 1992), the views of the genre theorists proved to be influential. Consequently, genre theories were a dominant feature of the National Literary Strategy Framework for Teaching (DfEE, 1998). There was an equal emphasis on fiction and non-fiction that had been informed by the view that there was too much story writing happening in primary schools. The goals for written composition no longer emphasised personal choice, writing to interest and excite readers, finding a vehicle for expression, writing to explore cross-curricular themes, writing as art, but were much more about the analysis of genre structures. The importance of writing for real purposes and reasons in order to communicate meaning was replaced by an emphasis on textual analysis as the main stimulus for composition.

Building on genre theories, the work of Wray and Lewis (1997) had a significant influence on the writing pedagogy of the NLS. They identified a four-stage model:

1   Demonstration – The teacher 'thinks aloud' as they demonstrate the writing process. This includes mental processes that go through the head while writing as well as information and skills. Examples are shown to the children.
2   Joint activity – Teacher and child(ren) engage in shared writing. Children are encouraged to contribute as much as possible to the writing under the guidance of the teacher.
3   Supported activity – The teacher sets a task but continues to support children as they need help.
4   Individual activity – Children write independently with minimal support when required.

However, Wray and Lewis pointed out that:

> It is, arguably, equally as damaging to hold back learners by insisting they go through the same programme of support and practice as everyone else as it is to rush learners through such a programme when they need a more extensive programme of support.
>
> (ibid.: 23)

This message was not heeded well enough, resulting in an approach to writing that at times became a mantra. The standards of writing over the period showed only modest gains, less than those for reading which were also modest, so it seems that more work needs to be done to better understand writing pedagogy.

The PNS Framework retains many of the features of the NLS approach, particularly the emphasis on analysis of text types, but with some additions. The dominant model consists of four phases:

1   Read and analyse features of the text type.
2   Explore the text type through a range of activities including oral ones.
3   The teacher demonstrates writing.
4   Children write the featured text type and evaluate their writing based on the teacher's criteria.

One of the dangers of any well-specified approach is that it can become a rather inflexible model. There is also the important question of what evidence there is to support such an approach.

One of the characteristics of the more recent research on writing pedagogy is that much has been done by looking at non-fiction genres but less on the writing of fiction and very little on forms of writing such as poetry. Andrews *et al.*'s (2006) systematic review looked at the writing of argumentative non-fiction writing. Their main findings with regard to the context for writing teaching were that the following were important:

•   A writing process model in which students are encouraged to plan, draft, edit and revise their writing.
•   Self-motivation (personal target-setting as part of self-regulated strategy development).
•   Some degree of cognitive reasoning training in addition to the natural cognitive development that takes place with maturation.
•   Peer collaboration, thus modelling a dialogue that (it is hoped) will become internal and constitute 'thought'.

(Andrews *et al.*, 2006: 32)

They also suggested some specific interventions that were successful, including support to use the structures and devices that aid the composition of argumentative writing; the use of oral argument to inform the written argument; identification of explicit goals including the audience for the writing; teacher modelling; and the teacher coaching writing during the process. These lists of aspects which are part of effective pedagogy do in some ways relate to the PNS model but the research shows this is a much more complex and subtle picture. Andrews *et al.* also point out that the recommendations were not universally shared by the studies that they looked at. One of the limitations of these outcomes is that the recommendations for practice cannot be related to the writing of fiction or poetry. At the heart of these and other forms is the use of imagination, and the extent of the originality and quality of ideas are paramount concerns. But these are only measureable if children are actually given choices over the topic and form of their writing. The links between genre theories, structured teaching and individuality were explicitly addressed by Donovan and Smolkin (2002). Their study examined the use of scaffolding in a range of writing tasks including story writing and non-fiction writing. One of their key findings based on evidence that writers' personal interests could result in improved writing was about the importance of author aim, which was explained as a keen sense of the audience for the writing linked with personal intentions and motives:

> Author aim reintroduces individuality to the writing landscape, a point with which certain Systemic Functional linguists [the theoretical tradition to which the genre theorists were linked] were not particularly comfortable . . . we are not distressed by the idea of instructing children in form. We are, however, concerned that individuals, authors, and their aims receive so little focus in considerations of structure-based instruction.
>
> (ibid.: 462)

There is very little evidence in the PNS that author aim is a central concern nor are children to be regularly encouraged to exercise individual choices. The question as to whether opportunities to make choices is important can, as we have shown, be addressed by research. However, this matter is also a question of values. You may feel that offering genuine choices periodically during a child's early years and primary schooling is ethically necessary and that this could result in children being more motivated to write.

Practice points

- Improve your observation and interaction skills by increasing your knowledge of writing development.
- Make decisions on how and when you will offer choices.
- Use your observations to adjust your planning for writing so that children's actual needs are met.

Glossary

Construct – in this context the word is a noun – as opposed to a verb – and means a specific way of thinking about something.
Pedagogy – approaches to teaching.
Transactional writing – concerned with getting things done, e.g. information, instructions, persuasion, etc.

References

Allen, D. (1980) *English Teaching Since 1965: How Much Growth?* London: Heinemann Educational Books.
Andrews, R., Torgerson, C. J., Low, G., McGuinn, N. and Robinson, A. (2006) 'Teaching argumentative non-fiction writing to 7–14 year olds: a systematic review of the evidence of successful practice', Technical report. *Research Evidence in Education Library*. Retrieved 29 January, 2007, from http://eppi.ioe.ac.uk/cms/

Barrs, M. (1991) 'Genre theory: what's it all about?' *Language Matters*, 1991/92(1): 9–16.

Britton, J. (1970) *Language and Learning*. Harmondsworth: Penguin.

Browne, A. (1996) *Developing Language and Literacy 3–8*. London: Paul Chapman.

Cairney, T. (1992) 'Mountain or mole hill: the genre debate viewed from "Down Under" '. *Reading*, 26(1): 23–29.

Clegg, A. B. (1964) *The Excitement of Writing*. London: Chatto and Windus.

Czerniewska, P. (1992) *Learning about Writing*. Oxford: Blackwell.

Department for Education and Employment (DfEE) (1998) *National Literacy Strategy Framework for Teaching*. London: DfEE.

Donovan, C. and Smolkin, L. (2002) 'Children's genre knowledge: an examination of K–5 students' performance on multiple tasks providing differing levels of scaffolding', *Reading Research Quarterly*, 37(4): 428–465.

Graves, D. H. (1983) *Writing: Teachers and Children at Work*. Portsmouth, NH: Heinemann Educational Books.

Hall, N. (1987) *The Emergence of Literacy*. Sevenoaks: Hodder & Stoughton.

Harste, J. C., Woodward, V. A. and Burke, C. L. (1984) *Language Stories and Literacy Lessons*. Portsmouth, NH: Heinemann Educational Books.

Martin, J. R., Christie, F. and Rothery, J. (1987) 'Social processes in education: a reply to Sawyer and Watson (and others)', in I. Reid (ed.) *The Place of Genre in Learning*. Victoria: Deakin University.

Protheroe, R. (1978) 'When in doubt, write a poem', *English in Education*, 12(1): 9–21.

Shayer, D. (1972) *The Teaching of English in Schools 1900–1970*. London: Routledge and Kegan Paul.

Smith, F. (1982) *Writing and the Writer*. Portsmouth, NH: Heinemann Educational Books.

Wray, D. and Lewis, M. (1997) *Extending Literary: Children Reading and Writing Non-fiction*. London: Routledge.

Wyse, D. (1998) *Primary Writing*. Buckingham: Open University Press.

Annotated bibliography

Andrews, R., Torgerson, C. J., Low, G., McGuinn, N. and Robinson, A. (2006) 'Teaching argumentative non-fiction writing to 7–14 year olds: a systematic review of the evidence of successful practice', Technical report. *Research Evidence in Education Library*. Retrieved 29 January, 2007, from http://eppi.ioe.ac.uk/cms/
Offers conclusions on effective pedagogy for the teaching of written argument.
L3 ***

Bissex, G.L. (1980) *GNYS At WRK: A Child Learns to Write and Read*. Cambridge, MA: Harvard University Press.
An extremely thorough and insightful account of one child's development.

A rich picture is combined with knowledgeable academic analysis: an important book.
L2 **

Czerniewska, P. (1992) *Learning about Writing*. Oxford: Blackwell.
Summarises many of the experiences of the National Writing Project which was so influential during the 1980s.
L2 *

Donovan, C. and Smolkin, L. (2002) 'Children's genre knowledge: an examination of K–5 students' performance on multiple tasks providing differing levels of scaffolding', *Reading Research Quarterly*, 37(4): 428–465.
L3 ***

Chapter 12

Composition

The process of writing can be seen as a distinction between composition and transcription. This chapter focuses particularly on the composition of writing. Ways of stimulating writing can be seen on a continuum between open and closed approaches. We explore ways that writing can be stimulated using a range of approaches.

Frank Smith (1982: 20) made the distinction shown in Box 12.1 between the composition of writing and transcription. The PNS framework for literacy separates composition and transcription through its different strands. The transcription strands are: Strand 5 – Word recognition: decoding (reading) and encoding (spelling); Strand 6 – Word structure and spelling; Strand 11 – Sentence structure and punctuation; and Strand 12 – Presentation. The composition strands are: Strand 9 – Creating and shaping texts; and Strand 10 – Text structure and organisation. Strand 9 has the aim that children will 'Write independently and creatively for purpose, pleasure and learning.' An important

---

Box 12.1 *The composition and transcription of writing*

Composition (author)	Transcription (secretary)
Getting ideas	Physical effort of writing
Selecting words	Spelling
Grammar	Capitalisation
	Punctuation
	Paragraphs
	Legibility

Source: Reproduced from Smith (1982: 20). Used with permission.

question to consider is to what extent do the framework and its guidance really support independent and creative composition.

One aspect of composition is the extent to which children should be required to plan their writing. The process that professional writers go through sheds light on the issue of planning. Carter (1999) collected together the thoughts of a number of fiction writers and included reflections on the routines that they used for writing. Helen Cresswell, a prolific and talented author for both children and adults, describes her way of composing:

> With most of my books I simply write a title and a sentence, and I set off and the road leads to where it finishes. All my books are like journeys or explorations. Behind my desk I used to have this saying by Leo Rosten pinned up on the wall that went 'When you don't know where a road leads, it sure as hell will take you there.' When I first read that, I thought, that's exactly it! That's what happens when I start on my books – I really don't know what's going to happen; it's quite dangerous, in a way. I often put off starting because it seems a bit scary. Yet at the end of the day, I feel that a story has gone where it's meant to have gone.
>
> (Carter, 1999: 118)

There are other writers who carry out written plans in detail before they write a word:

> Unlike novelists like Brian Moore, who write to discover what happens to their characters, Iris Murdoch writes nothing until she knows how the story will develop:
> 'I plan in enormous detail down to the last conversation before I write the first sentences. So it takes a long time to invent it.'
>
> (Harthill, 1989: 87)

As you can see, professional writers have different approaches to planning, so it is logical to assume that children need a range of ways into writing. It is not a good idea to insist that every piece of writing that children do should be preceded by a written plan. Many will benefit from the opportunity to get stuck into their writing with the minimum of delay.

In relation to adult writing, Wyse (2006) established the concept of *retrospective planning* which is planning that is carried out *after* the writing has been started. This is particularly useful with longer pieces where the sequence of the overall structure, principally the sections and paragraphs, needs to be improved. Children could be encouraged to read through their early drafts and then write a retrospective plan which you feel is the most appropriate to the kind of writing been done. For example, there is no reason why a story plan couldn't be applied retrospectively so the early motivation for writing a story is not frequently lost to a mundane and repetitive planning process.

Stimuli for writing

One of the key questions when planning the teaching of writing is 'what kind of stimulus should I offer?' In other words, the teacher has to decide what kind of encouragement, activities and experiences children need in order to help them to write. These decisions should be affected by consideration of children's motivation. Most teachers make the sensible assumption that when children are not motivated, they do not learn as well as they could.

When planning the kind of activities to stimulate children's writing it is helpful to think of a continuum between open and closed approaches (see Figure 12.1). The PNS Framework strongly emphasises writing which is modelled on other texts. For example, in Year 2, children have to be taught to 'Draw on knowledge and experience of texts in deciding and planning what and how to write' (PNS, p 57). In Year 5, they have to 'Adapt non-narrative forms and styles to write fiction or factual texts, including poems' (ibid.). The PNS Framework also emphasises closed activities such as decontextualised ☞ phonics work or the sentence work derived from the *Grammar for Writing* resource.

As an example of open approaches the *process approach* has an enviable track record in motivating children to write and is based on establishing authorship in the classroom supported by a publishing process (➡ Chapter 11 for a fuller explanation of the process approach). The most important feature of the 'process approach' to teaching writing is that children choose what to write. This is not just choice within a genre ☞ prescribed by the teacher but real choice over the topic and type of writing. One of the classic techniques is to ask children to generate a list of five things that they would like to write, then to choose one and get writing.

The use of artefacts and first-hand experiences is also a well-established means of stimulating writing through a creative writing approach which the three following examples illustrate.

1   Kirklees Local Education Authority had an extensive range of boxed artefacts and books available from the library service that supported cross-curricular work. One of the highlights was 'granny's attic' which contained

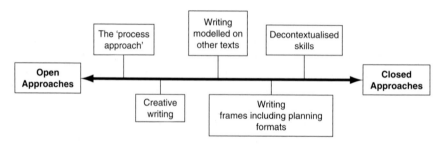

Figure 12.1 Writing approaches continuum.

a treasure trove of historical artefacts and documents that could be used as the basis for children's stories about the origins of the objects and a wide range of historical work.

2   A maths lesson was postponed for an hour when it began to hail and the children's collective attention was focused on the sudden change in light, the noise, the heightened sense of unease and danger. Standing outside, underneath a canopy, they began to write what they saw. Rebecca (8) wrote:

Hail

Suddenly, the light changed
Crisp, bright, yellow
I rushed outside and stood
Waiting impatiently
Just as the hail fell
Heavy ricochets
The air smelt, strangely
And the breath was sucked
From my lips
The wind changed the weather vane
And made the bushes dance
In a moment it was gone
The air hung grey empty
The clanging flagpole signalled
All clear

3   Many children are not able to sustain observational writing in this way, but they should still feel their work has worth and potential. A class of children on a field trip to the Northumbrian coast sat beside the harbour watching the day developing. One girl wrote a series of unrelated observations which neither inspired nor interested her. She was asked to select two or three elements of her writing which might 'feel right' together, and to express them in the smallest space which achieved what she wanted to say. Charlotte wrote:

Soon the tide
And the birds will follow

It took Charlotte some considerable time to arrive at these two lines, and it brings to mind an anecdote from Oscar Wilde. He once said that he had spent the morning working on a piece of writing and by lunch had added a comma. In the afternoon he took it out again.

Moving further towards the closed end of our writing continuum, writing frames offer a way of stimulating writing particularly in the context of non-fiction writing.

Writing frames

The research from the 'Exeter Extended Literacy Project' (EXEL) developed the idea of 'frames' as a way of supporting children's non-fiction writing. Lewis and Wray explain the notion of writing frames:

> Writing frames are outline structures, enabling children to produce nonfiction writing in the different generic forms. Given these structures or skeleton outlines of starters, connectives and sentence modifiers, children can concentrate on communicating what they want to say. As they practise building their writing around the frames, they become increasingly familiar with the generic forms.
>
> (Lewis and Wray, 1995: 53)

One of the important ideas behind writing frames is that they are intended to support writing done in meaningful contexts; the sort of contexts where appropriate audiences and purposes have been facilitated. Lewis and Wray are quite clear that 'using the frames for the direct teaching of generic structures in skills-centred lessons' is inappropriate.

There are six writing frames: recount, report, procedure, explanation, persuasive argument, discussion. Of these, it is perhaps the writing of argument that has proved the most demanding for teachers and children alike. The following example shows how a child used the writing frame: the child's text is in italic and the frame text is normal:

Although not everybody would agree, I want to argue that
Children should not wear school uniform.

I have several reason for arguing for this point of view. My first reason is
That they feel more comfortable in clothes which they choose to wear. They would feel more relaxed and be able to work better and concentrate more on their work.

Another reason is
There wouldn't be the problem of parents not wanting to buy uniforms because they think they are too expensive.

Furthermore
Sometimes you might wake up and find your two lots of uniform in the wash.

Therefore, although some people argue that
Children might take it past the limits.

I think I have shown that
Children should be able to choose their clothing just as adults do, as long as they wear sensible clothes.

(ibid.: 85)

It is pointed out that prior to using this kind of structure, teacher modelling ☞ and shared construction of texts are important. We would also point out that children need to experience the extensive reading of any genre that they are trying to write themselves.

The writing frames are designed to be flexibly applied, and it is intended that children should move towards independence. This means that the form of the frame can be modified to offer a different level of support. If we return to written argument, Box 12.2 gives an example that includes a list of connectives ☞:

Box 12.2 *Part of writing frame with suggested connectives*

I would like to persuade you that

There are several points I want to make to support my point of view. Firstly

> These words and phrases might help you:
> because
> therefore
> you can see
> a supporting argument
> this shows that
> another piece of evidence is

Source: Lewis and Wray (1995: 133)

Practice points

- Make a clear distinction between composition and transcription when teaching writing.
- In the early stages of writing, composition is most important. Without composition there is no transcription.
- Use a range of approaches to stimulate writing.

Glossary

Connectives – words and phrases whose main purpose is to connect phrases, sentences and other large units of text

Decontextualised work – teaching and/or activities that focus on language (frequently words or parts of words) removed from a normal whole-text context.

Genre – a form of writing such as newspaper, story, poem. In education can refer to spoken forms as well as written forms.

Teacher modelling – the teacher shows by demonstration and speaking their thoughts aloud how writing is composed.

References

Carter, J. (1999) *Talking Books: Children's Authors Talk about the Craft, Creativity and Process of Writing.* London: Routledge.

Harthill, R. (1989) *Writers Revealed: Eight Contemporary Novelists Talk about Faith, Religion and God.* New York: Peter Bedrick Books.

Lewis, M. and Wray, D. (1995) *Developing Children's Non-Fiction Writing: Working with Writing Frames.* Leamington Spa: Scholastic.

Smith, F. (1982) *Writing and the Writer.* Oxford: Heinemann Educational.

Wyse, D. (2006) *The Good Writing Guide for Education Students.* London: Sage.

Annotated bibliography

Bereiter, C. and Scardamalia, M. (1987) *The Psychology of Written Composition.* Hillsdale, NJ: Lawrence Erlbaum Associates. Quoted in R. Beard (ed.) *Teaching Literacy Balancing Perspectives.* London: Hodder & Stoughton, 1993: 159, 162.

Collins, F. M. (1998) 'Composition', in J. Graham and A. Kelly (eds) *Writing Under Control: Teaching Writing in the Primary School.* London: David Fulton.
This chapter looks in more depth at a number of the issues that we discuss. Includes useful reminders about bilingual children and the use of drama to stimulate writing.
L2 *

Crick software. Available from: http://www.cricksoft.com/uk/products/clicker/
Clicker software allows children to click onscreen cells to insert text and pictures to support the composing of documents. The site includes clicker screens (called grids) that can be downloaded and used to support teaching.
L1 *

Lewis, M. and Wray, D. (1995) *Developing Children's Non-Fiction Writing: Working with Writing Frames.* Leamington Spa: Scholastic.
A thorough account that includes the rationale for the use of writing frames and examples of practice.
L2 *

Riley, J. and Reedy, D. (2000) *Developing Writing for Different Purposes: Teaching about Genre in the Early Years*. London: Paul Chapman.
Useful reminder of many of the main issues in the teaching of writing. Includes interesting six-point theory on the teaching of writing developed in New Zealand.
L2 **

Chapter 13

Spelling

Margaret Peters' distinction between spelling being 'caught or taught' leads us into the strategies that are used when teaching spelling. A five-stage model of spelling development is presented and the chapter concludes with reflections on the pros and cons of spelling tests.

Here are two lovely examples of children's spelling attempts. Can you work them out?

my klone

ches and unen

The first is a famous footballer originally from Liverpool; the second is a flavour of crisps. It is the irregularities of English that make it demanding for children to learn and for teachers to teach.

In her seminal book *Spelling: Caught or Taught?* Peters (1985) argued that in the past spelling had not been taught effectively. She suggested that spelling is a particular skill, or set of skills, that requires direct instruction for the majority of school pupils. Children who are not taught to spell properly often develop a poor self-image as far as spelling is concerned and lack self-confidence in their writing as a whole. Crucially, she emphasised the significance of children acquiring visual strategies ☞ rather than auditory strategies ☞ in learning to spell, though she also acknowledged the usefulness of kinaesthetic strategies ☞. She strongly recommended the 'Look–Cover–Write–Check' approach:

1 Look carefully at the word, noting particular features such as familiar letter strings, suffixes, etc. and memorise it by saying the word silently, thinking of the meaning of the word and trying to picture it in the mind's eye.
2 Cover the word.
3 Write the word from memory.

4   Check that the word written is correct by matching it with the original. If the spelling is incorrect, the whole process should be repeated.

Peters' research also led her to believe that there is a direct correlation between confident, clear and carefully formed handwriting and the development of competent spelling (➡ Chapter 14, 'Handwriting').

Mudd (1994) points out that some children, often poor spellers, can have a visual memory deficit which requires remediation through multi-sensory techniques ☞ or mental linking by remembering sets of objects placed within their sight. One of the important issues addressed by Mudd concerns the teaching of spelling rules. Her view is that generalisations, not rules, should form the basis for instruction in school. Rules suggest immutability and correctness whereas generalisations allow for the possibiity of exceptions. The so-called 'Magic E' (or modifying E) rule, for instance, is better taught as a generalisation because there are so many exceptions to it such as *one, have, give, where*. Children can be taught to perceive this as a generalisation rather than a rule and be urged to discover words which confirm or disprove it. Another example is the adding of one consonant or two when adding '-ing' to verbs that end in a consonant preceded by a short or long vowel, such as 'run' and 'shop' or 'sleep' and 'eat'. This necessitates children being able to distinguish between long and short vowels and, ideally, being able to hear whether the preceding syllable is stressed or not. Mudd clearly has doubts about this and suggests that most novice spellers will need very specific, clearly worded teaching on this to avoid confusion.

Spelling development

A number of writers cite the importance of the work of Gentry (1982) in relation to the five stages of development for spelling.

The first stage is the *pre-communicative* stage, when young children are making their first attempts at communicating through writing. The writing may contain a mixture of actual letters, numerals and invented symbols and, as such, it will be unreadable though the writer might be able to explain what they intended to write.

When children are at the second stage, that is the *semi-phonetic* stage, they are beginning to understand that letters represent sounds and show some know-ledge of the alphabet and of letter formation. Some words will be abbreviated or the initial letter might be used to indicate the whole word.

At the *phonetic* stage children concentrate on the sound–symbol correspond-ences, their words become more complete and they gain an understanding of word division. They can cope with simple letter strings such as -*nd*, -*ing* and -*ed* but have trouble with less regular strings such as -*er*, -*ll* and -*gh*.

During the *transitional* stage children become less dependent on sound–symbol strategies. With the experience of reading and direct spelling instruction they become more aware of the visual aspects of words. They indicate an awareness of the accepted letter strings and basic writing conventions of the English writing system and have an increasing number of correctly spelt words to draw upon.

Finally, the fully competent speller emerges at the *correct* stage. Correct spellings are being produced competently and confidently almost all the time and there is evidence of the effective use of visual strategies and knowledge of word structure. Children at this stage have an understanding of basic rules and patterns of English and a wide spelling vocabulary. They can distinguish homographs ☞, such as 'tear' and 'tear' and homophones ☞, such as 'pear' and 'pair' and they are increasingly able to cope with uncommon and irregular spelling patterns.

Teachers will be able to use the model to identify what stage individual pupils are at, what sort of expectations they might have of these individuals, what targets they might set for these children and what teaching strategies they might usefully employ at any one time.

Beard (1999) refers to Gentry's model as being very influential, but he does raise several notes of caution. He maintains that the different stages represent 'complex patterns of thinking and behaviour' and aspects of several stages might be evident in one piece of writing. The teacher therefore needs to evaluate the individual's progress through the stages on the basis of a wide sample of writing each time. He also points to the importance of parental support (making reference to the case-study of Paul Bissex which was used as the basis for Gentry's stages: ➡ Chapter 11, 'The development of writing') and the significance of effective teaching of spelling in school. The rate of children's progression through the stages will vary greatly depending on these factors and, of course, individual differences.

Spelling and the PNS Framework

The PNS Framework heavily emphasises the role of phonics in the early stages of learning to spell:

Most Children Learn:

- that segmenting words into their constituent phonemes ☞ for spelling is the reverse of blending phonemes into words for reading
- to spell words accurately by combining the use of grapheme–phoneme correspondence knowledge as the prime approach, and also morphological knowledge and etymological information

Although the research on learning to read is persuasive about the specific but limited benefit of phonics teaching, it is far from clear whether phonics is the best way to help spelling. Although there clearly are links between reading and

writing, they are such different processes that we doubt that the kind of synthetic phonics advocated by the PNS Framework will be the best way to help
spelling.

There is a welcome range of spelling strategies outlined in the objectives
from Year 2 to Year 6 but the location of objectives in the sequence does not
adequately represent the way that spelling develops. For example, the helpful
objective in Year 4 that children should learn to 'Develop a range of personal
strategies for learning new and irregular words' is applicable for children of
most ages not just Year 4.

Most of the following are covered by the framework:

- Visual strategies include checking critical features of the word such as shape
  and length (asking 'Does it look right?'), looking for words within words,
  e.g. *for* in *before*, *the* in *they*, recognising tricky bits in different words, e.g.
  oo in *book*, *ai* in *said* and using the 'Look–Cover–Write–Check' procedure.
- A morphemic and word analogy approach using known spellings as a
  basis for correctly spelling other words with similar patterns or related
  meanings, and building words from awareness of the meaning or derivation
  of known words: here, there, everywhere; light, sight, bright; the, them,
  theme, thematic.
- Knowing about the serial order of letters in the language, that is the order
  in which letters in a word are likely to occur. For example, what letter is
  likely to follow Q? You probably sensibly guessed U, but there are a couple
  of words without the U such as 'qadi'.
- Mnemonic approaches involve inventing and using personal mnemonic
  devices for remembering difficult words, such as 'two ships on the sea', 'one
  collar and two sleeves' – necessary; 'there's an "e" for envelope in the middle
  of stationery'; or 'an "i" (eye) in the middle of "nose" makes a noise', etc.
- Thinking about and investigating spelling 'rules' and their exceptions.

The NLS resource *Spelling Bank* offers activities for Key Stage 2 that were
designed to meet the requirements. Despite the useful range of activities in
the Spelling Bank, it seems particularly unfortunate that the use of games is
not encouraged. Games such as Scrabble, hangman, crosswords, word searches,
Boggle, Countdown, etc. can all be useful in stimulating and motivating children's interest in words and spelling.

Assessing spelling

Weekly spelling tests are one of the most common ways that children's spelling
is assessed. It is tempting to ask why this is so prevalent when there is very little
evidence about its effectiveness. However, historical tradition, and particularly the spelling test requirement in the statutory tests are the likely driving
forces behind the practice. It is important to consider what the pros and cons of

spelling tests are. A potentially positive feature of spelling tests is that lists of words are sent home to be learned. If this is carefully thought through, word lists can provide an activity that many parents feel confident to support their children with (although not all parents will feel confident about this). These lists of words are often differentiated into three ability levels. Unfortunately teachers rarely individualise the work, for example, by encouraging children to identify problem words from the ones they have been writing as part of their lessons or words that are of particular interest. It is common for teachers to encourage children to put the words into a sentence context or even a paragraph context as part of the homework.

However, when word lists and spelling tests represent the main approach to spelling and when the lists are sent home *every* week, then the likelihood is that children will become very demotivated about writing. There is no reason why spelling homework cannot feature a wide range of activities such as the ones covered in this chapter. One activity that is overlooked is the simple but potentially valuable one of bringing home a draft of writing and asking for help with proof-reading. It is often suggested that spelling tests are used to enhance standards of spelling, but as you have seen there are many other strategies that might achieve this more effectively. Daw *et al.* (1997) used their experiences as advisory teachers to argue that there were 11 key strategies that effective schools used to enhance standards of spelling including: 'Teaching methods and resources are deployed in ways that encourage pupils to experiment and become quite independent as spellers from an early age' (ibid.: 44).

The claim that spelling tests are used as an assessment tool is questionable. The biggest problem is that the true test of learning a spelling is whether it is written correctly in the course of normal writing. Every piece of writing that a child carries out gives teachers an opportunity to assess their spelling, and it should be remembered that the kind of writing that the child is doing will affect the nature of their spelling mistakes. A diary, for example, will create different challenges from a piece of scientific writing. In addition, however sensitively tests are handled, there will always be children who are poor spellers whose self-esteem will be damaged each time they have to carry out a spelling test. The most useful assessment of children's spellings will, arguably, take place at the time that the children are actually engaged in the writing process in the classroom.

Practice points

- In the early stages the use of phonological understanding ☞ should be encouraged but in time children need to understand the importance of visual strategies for standard spelling.
- Every piece of writing provides an opportunity for the assessment of a child's spelling.

- There needs to be a careful balance between encouraging invented spelling which can aid composition and standard spelling which is the final goal.

Glossary

Auditory strategies – the use of sounds to help spelling of unknown words.

Homographs – words with the same spelling as another but different meaning: 'a lead pencil/the dog's lead'.

Homophones – words which sound the same, but have different meanings or different spellings: 'read/reed'; 'right/write/rite'.

Kinaesthetic strategies – the use of the memory of physical actions to form words.

Multi-sensory techniques – the use of as many senses as possible through movement, vision, touch, and hearing in order to remember words.

Phoneme – the smallest unit of sound in a spoken word, e.g. the /b/ in 'bat'.

Phonological understanding – understanding the way that letters represent speech sounds.

Visual strategies – the use of visual memory of words including common patterns of letters.

References

Beard, R. (1999) *National Literacy Strategy: Review of Research and Other Related Evidence*. London: DfEE.

Daw, P. with Smith, J. and Wilkinson, S. (1997) 'Factors associated with high standards of spelling in years R-4', *English in Education*, 31(1): 36–47.

Gentry, J. R. (1982) 'An analysis of developmental spelling in *GNYS AT WRK*', *Reading Teacher*, 36: 192–200.

Mudd, N. (1994) *Effective Spelling: A Practical Guide for Teachers*. London: Hodder & Stoughton.

Peters, M. L. (1985) *Spelling: Caught or Taught: A New Look*. London: Routledge and Kegan Paul.

Annotated bibliography

Brooks, P. and Weeks, S. (The Helen Arkell Dyslexia Centre) (1999) *Individual Styles in Learning to Spell: Improving Spelling in Children with Literacy Difficulties and All Children in Mainstream Schools*. London: DfEE.
A very significant piece of research. In common with other research demonstrates that important aspects of literacy learning need to be individualised. Includes fascinating ideas on 'neurolinguistic programming'. L3 ***'

Mudd, N. (1994) *Effective Spelling: A Practical Guide for Teachers*. London: Hodder & Stoughton.

As the title suggests, this book gives sensible, systematic, practical guidance to the effective teaching of spelling at Key Stages 1 and 2, as well as providing some interesting insights into the history of the English language and past and present approaches to spelling in school.
L1 *

Peters, M. L. (1985) *Spelling: Caught or Taught: A New Look*. London: Routledge and Kegan Paul.

First published in 1967, *Spelling: Caught or Taught* was a seminal work based on doctoral research in the 1960s arguing for teacher intervention in the field of spelling and young children and setting out certain strategies, particularly visual strategies, for teaching spelling in school. In this later work she covers similar ground and brings to bear additional research carried out with various colleagues.
L2 **

Torgerson, C. J. and Elbourne, D. (2002) 'A systematic review and meta-analysis of the effectiveness of information and communication technology (ICT) on the teaching of spelling', *Journal of Research in Reading*, 25(2): 129–143.

Found only six studies addressing the issue of the benefits of ICT for spelling teaching that were randomised controlled trials. The evidence for use of dedicated spelling packages is not particularly convincing.
L3 ***

Chapter 14

Handwriting

Handwriting is an important transcriptional skill. The development of a fluent, comfortable and legible style helps children throughout their schooling, not least in exams. The basic concepts of handwriting are described and these are followed by a discussion of handwriting in the National Curriculum and a section on handwriting problems.

Venerable Will played jazz sax 'til 3 o'clock in the morning before he quit.

The five boxing wizzards jump quickly.

(Jarman, 1989: 101)

These examples that contain all the letters of the alphabet serve to remind us that quick brown foxes are not the only subjects for such sentences. They are of course quite a handy way to cover the formation of all the letters of the alphabet in one meaningful sentence.

Learning to form the individual letters of the alphabet and produce legible handwriting at a reasonable speed, involves a complex perceptuo-motor skill ☞. The goal of handwriting teaching is a legible, fluent and comfortable style. Legibility will have different levels according to the purpose of the writing. Sassoon (1990) points out that children cannot be expected to produce their neatest handwriting all the time, so she advocates different levels of handwriting. A calligraphic ☞ standard for special occasions might require a careful, deliberate approach which will be more time-consuming than a legible day-to-day hand. There will also be times when pupils are drafting text or making notes that they alone will read where a lower standard of legibility is appropriate. The importance of fluency is particularly important in tests and exams when time pressures are present. A comfortable style requires an appropriate grip, appropriate seating and a good posture.

Posture and working space are important elements of handwriting. For right-handed pupils, the paper is tilted to about 45° anticlockwise. It is important that the writing implement is not gripped too hard as this can also lead to muscle tension in the shoulder and pain in the wrist and hand. It is important that you are aware of all the left-handed children in your class from the beginning of the year. As far as handwriting is concerned, left-handed children have particular needs. Their writing moves inwardly, that is, in towards their bodies thus tending to make it difficult for them to read what they have just written. Left-handers should be encouraged to turn their paper *clockwise* (to about 45°), not to hold their pen or pencil too near to the actual point and to sit on a chair that is high enough to allow them good visibility. Left-handers can be helped by ensuring that they sit to the left of a right-hander so that their elbows are not competing for space.

Basic handwriting concepts

Sassoon (1990) puts forward the concepts behind our writing system. Direction, movement and height are all crucial: left to right and top to bottom; the fact that letters have prescribed flowing movements with specific starting and exit points; the necessity to ensure that letters have particular height differences. In addition, the variance between upper and lower case must be recognised and correct spacing consistently applied. She also stresses the importance of taking particular care when teaching certain letters that have mirror images of each other, such as *b-d*, *m-w*, *n-u* and *p-q* to avoid confusion for young learners. She suggests that speed – but not too much speed – is important as this can lead to fluency and greater efficiency. Modern classroom situations do require pupils to think, work and write reasonably quickly.

For teachers there are a small number of technical terms that are useful when talking about handwriting. *Ascenders* are the vertical lines that rise above the mid-line (or x-line) on letters like 'd'; *descenders* are the vertical lines that hang below the baseline on letters like 'g'. Letters have an *entry stroke* where you start the letter and an *exit stroke*. The letter 't' is interesting in that its horizontal line is called a *crossbar* and the height of the letter should only be three-quarters. This means that the top of the letter finishes between the mid-line and the ascender line. There are four important horizontal lines: the *descender line*, the *baseline*, the *mid-line* and the *ascender line*. For adults only the baseline is visible; for children other lines have to be used carefully because there is a danger that they can measure the length of a stroke by the distance to the line not by understanding the differences in letter size. Children need to understand these concepts if they are to have legible and fluent handwriting.

Jarman (1989), like Sassoon, suggests that letters can be taught in families that are related by their patterns of movement. There are slight differences between their approaches, but both underline the importance of the idea of letter families. Jarman links specific patterns – which he regards as beneficial – with the families of letters. He also suggests that there are two kinds of join or 'ligature': horizontal joins and vertical joins. He points out that it is sensible to leave some letters unjoined, such as b g j p q and y when joined to most vowels. Sassoon links together the following letters:

1 i l t u y j
2 r n m h b p k
3 c a d g q o e
4 s f
5 v w x z.

Handwriting, spelling and cursive writing

According to Bearne (1998), the connection between handwriting and spelling relates to kinaesthetic ☞ memory, that is the way we internalise things through repeated movements. Forming letter shapes in the air, or in sand, with paint, with a finger on the table, on paper with a pencil or pen, or even writing out misspellings several times encourages the kinaesthetic memory for the particular movements. Peters (1985) similarly discussed perceptuo-motor ability and argued that carefulness in handwriting goes hand in hand with swift handwriting, which in turn influences spelling ability. Children who can fluently write letter-strings such as -*ing*, -*able*, -*est*, -*tion*, -*ous* are more likely to remember how to spell words containing these strings.

> Quality of handwriting is highly correlated with spelling attainment, so also is the speed of handwriting, for it is a myth that the slow writer is the careful writer and vice versa. The slow writer is often one who is uncertain of letter formation . . . and . . . often . . . makes a random attempt at the letter he is writing. The swift writer is one who is certain . . . [and] can make a reasonable attempt at a word he may never have written before.
>
> (ibid.: 55)

It was also Peters' view that the teaching of 'joined up' or cursive writing, should begin long before the junior school, that is to say at Key Stage 1 rather than 2. The main advantages of this are: (1) the concept of 'a word' (and the spaces between words) is acquired from the outset as distinct from 'a letter' (and the spaces between letters); (2) correct letter formation with appropriate exit strokes is learned from the beginning; (3) the movement of joined-up writing assists successful spelling and is quicker than printing; (4) children do not have to cope with changing from one to the other at 7 or 8 years of age. Sassoon (1990) suggests that with sufficient preparation in the 'movement' of letters and the different exit strokes required, pupils can begin to join up the simple letters by the end of the reception year or Year 1 at least. She advocates the teaching of the letters and the joins in family groups and puts forward a clear analysis as to how this might be achieved in school.

The National Curriculum treats handwriting as a 'key skill'. At Key Stage 2 the emphasis is not just on legibility, fluency and confidence, but also on adaptability. Handwriting should be adaptable to a range of tasks such as presenting clear, neat final copy, taking notes, printing headings and subheadings, labelling diagrams, lettering for posters, presenting information in tabular form, map making, and so on. There is also an emphasis on presenting work in a variety of ways. This includes different kinds of handwriting for different purposes and the use of other devices such as a range of computer-generated fonts, bullet points, borders, shading, etc. and even pictures and moving images. The PNS Framework objectives progress through Key Stage 2 as follows:

Presentation
Most children learn to:

- develop a clear and fluent joined handwriting style
- use keyboard skills and ICT tools confidently to compose and present work

Year 4
Write consistently with neat, legible and joined handwriting
   Use word processing packages to present written work and continue to increase speed and accuracy in typing

Year 5
Adapt handwriting for specific purposes, e.g. printing, use of italics
   Use a range of ICT programmes to present texts, making informed choices about which electronic tools to use for different purposes

Year 6
Use different styles of handwriting for different purposes with a range of media, developing a consistent and personal legible style
   Select from a variety of ICT programmes to present text effectively and communicate information and ideas

Diagnosis of problems

Pupils entering the Key Stage 2 phase of schooling sometimes arrive with handwriting problems. These might have been caused by indifferent teaching or they might, according to Sassoon (1990), be symptomatic of pupils' particular condition or set of circumstances. They might be considered 'dyspraxic', that is prone to particular motor coordination problems. For example, they might not be able to catch a large ball, or cope easily with gymnastics or play games using the simplest of equipment. For these children, neat, regulation handwriting might be impossible. Teachers need to acknowledge this, not continually chastise them but help them to develop handwriting that is reasonably swift and legible.

Sassoon argues that handwriting can be regarded as a diagnostic tool in itself, indicating certain problems that pupils have and teachers need to address. Hesitancy and a lack of confidence in spelling will interrupt the flow of handwriting. If this is accompanied by frequent attempts at correcting mistakes, the result is 'messy' handwriting that many teachers find unacceptable. This may well bring to their attention that these children need help in spelling as well as handwriting. Occasionally, children have psychological problems to cope with, too, such as bullying, bereavement, divorce, and so on, which, in addition to a range of behavioural changes, can be evident in their handwriting. Often the writing becomes very variable and sometimes illegible, when previously it was conventional.

Some children with poor handwriting skills are found to have weak auditory, perceptual and memory skills and are not able to remember sequences of movements or sequences of verbal instructions. Difficulties with handwriting might indicate poor eyesight or a squint and perhaps the need for spectacles for an individual child. Children suffering from fatigue due to the after-effects of an illness, a physical disability or just insufficient sleep at night might also reflect this in their handwriting. Finally, poor handwriting might bring the teacher's attention to the poor posture of some children when writing or even generally. Thus alerted and made aware of any of these cognitive, psychological or physical problems, teachers will be able to take steps, possibly with support from other professionals, to remedy them and aim to improve, not just children's handwriting, but other important features of their pupils' learning and development in school.

Practice points

- The individual support for handwriting during the writing process should be supplemented by whole group handwriting sessions on a weekly basis.
- A balance needs to be found between emphasis on standard letter formation and encouraging legibility and fluency.
- Joined-up writing should be encouraged as early as possible.

Glossary

Calligraphic – description of a particularly skilled way of writing. Handwritten italic script is often seen as calligraphy.

Kinaesthetic – our sense and memory of movement/muscular control.

Perceptuo-motor skill – skills that rely on use of the senses, the brain and learned physical movement.

References

Bearne, E. (1998) *Making Progress in English*. London: Routledge.

Jarman, C. (1989) *The Development of Handwriting Skills: A Resource Book for Teachers*. Oxford: Basil Blackwell.

Peters, M. L. (1985) *Spelling: Caught or Taught: A New Look*. London: Routledge and Kegan Paul.

Sassoon, R. (1990) *Handwriting: A New Perspective*. Leckhampton: Stanley Thornes.

Annotated bibliography

The British Institute of Graphologists (2007) Homepage. Retrieved 18 January, 2007, from http://www.britishgraphology.org/
Includes a monthly analysis of someone's handwriting. An interesting view of how some people believe that it is possible to make judgements about character based on handwriting.
L1 *

Department for Education and Skills (DfES) (2004) *Key Stage 3 National Strategy: Handwriting and Presentation*. Retrieved 18 January, 2007, from http://www.standards.dfes.gov.uk
Although this resource was developed for Key Stage 3 it has some useful ideas that could be modified for Key Stage 2. It includes careful analysis of pupils' writing and detailed planning of lessons.
L1 *

Jarman, C. (1989) *The Development of Handwriting Skills: A Resource Book for Teachers*. Oxford: Basil Blackwell.
Jarman makes a strong case for the teaching of eight specific patterns which he suggests account for all lower case letters. The book includes fascinating information about a range of handwriting-related topics. The main part of the book consists of photocopiable handwriting sheets.
L1 *

Medwell, J. and Wray, D. (2007) 'Handwriting: what do we know and what do we need to know?' *Literacy*, 41(1): 10–15.
A timely and very useful overview of research in an area that receives limited attention.
L1 *

Sassoon, R. (1999) *Handwriting of the Twentieth Century*. London: Routledge.
Rosemary Sassoon has contributed a huge amount to our understanding of handwriting. This book, her most recent, gives a recent historical perspective on the teaching of handwriting. Her book *Handwriting: The Way to Teach It* (Sassoon, 1990b) focuses more on classroom practice.
L1 *

Chapter 15

Punctuation

A brief reminder about some of the aspects of punctuation that are tricky for children and adults alike is followed by reflections on the ways that children learn to punctuate. The chapter concludes with examples of how punctuation can be taught.

Lynn Truss's bestselling book *Eats, Shoots and Leaves* (2003) proved that punctuation is a fascinating subject for hundreds of thousands of people. Highlights of her book included the amusing idea of the subordinate clause as one of Santa's little helpers. The title of the book is also based on a joke. The educationist Nigel Hall who has done some useful research on children's punctuation gave Lynn Truss this:

> A panda walks into a restaurant, sits down, and orders a sandwich. He eats the sandwich, pulls out a gun, and shoots the waiter dead. As the panda leaves, the manager shouts, 'Stop! Where are you going? You shot my waiter!'
> 'I'm a PANDA!' the panda shouts back. 'Look it up!'
> The manager opens his dictionary and reads:
>
>> **Panda** A rare mammal akin to a bear with black and white markings native to a few mountainous areas of forest in China and Tibet. Eats shoots and leaves.

Part of the intrigue of punctuation is spotting the frequent 'errors' that occur. The apostrophe is a bit of a classic in this regard. The following professionally printed banner appeared on a pub wall:

> Qs monster meals won't scare you but the portion's might

Well, one out of three for the apostrophes in that one! It is worth reminding ourselves of the common types of apostrophe: (1) contraction: didn't = did not; (2) possession singular: the cat's tail, the child's book; (3) possession plural: the cats' tails, the children's books (as 'children' is an irregular plural form, the apostrophe comes before the 's'); (4) possession with name ending in 's': Donald Graves's book. Common errors include: this first happened in the 60's. – 60s is plural not a contraction; was that it's name? – because of the confusion with *it's* (as in: It's (it is) my party and I'll cry if I want to) this possessive form is irregular and does *not* have an apostrophe (was that its name?).

Semicolon ;

The use of colons and the semi-colons can also be particularly problematic so it is important to be as clear as one can be about their use.

The semicolon separates main clauses that are not joined by a coordinator ☞ which the semicolon replaces. The two parts of the sentence feel equally important. This represents a break in the flow of the sentence which is stronger than a comma but weaker than a full stop, e.g. the students in the first study were hard working; those in the second were lazy.

Colon :

The colon separates a first clause, which could stand as a sentence, from a final phrase or clause that extends or illustrates the first clause. Most commonly used to introduce things, like lists or an example. If in doubt, don't use a colon mid-sentence, reword or try a comma instead.

Children learning to punctuate

An early piece of punctuation research was carried out by Hutchinson (1987) who worked closely with a child on a piece of writing that was a re-enactment of *Come Away from the Water Shirley* by John Burningham (1977):

> shirley and her mum and dad were going to the seaside and her dad told her to go and play with the other children and her dad didn no she went saling with a dog and a pirate ship was foiling and the pirates corght her.

Hutchinson made the point that Danny's reliance on speech results in the use of conjunctions ☞ where full stops would be more appropriate in writing. However, he also points out that an analysis based on one text is not sufficient for assessing understanding. The following day when they reloaded the writing, Danny decided to put a full stop after the title. When asked if he could put some more in, he demonstrated a better knowledge than he had the day before. The importance of redrafting is clearly indicated in this example. One of the points to emerge was the way that the child used his speech to support his structure of the writing. An important aspect of teachers' knowledge is recognising the significant differences between speech and writing.

Hall's (1998) work was one of the first to look closely at the teaching and learning of punctuation. His book includes an overview of the history of punctuation. For example, in 1700, Richard Browne said: 'What is the use of stops or points in reading and writing? To distinguish sense; by resting so long as the stop you meet with doth permit' (Hall, 1998: 2). In Roman times it was the readers who inserted the punctuation into texts not the writers: this was related to the need to declaim texts orally. Since that time the function of punctuation has changed. However, the idea that punctuation is primarily designed to support oral reading – through pauses – still persists. Hall reiterates that punctuation is no different to writing in general in that the generation of *meaning is* the primary function of written language: one of the main points that he makes is that punctuation is learned most successfully in the context of 'rich and meaningful writing experiences' (1998: 9).

He usefully differentiates between 'non-linguistic punctuation' and 'linguistic punctuation'. An example of non-linguistic punctuation is where a child puts full stops at the end of every line of a piece of writing rather than at the end of the sentences. This illustrates the child's belief that punctuation is to do with position and space rather than to indicate meaning and structure. With regard to non-linguistic punctuation the idea of 'resistance to punctuation' is discussed. One of the reasons that children can remain resistant to using punctuation appropriately is exacerbated by teachers whose comments are often directed to naming and procedures rather than explanation:

> As already indicated, teacher comments which are simply directed to the placing of punctuation rather than to explaining its function can leave the child with no sense of purpose. Yet research suggests that teacher practices are, probably quite unconsciously, dominated by procedure rather than explanation.
>
> (ibid.: 5)

Standard punctuation is linked with grammar and sentence structure. The necessary understanding of these complex concepts does not happen suddenly. Children gradually begin to realise that spatial concepts either do not work or do not match what they see in their reading material. Hall illustrates this with an example from his research:

> three children who were jointly composing a piece of text which was being scribed for them . . . After two lines, one child insisted on having a full stop at the end of each line. The rest of the piece was written with no more punctuation. Then there was a scramble for the pen and one child wanted to put a full stop after 'lot' on line three.
>
> *Derek:* You're not supposed to put full stops in the middle.
> *Rachel:* You are!

Derek: No, they're supposed to be at the end, Ooh!
Rachel: You are, Derek.
Fatima: Yeah. So that's how you know that (meaning the 'and' at the end of line 3) goes with that (meaning line 4).

(ibid.: 12)

The PNS Framework introduces punctuation marks at the following stages:

Year 1
Use capital letters and full stops when punctuating simple sentences

Year 2
Use question marks, and use commas to separate items in a list

Year 3
Clarify meaning through the use of exclamation marks and speech marks

Year 4
Use commas to mark clauses, and use the apostrophe for possession

Year 5
Punctuate sentences accurately, including using speech marks and apostrophes

Year 6
Use punctuation to clarify meaning in complex sentences

It is unfortunate that in Year 4 the use of commas is seen as marking clauses rather than as a way to clarify meaning and to avoid ambiguity, which is their primary role.

Waugh (1998) looks at some practical approaches to teaching punctuation in the primary school and he makes an important point about 'response partners'. One of the most effective ways of improving punctuation is to work with someone who is proficient at proofreading. All professionally published materials pass through a proofreading stage: this book will be passed to a proofreader and a copy-editor; newspaper articles go to sub-editors who work on style and presentation, etc. This is in part a recognition that proofreading is often more efficient if it is not solely carried out by the author who often is primarily concerned with the composition. This also reflects the idea that it is sensible to separate composition and transcription in the various stages of the writing process.

Other suggestions that Waugh makes include the use of comic strips and speech bubbles which can then be converted to text only. Reading punctuation aloud can be done by giving the name of the mark when it is read or by having different sounds for different marks (you can listen to the comedian Victor Borge doing this at www.geocities.com/). Waugh also suggests 'walking and reading' where the reader has to stop walking at a punctuation mark. One of the main uses of punctuation is to avoid ambiguity, and some useful examples are offered where children can change the punctuation to create different meanings:

PRIVATE. NO SWIMMING ALLOWED.

PRIVATE? NO! SWIMMING ALLOWED.

Practice points

- Children should be taught that one of the main reasons for punctuation is to improve clarity and avoid ambiguity.
- As teachers you should be clear that punctuation is more about meaning than about pauses when reading aloud.
- The use of the full stop and the comma require complex knowledge, but they should be the first priority.

Glossary

Conjunction – a type of word that is used mainly to link clauses in a sentence, e.g. She was very happy *because* John asked for help with his maths.
Coordinator – a word that links parts of a sentence. The most common coordinators are 'and', 'or' and 'but'. Some people call these conjunctions.

References

Burningham, J. (1977) *Come Away from the Water, Shirley!* London: Cape.
Hall, N. (1998) *Punctuation in the Primary School.* Reading, University of Reading, Reading and Language Information Centre.
Hutchinson, D. (1987) 'Developing concepts of sentence structure and punctuation', *Curriculum*, 8(3): 13–16.
Truss, L. (2003) *Eats, Shoots and Leaves: The Zero Tolerance Approach to Punctuation*, London: Profile Books.
Waugh, D. (1998) 'Practical approaches to teaching punctuation in the primary school', *Reading*, 32(2): 14–17.

Annotated bibliography

Hall, N. and Robinson, A. (1996) *Learning About Punctuation.* Clevedon: Multilingual Matters.
A range of contributors offer their thoughts on the teaching of punctuation. Includes a study that looked at the development of a group of 8- and 9-year-old children.
L2 **

Kress, G. (1982) *Learning to Write*. London: Routledge and Kegan Paul.
An important text that looks closely at the differences between speech and writing. Also contains well-thought-out views on children's 'errors'.
L3 **

Wyse, D. and Shelbourne, H. (2005) 'Marks that make meaning (1)', *Primary English Magazine*, 11(1): 24–27.
The first of three articles (see volumes 11(2) and 11(3)) that expand some of the ideas touched on in this chapter.
L1 *

Chapter 16

Grammar or knowledge about language (KAL)

The value of many forms of grammar teaching continues to be in doubt. This chapter reminds us that questions about grammar teaching have been around for some time. We outline the difference between 'descriptive' grammar and 'prescriptive' grammar. An examination of the important idea of 'knowledge about language' is followed by reflections on the approach adopted in the PNS Framework.

The word 'grammar' itself is used in two very distinct ways: prescriptively and descriptively. Prescriptively, the term is used to prescribe how language should be used; descriptively the term is used to describe how the language actually is used. Prescriptive grammarians ☞ believe that English grammar is a fixed and unchanging series of rules which should be applied to the language. For prescriptive grammarians expressions like: *I ain't done nothing wrong*, or *We was going to the supermarket*, are quite simply wrong. To understand this a bit better it is necessary to consider two other related questions that often get muddled up with grammar in the public discourse ☞, and they are the question of style and the question of Standard English

Many complaints about incorrect grammar are actually complaints about style. Split infinitives ☞ are a case in point. There is nothing *grammatically* wrong with a sentence like: *I am hoping to quickly finish writing this paragraph*. It makes perfect sense, but it might be thought stylistically preferable to write: *I am hoping to finish writing this paragraph quickly*, or even to write: *I am hoping quickly to finish writing this paragraph*. However, if I were to write: *Hoping writing I paragraph finish to quickly am*, there would be something grammatically wrong with that!

So far as Standard English is concerned, an accident of history meant that, when printing developed, it was the Anglian regional dialect that was written down (➡ Chapter 1, 'The history of English, language and literacy'). Because it was written, it became the 'standard'. It would thus be more accurate to describe Standard English as the standard *dialect*. Other dialects are then described as 'non-standard'. Standard English is distinguished from non-standard dialects by features of vocabulary and features of grammar. In addition middle-class speech tends to keep some of the grammatical features of the written form, particularly with regard to the use of negatives and the use of some verb forms. Thus matters of class and matters of dialect have come to be linked.

From the point of view of *prescriptive* grammarians, the grammar of Standard English is 'good' or 'correct' grammar, and the grammar of non-standard dialects is 'bad' or 'incorrect' grammar. So, for example, children who say I *ain't done nothing*, often have their language 'corrected' by their teachers, and even by their own parents, on the ground that it is 'bad' grammar, or indeed, more generally, that it is just 'bad' English.

Descriptive grammarians are interested in describing how the language actually is used rather than how it ought to be used. Thus a descriptive grammarian will note that a middle-class speaker, using the standard dialect known as Standard English, may say: *We were pleased to see you*, and that a working-class speaker using a working-class cockney dialect may say: *We was pleased to see you*. Both examples are grammatical within their own dialects, both examples make perfect sense, and in neither example is there any ambiguity. The idea that a plural subject takes a plural verb is true only of the middle-class standard dialect, not of the working-class Cockney dialect. To put it another way, the plural form of the verb in middle-class standard is *were*, while the plural form of the verb in working-class Cockney is *was*.

Let us now offer this simple working definition: *Grammar is an account of the relationship between words in a sentence*. In the light of this definition what the grammarian has to do is to look for regular patterns of word use in the language, and give labels to them. However, some of the relationships are pretty complicated, and describing them is not easy. The definitions many of us half-remember from our own primary school days – 'a noun is a naming word', 'a verb is a doing word' – are at best unhelpful and at worst downright misleading. Though meaning has a part to play in determining the relationship between words, parts of speech are not defined in terms of word meaning, they are defined, rather, in terms of the function of the words within the sentence. As an example of what we mean, think about the word *present*.

Present can be a verb:

I **present** you with this tennis racket as a reward for your services.

or a noun:

Thank you for my birthday **present**, I've always wanted socks!

or an adjective:

In the **present** circumstances I feel unable to proceed.

It will be clear, then, that teaching grammar has its problems. Confusion can occur at a number of levels: between prescriptive and descriptive approaches, between questions of grammar proper and questions of style, and around issues of variation between standard and non-standard dialects.

Grammar or knowledge about language (KAL)

The teaching of reading and writing, of spelling and punctuation requires the continual use of everyday language about language: words such as *alphabet, letter, word, spelling, sentence, full stop* are all language about language (the technical term for this is metalanguage or metalinguistic). In addition, many teachers take the opportunities offered by reading and writing to draw children's attention to specific items of vocabulary. Much of this specific attention to language itself is at the word and sentence level.

The proposal to teach children explicitly about language raises some questions:

- What are the reasons for teaching primary children about language?
- What are the benefits to be gained?
- What should be taught, and at what ages?
- How should it be taught?
- What is the place of terminology?
- Where does grammar fit into all of this?

Cox (1991) suggested that there are two justifications for teaching children explicitly about language. The first is that it will be beneficial to their language use in general. The second is that it is essential to children's understanding of their social and cultural environment, given the role language plays in society. A third suggestion, related to the second, is that 'language should be studied in its own right as a rich and fascinating example of human behaviour' (LINC, 1992: 1).

Prior to the PNS Framework sensible cautions were expressed about the likelihood that grammar teaching would have a beneficial effect on children's reading and writing:

> Language study can influence use, but development of the relationship between learning about language and learning how to use it is not a linear one but rather a recursive, cyclical and mutually informing relationship.
>
> (Carter, 1990: 4)

The PNS Framework objectives for grammar are:

- • vary and adapt sentence structure for meaning and effect
- • use a range of punctuation correctly to support meaning and emphasis
- • convey meaning through grammatically accurate and correctly punctuated sentences.

Year 1
Compose and write simple sentences independently to communicate meaning

Year 2
Write simple and compound sentences and begin to use subordination in relation to time and reason
Compose sentences using tense consistently (present and past)

Year 3
Show relationships of time, reason and cause through subordination and connectives
Compose sentences using adjectives, verbs and nouns for precision, clarity and impact

Year 4
Clarify meaning and point of view by using varied sentence structure (phrases, clauses and adverbials)

Year 5
Adapt sentence construction to different text-types, purposes and readers

Year 6
Express subtle distinctions of meaning, including hypothesis, speculation and supposition, by constructing sentences in varied ways

The three overall objectives with their focus on meaning are entirely appropriate. However, the further specification of these in the objectives for each year leads to a mismatch. The Year 3 objectives are particularly problematic. Appropriate grammar for a piece of writing is dependent on the intentions of the writer, the genre, and the extent to which the various elements cohere. Whether the writing shows subordination or parts of speech as specified in Year 3 is not particularly relevant. It is very difficult to see a sensible rationale for this kind of grammatical requirement except as an awkward compromise between the old NLS Framework for Teaching and the current PNS Framework, which still recommends the *Grammar for Writing* resource (Department for Education and Employment, 2000).

While it looks possible that the right sort of detailed attention to language itself may be more widely beneficial, research has clearly shown that grammar teaching does not have a positive effect on children's writing (➡ Chapter 11). We must look, therefore, to the other justification for language study: that it is a subject of inherent interest both in its own right and in the role that it plays in wider social and cultural life. The question immediately arises as to the appropriate age range for language study and, while earlier reports delayed any systematic attention to language until the later primary years, in the current orders for English in the National Curriculum explicit attention to language is seen as appropriate from the reception year.

Although the Language in the National Curriculum (LINC) project was carried out many years ago now, its recommendations about teaching knowledge about language are still valid. The starting point is that children should be encouraged to discuss language use in meaningful contexts that engage their interest. Here are some examples of work done in primary schools under the auspices of the LINC project, all of which were extremely productive in getting children to think and talk about language itself (all examples from Bain *et al.*, 1992):

- Making word lists.
- Compiling dictionaries including slang and dialect dictionaries.
- Discussing language variation and social context. For example, how does a mobile phone text message compare with a formal letter?
- Discussing accent, and Standard English.
- Compiling personal language histories and language profiles.
- Capitalising on the language resource of the multilingual classroom beginning with in-depth knowledge of languages spoken, read, written and their social contexts including religious ones.
- Role play and drama particularly to explore levels of formality and their links with language.
- The history and use of language in the local environment.
- Collecting and writing jokes.
- Collaborative writing which involves discussion about features of writing and language.
- Media work including the language of adverts.
- Book making.

One of the aspects of language variation is the way that spoken language differs from written language as Table 16.1 shows.

Many of the examples in the list above could be and indeed were done with the youngest children, and terminology was learned in context as and when the children needed it in their work.

Effective grammar teaching will involve pupils playing with language, and exploring language in ways that are meaningful and fun. Teachers will need both to understand the issues and to be confident in naming terms themselves, so that they can then use them with confidence in everyday discussion with

Table 16.1 Differences between speech and print

Speech	Print
Requires other speakers to be present at time of speech (unless recorded)	Readers are not present at time of writing
Speakers take turns	Primary writer works alone
Instant and cannot be changed	Can be composed and reworked
Can be incomplete but make sense because of shared understanding of conversation	Writing usually doesn't make sense if it is not complete
Intonation, pitch and body language used to support meaning	Fonts effects such as italics used to support meaning
Organised in communicative units	Organised in sentences
Separated by pauses in flow of sounds	Separated by punctuation
Words integrated within stream of sounds	Words demarcated by spaces
Consists of phonemes (sounds)	Consists of graphemes (letters)
Accent and dialect recognisable feature of speakers	Accent and dialect not a feature unless used as deliberate device in fiction or poetry
Tends to be informal	Tends to be formal

pupils. If teachers use the terms correctly with the children all the time, the children will learn what the terms refer to, even if they are not able to define them to the satisfaction of a linguistics expert until they are older. Dry as dust decontextualised old-fashioned grammar exercises of the *underline the noun* variety do not work and put more children off than they help. In addition, text-books that do not discuss dialect variation, that confuse matters of style with matters of grammar, and that take a prescriptive 'correct English' approach throughout are to be avoided.

Practice points

- The main point of grammar teaching should be to enthuse an interest in the way that language works.
- Engage children's curiosity about language through work on, for example, accent and dialect.
- Use metalanguage only if it actually helps learning.

Glossary

Grammarian – someone who studies grammar.
Infinitive – part of a verb that is used with 'to': e.g. to *go* boldly.

Public discourse – discussions and debates in the public domain particularly seen through the media.

References

Bain, R., Fitzgerald, B. and Taylor, M. (1992) *Looking into Language: Classroom Approaches to Knowledge about Language*. Sevenoaks: Hodder & Stoughton.
Carter, R. (ed.) (1990) *Knowledge about Language and the Curriculum: The LINC Reader*. London: Hodder & Stoughton.
Cox, B. (1991) *Cox on Cox: An English Curriculum for the 1990s*. London: Hodder & Stoughton.
Department for Education and Employment (DfEE) (2000) *The National Literacy Strategy: Grammar for Writing*. London: DfEE Publications.
Language in the National Curriculum (LINC) (1992) 'Materials for professional development', unpublished.

Annotated bibliography

Bain, R., Fitzgerald, B. and Taylor, M. (1992) *Looking into Language: Classroom Approaches to Knowledge about Language*. Sevenoaks: Hodder & Stoughton.
This is the book that describes some of the classroom activities that arose out of the LINC project. There are lots of excellent ideas here, some of which could even be adapted for use within a literacy hour, but others of which would be more suitable for extended language and literacy work.
L2 **
Carter, R. and McCarthy, M. (2006) *Cambridge Grammar of English*. Cambridge: Cambridge University Press.
A comprehensive account of English grammar that uses examples of oral and printed language in modern use (corpus data) in order to describe and explain the way the language works.
L3 **
Crystal, D. (1988) *Rediscover Grammar*. Harlow: Longman.
The best book of its kind if you want to learn about grammatical terms and concepts. Succinct and as straightforward as possible.
L1
Qualifications and Curriculum Authority (QCA) (1998) *The Grammar Papers: Perspectives on the Teaching of Grammar in the National Curriculum*. London: QCA Publications.
A collection of six papers from unnamed writers. In the examples they give there is an emphasis on the pupils' production of language in meaningful situations, and the sixth paper is a useful review of the research evidence about teaching grammar.
L3 ***

Wyse, D. (2006). 'Pupils' word choices and the teaching of grammar'. *Cambridge Journal of Education*, 36(1): 31–47.
This paper shows what Year 5 and Year 6 pupils say about their reasons for selecting unconventional grammar. It is suggested that unconventional grammar is directly linked to text-level concerns.
L3 ***

Chapter 17

Assessing writing

The main purpose of assessment is to feed into decisions about future teaching. We start by considering marking as an assessment tool. This is followed by thoughts on the vital job of formative assessment ☞. The section on summative assessment ☞ includes reflections on national tests and target setting. This chapter should be read in conjunction with Chapter 10, 'Assessing reading' and Chapter 22, 'Assessing talk', as some strategies – such as diaries of observations – are applicable to all three modes and other strategies are specific to one mode.

Some of the most important assessment of children's writing is carried out orally during the process of writing when the teacher sits with the child and offers advice. This kind of advice is likely to be most effective if the teacher has a clear idea of how children's writing should develop (➡ Chapter 11, 'The development of writing') and has a clear idea about how to interact. The other day-to-day activity that can be a vital assessment tool is marking: either with the child or after the event.

Formative assessment

One of the ideas about responding to children's work is that every single piece of written work should be marked. If we pause to consider the volume of writing that children produce in school, we quickly realise that this is not a realistic or manageable idea. If we take a class of 30 children and conservatively estimate that they might generate four pieces of writing every day, that would total 600 pieces of writing in one week alone. If you gave only 2 minutes to each piece of writing, that would mean 20 hours marking per week. The practical reality of these figures means that decisions need to be made on which work should be sampled for marking. Ideally these decisions should be agreed as part of a whole school marking policy.

The choice of pupils' writing for detailed feedback depends on the nature of the writing and your approach to assessment. One of the ways to select can be on the basis of range. So if on the last occasion you marked a story, then a piece of non-fiction might be appropriate the next time. Or if on the previous occasion you had commented on the presentation of a final draft, you might want to comment on an early draft. It is worth remembering that appropriate written comments can be collected together to form the basis of an assessment profile for a child.

One of the difficult aspects of marking children's work relates to the range of choices that are available for your response. One possible way to think about these choices can be to have a system for responding:

1 A specific positive comment about the writing.
2 A specific point about improving something that is individual to the child's writing.
3 A specific point about improving something that relates to a more general target for writing.

One of the common criticisms about marking is that ticks, stars, smiley faces, scores out of 10, etc., can be used too much. These give no information to the child about what in particular they did well or specifically how they could improve next time. However, for young children the extrinsic rewards such as stickers, smiley faces or merit awards can be an important way of rewarding hard work. As a teacher you need to be clear about the pros and cons of the different strategies. A tick at the end of a piece of work should perhaps only be used to indicate that you have checked that the child completed the work and it indicates that you have skim read the piece. A reward such as a sticker could be used to indicate that the child has worked particularly hard and ideally should accompany more detailed feedback which could be oral and/or written.

The terms *personalised learning* and *assessment for learning* have been promoted by government. Government has described personalised learning as 'the drive to tailor education to individual need, interest and aptitude' (Department for Education and Skills, 2004: 4). Assessment for learning is essentially about high-quality formative assessment as opposed to assessment *of* learning which is summative assessment. Formative assessment methods require your skills as a perceptive observers of children's development. If learning is really to be personalised, then it requires children to be given real choices about their education. To take the teaching of writing this could mean giving them choices over the kind of writing that they carry out. However, in reality, personalised learning can too easily become just another government phrase representing another version of the standards agenda which has been the driving force of education policy since 1997.

One of the dominant aspects of teaching in recent years has been the requirement to ensure that teaching is informed by lesson objectives. This is linked with the presumption that the best kind of assessment is that which assesses carefully against the objectives of the lesson. Box 17.1 is an example of objective-led assessment.

Although this kind of assessment ensures a careful focus on a pre-determined aspect of learning, the best kind of formative assessment of writing really is personalised. It involves the teacher sitting with the child, reading the writing and discussing it with the them (and or providing written feedback after the lesson).

Summative assessment

The most important feature of the statutory assessment system is the National Curriculum levels of attainment. These levels determine the kinds of summative judgements that are made about pupils' progress. The statutory tests and teachers' judgements are determined by the level descriptions ☞. When teachers decide on the National Curriculum level descriptions that best fit their children's writing they need to consider a range of writing. This often means that annotated portfolios ☞ of writing are kept and used as the basis of the teacher's judgements. The teacher's own written records can also usefully contribute to the judgement. One of the challenges for all assessment processes, including the SATs, is to make sure that the assessments are fair for all children: this requires moderation ☞.

Box 17.1 *Example of teacher-assessment format*

Objectives:

1. To construct an argument in note form or full text to persuade others of a point of view
2. Present the case to the class or a group
3. Evaluate its effectiveness

Names	1.	2.	3.	Observations
James Boyd	Δ	Δ	\	Strong key points and presentation but found evaluation difficult
Yasmin Akhbar	Δ	L	Δ	Not enough points made to convince the class but was able to recognise this when evaluating
Gemma Corkhill	Δ	Δ	L	Struggled with sequence of ideas but presentation was convincing
Etc.				

Key: Δ = objective achieved; *L* = further teaching required; \ = objective not achieved

---

The National Curriculum in Action website is a very useful resource for helping you to arrive at judgements about your pupils' work. It is possible to search for examples of pupils' work in different subjects and at different National Curriculum levels of attainment. The accompanying commentaries are detailed and explain why particular judgements have been made. For example, the writing of a child called Bethan is featured. The collection features several pieces of writing by Bethan showing a range of genres. In one example she responds to the book *Carrie's War* by writing a letter and a diary entry in role as Carrie. Here is the commentary:

Writing
Bethan's writing shows understanding of the letter form and a developing awareness of the diary form.

The letter is appropriately set out, suitably introduced and concluded, and contains well-selected details from the book. The tone and style are appropriate for an informal letter and the information has been structured into paragraphs.

Similarly, the diary entry contains lively information about their journey and arrival as evacuees ('I wanted to cry but I felt too old for that').

The diary has a literary style and retells the story from the point of view of the main character. However, it does not include other features characteristic of diaries, such as reflection and comment, and it is not paragraphed.

In both the letter and diary, Bethan gives clues to the writer's feelings rather than stating them obviously ('As I tried to get to sleep I kept thinking about how neat and tidy everything was. I wondered how I could get used to it'). She selects different information from the book for each task to avoid repetition.

Bethan uses appropriate tenses in both – a mixture of present and past in the letter, and past in the diary.

Bethan employs a good range of strategies to elaborate her statements and make them interesting in both her letter ('Nick got constapated because in the daytime we can't use the flush toilet') and her diary ('a plump little lady').

In her diary, she uses a variety of sentence conjunctions to order information concisely ('When we went upstairs we had to step on a large piece of white material'). Connectives in the diary link related points together and move the narration forward ('when we arrived . . . until there were only . . . then finally . . . just then . . . As I tried to get to sleep').

Most sentences are demarcated with capitals and full stops, and Bethan is beginning to use the comma within sentences to demarcate some adverbial clauses, though not phrases. Sometimes the comma is used instead of a full stop.

Apostrophes are used accurately in most instances for omission and possession. The punctuation of direct speech is often accurate but not paragraphed, and brackets are used in the diary entry to provide more information for the reader.

Bethan's writing matches some of the features expected for Level 4 in writing. To develop her writing, Bethan needs to:

- include reflection and comments the narrator might make about the events being described;
- organise her text into paragraphs;
- demarcate phrases and clauses within sentences.

Although this example represents a high quality of assessment, it also shows the amount of work that is involved. Nearly every sentence of the quote would require careful consideration by the teacher. It must be remembered that this assessment is only for writing and that the primary teacher has many other subjects and areas to assess. Once again it is important to reiterate that the best assessment has to be manageable in order to be of a high quality.

Statutory tests

The writing tests present a much more complex picture than the reading tests that we looked at in Chapter 10. Once again we refer to the 2006 test pack for our explanation. The first part of the writing test consists of what is called the 'Shorter Task' and a spelling test. The shorter task has to be completed in 20 minutes, including five minutes' thinking time. The task booklet begins with a writing prompt to help the pupils:

Endangered Creature
Imagine a creature called a Tongo Lizard.
  It is an endangered creature, which means that very few remain and it may become extinct.

[Picture of lizard.]

An information book about endangered creatures is being prepared.

Your task is to write the page about the Tongo Lizard

This was followed by a planning format like a topic map and four prompts for the children to think about. The mark scheme for the short task has two components: 'sentence structure, punctuation and text organisation' is worth a maximum of four marks, and 'composition and effect' is worth eight marks. When the seven marks for the spelling test are added there are a total of 19 marks available for the short task.
  The longer task had this prompt:

Dear Diary . . .
A brother and sister went on a day out with their family.

Tom really enjoyed the outing, but Sara did not.

[Picture of boy and girl with speech bubbles expressing their different views.]

When they returned home, Tom and Sara wrote about the day in their diaries.

Your task is to write Tom and Sara's diary entries.

The longer task has a maximum of eight marks for sentence structure and punctuation, eight marks for text structure and organisation, twelve marks for composition and effect, and three marks for handwriting. In order to achieve the highest marks the criteria are:

Sentence structure and punctuation
Band A5
- Length and focus of sentences varied to express subtleties in meaning and to focus on key ideas. Sentences may include embedded subordinate clauses, sometimes for economy of expression; word order used to create emphasis/conversational effect.

8 marks

Text structure and organisation
Band B5
- The structure of the text is controlled and shaped across the two diary entries. Sequencing of sections or paragraphs contributes to overall effectiveness, e.g. strategic placing of most significant event common to both entries.
- Sections or paragraphs varied in length and structure, ideas connected in a variety of ways, e.g. an event given prominence in one diary is deliberately dealt with briefly in the other.

8 marks

Composition and effect
Band C5
- Choice and placing of content adapted for effect, e.g. contrast in characters subtly revealed by what is prioritised or dealt with briefly.
- Viewpoint well controlled and convincing, e.g. writer manages two contrasting positions and develops attitudes of both characters through reflection.

- Stylistic devices fully support purpose and engage, e.g. Tom's and Sara's language is stylistically distinct.

12 marks

Handwriting
Band F3
The handwriting is consistent and fluent with letters and words appropriately placed. The handwriting maintains a personal style to engage the reader.

3 marks

One of the key features of the tests is that they are supposed to assess the child's National Curriculum level for the different subjects. The average level for children's writing at the end of Key Stage 2 is Level 4:

Level 4
Pupils' writing in a range of forms is lively and thoughtful. Ideas are often sustained and developed in interesting ways and organised appropriately for the purpose of the reader. Vocabulary choices are often adventurous and words are used for effect. Pupils are beginning to use grammatically complex sentences, extending meaning. Spelling, including that of polysyllabic words that conform to regular patterns, is generally accurate. Full stops, capital letters and question marks are used correctly, and pupils are beginning to use punctuation within the sentence. Handwriting style is fluent, joined and legible.

Some children will achieve Level 5:

Level 5
Pupils' writing is varied and interesting, conveying meaning clearly in a range of forms for different readers, using a more formal style where appropriate. Vocabulary choices are imaginative and words are used precisely. Simple and complex sentences are organised into paragraphs. Words with complex regular patterns are usually spelled correctly. A range of punctuation, including commas, apostrophes and inverted commas, is usually used accurately. Handwriting is joined, clear and fluent and, where appropriate, is adapted to a range of tasks.

To ensure that there is a match between these National Curriculum levels and the marking criteria for the tests, 'assessment focuses' are shown for the different marking categories shown above. So 'composition and effect' includes the assessment focus 'write imaginative, interesting and thoughtful texts', yet nowhere in the detail of the criteria is the marker required to make a judgement about whether the writing is 'imaginative' or 'interesting'. Nowhere! And therein lies the problem with the writing tests. Surely one of the most important features about nearly every piece of writing is that it is interesting. For fiction and poetry, in particular, the imagination of the writer is absolutely central to the success of the writing. Given that both the short test and the long test required the children to 'Use your imagination', it is doubly remiss that the criteria did not require the markers to make a judgement about this.

If the criteria included judgements about things like imagination, interest and thoughtfulness perhaps the marks for the following example test responses might be different:

> I had an awful day . . . we went to a Roman museum, I've always wanted to go there. Oh, how could you tell I was being sarcastic? It was so boring. I begged and pleaded not to go right from the beginning. My feet hurt where we trampled round every tiny inch of the museum. I decided to cheer myself up by helping Tom build the tapestry but it just got me down even more because it was far too hard, but Tom managed to do it and he's younger than me! By the time we got to write our name in Roman I was bored stiff. What a stupid idea it was to write our name in Roman. Only people from sadland would do that! Oh, to make matters worse we stopped at every single fact sheet, and there were 200 of them. I was tired, bored and just over all FED UP! I mean we must have been the first family to stand there and look at every single fact sheet. I hope we never go back there again.

> I had an awful day . . . my little brother threw sand at me. My dad threw me under the water. My mum pulled my hair and when I had an ice-cream my brother made me drop it so that I couldn't have one. The best bit was when we had lunch because I had more than my brother. But when we went on the jet skis I fell off and nearly drowned. Then we went home we fell asleep in the car. When we woke up my brother came over and gave me a cuddle and he brought me an ice-cream with his money. My mum took me out shopping with my friends and I got 2 dresses and 2 tops.

There are many things about the second piece that we like. The images are instantly recognisable, powerful and presented in quick succession. This is a writer using their senses and their authentic memories of childhood: sand in the eyes; struggling to breathe underwater; the disappointment of the upturned ice-cream; and the real danger of drowning. And what a wonderful touching moment when the brother gives his sister a cuddle – read Anthony Browne's book *Tunnel* for a powerful exploration of these emotions. It's a shame that the repetition of 'when/then we' wasn't varied more towards the end of the piece.

The writer of the first piece does use devices well, and we liked the idea of 'sadland' particularly. But, just as the writer was bored, well, I'm afraid we got bored reading about them being bored. It also made us want to say, you ungrateful child, you don't deserve to be taken to a museum. But perhaps that is a sign that the writer had engaged our emotions!

And the marks for these pieces of writing for composition and effect, shown in the test marking guide for 2006? – Twelve marks for the first piece and *three marks* for the second piece.

Practice points

- Improve your interaction with children to enhance formative assessment skills.
- Keep diaries of observations of children's English development.
- Keep a balance between high-quality in-depth assessment and simpler day-to-day quick assessment.

Glossary

Formative assessment – ongoing assessment that is used to inform teaching, interaction and planning.

Level descriptions – short paragraphs in the National Curriculum that describe the understanding that children should have gained in order to attain a particular level.

Moderation – the process of agreeing assessment judgements with other people.

Portfolio – a collection of children's work that often includes forms for teachers' comments.

Summative assessment – assessment that sums up progress at a particular point in time.

References

Department for Education and Skills (DfES) (2004) 'A national conversation about personalised learning', retrieved 9 January, 2006, from http://www.standards.dfes.gov.uk/personalisedlearning/?version=1

Qualification and Curriculum Authority (QCA) (2001) 'Letter and diary entry ("Carrie's War") – Bethan', retrieved 9 January, 2007, from http://www.ncaction.org.uk

Annotated bibliography

Gipps, C., McCallum, B. and Hargreaves, E. (2000) *What Makes a Good Primary School Teacher*. London: RoutledgeFalmer.
The assessment chapter in this book covers the whole curriculum but many of the suggestions are relevant to the assessment of writing.
L2 **

Gipps, C. and Murphy, P. (1994) *A Fair Test? Assessment, Achievement and Equity*. Buckingham: Open University Press.
This award-winning book looks in detail at some of the issues that underpin assessment. Gipps has developed great expertise in this field so many of her publications are worth reading.
L3 **

Harlen, W. and Deakin Crick, R. (2002) 'A systematic review of the impact of summative assessment and tests on students' motivation for learning (eppi-centre review, version 1.1*)', *Research Evidence in Education Library. Issue 1.* Retrieved 9 January, 2007, from http://eppi.ioe.ac.uk/cms/Default.aspx?tabid=108
This review clearly shows the negative aspects of high stakes testing systems.
L3 ***

Qualification and Curriculum Authority (QCA) (2001) 'Letter and diary entry ("Carrie's War") – Bethan', retrieved 9 January, 2007, from http://www.ncaction.org.uk
Very useful examples of children's writing and commentaries explaining assessment judgements.
L1 *

Part IV

Speaking and listening

Chapter 18

The development of language

Stages of language acquisition are described as several dimensions. Educational policy for language in the Foundation Stage and speaking and listening in the National Curriculum are explored. It is argued that the term language should be used to describe speaking and listening for both Foundation Stage and National Curriculum documents.

By the age of 5, provided they do not have language difficulties, all children have acquired the adult grammar for the main constructions of their native language (Peccei, 2006). This is true across all cultures and in all languages. The term 'acquired' in this context is important because linguists make a distinction between emergent language constructions and ones which are fully acquired.

Nature versus nurture arguments are still a potent force in discussions about how child language develops. One of the most famous advocates of the idea that language development is natural was Noam Chomsky. In his early work he hypothesised that children made use of a Language Acquisition Device (LAD). This device, he argued, is a special capacity of the brain that enables children to use the rules systems of their native language. Jerome Bruner countered that Chomsky's theory correctly identified this aspect of the child's capacity but that this was only part of the process of language acquisition:

> The infant's Language Acquisition Device could not function without the aid given by an adult who enters with him into a transactional format. That format, initially under the control of the adult, provides a Language Acquisition Support System (LASS). It frames or structures the input of language and interaction to the child's Language Acquisition Device in a manner to 'make the system function'. In a word, it is the interaction between the LAD and the LASS that makes it possible for the infant to enter the linguistic community – and, at the same time, the culture to which the language gives access.
>
> (Bruner, 1983: 19)

Messer (2006) shows the ways that such debates have continued to be an important part of thinking about children's language acquisition. Chomsky's later work involved theories of minimalism. One of the important features of minimalist theory is the idea that many aspects of grammar are contained in the vocabulary of a language, and its semantic information. Previous theories proposed that grammatical representations were independent of the vocabulary. Minimalist ideas and other developments in the field have resulted in language development theorists focusing on the way that the human brain operates more generally. Neuro-scientists have defined the brain's activity in terms of connectionist networks, neural networks or parallel distributed processes, which are different terms describing the same general phenomena. Connectionist networks have been explored by encouraging computers to learn grammatical features such as past tense. Computers have had success with both regular and irregular past tense forms. The point of such work is to research the extent to which language features are innate, hence not learnable by computers, or can be learned. However, as Messer cautions, there has also been a welcome resurgence of interest in how adults speak to children and scepticism about all-encompassing grand theories such as Chomsky's LAD. As you will see later in this chapter, language development seems to progress along several routes simultaneously.

One of the important ideas in relation to children's language acquisition was the concept of *motherese*, the impact, appropriateness and helpfulness of language interactions particularly between mothers and their children (see Tizard and Hughes, 1984). This is now called Child Directed Speech (CDS) in recognition of the fact that it is not just mothers who modify their speech when talking to young children. Peccei (2006) points out that there is no clear evidence that CDS should be seen particularly as a teaching tool. She accurately observes that CDS is probably just a natural response to the fact that young children use talk which is semantically and syntactically simple; therefore if an adult is to communicate effectively with them they need to use a similar kind of language. This perhaps suggests that natural forms of communication between adults and children, commensurate with the child's language at different stages, are beneficial.

Language acquisition

One of the most important aspects of learning to talk is the ability to hold a sustained conversation. Discourse development requires the learning of many sophisticated understandings. In education settings the ability to take turns, and having to signal that you want to speak by putting your hand up, is one of the important areas that differs significantly from the home language environment. There are also many conventions, such as manners, that have to be learned. Children also learn that language differs according to who they are talking to. So a conversation with an adult will be different from talk with their peers. Discourse development, which is a particularly important aspect of language, is served by development in all the other areas listed in Table 18.1 which are explained below (Table 18.1 and the following information is summarised from Peccei, 2006).

The main stages of children's syntactic development begin with single words and then move on to two-word phrases. After this, children's syntax develops rapidly and on many fronts. Negative sentences such as 'I am not walking' and the use of complex sentence types will be areas that develop during the nursery stage. The ability to ask questions is another aspect of syntax that develops at this time.

The word morphological comes from morpheme. A morpheme is the smallest unit of language that can change meaning. For example, if we take the singular 'apple' and turn it into the plural 'apples', then the letter 's' is a morpheme because it changes the meaning from singular to plural. Morphemes that can stand alone, such as 'apple', are called *free morphemes*, and those which cannot, such as -s in apples, are called bound morphemes. Children's development of morphological understanding can be seen in their capacity to invent words, such as 'carsiz' (cars).

Lexical ☞ development is concerned with the development of vocabulary so is not something that has a particular end point because we continue to add vocabulary throughout our lives. One of the features of children's lexical development is over-extension. An example of over-extension is where children call all meats chicken because they are familiar with that word but not others such as beef, pork, etc. Another feature of lexical development is learning about the way that the meaning of words relate to each other, something called sense relations. Synonyms such as 'happy/joyful' and antonyms such as 'happy/sad' are part of this. This means that children can learn about vocabulary from words that they know without having to directly experience the concept of the word in question.

Phonological development ☞ has been much studied, partly because of its link with learning to read. As far as talk is concerned, there are some understandings and skills that have to be acquired before those which are beneficial for literacy. For, example the young child learns to control their vocal chords. The sound/airflow which passes from the vocal chords is obstructed in various ways in order to form phonemes (sounds). The place of articulation involves use of the teeth, lips, tongue, mouth and glottis. The manner of articulation involves obstructing the airflow to varying degrees such as completely stopping it or allowing some to pass through the nose.

Table 18.1 is a summary of Peccei's (2006) introductory chapters on children's language development. It shows the typical ages when significant developmental milestones in the areas described above occur.

Table 18.1 Summary of stages of children's language acquisition based on information from Peccei (2006)

Age	Phonological development	Sense relations	Vocabulary	Morphological development	Syntactic development	Discourse development
Birth to two months	Vowel-like sounds such as crying and grunting					
Two to four months	Cooing					
Four to six months	Vocal play including rudimentary syllables such as /da/ or /goo/					
Six months	Babbling such as /ba/ba/ba/ or /ga/ba/ da/do					
One year	First meaningful words					
Nine months to one year three months						Prelinguistic directive such as speech sounds and pointing
One year and six months to one year and eight months			First 50 words acquired			
One year three months to two years						Telegraphic directives: e.g. 'that mine', 'gimme'

Age			
Two years	Average vocabulary = 200–300 words		Begin to put words together in sentences. Noun phrases with pre-modification of the noun: e.g. 'more biscuit'. Pronouns appear: e.g. 'me want that'
Two years and three months		Past tense inflection appears	
Two years to two years four months			Limited routines: 'Where's my X?', 'What's that?'
Two years and six months		Starting to acquire rules for inflecting nouns and verbs: e.g. 'breaked it' or 'mouses'	Multiple pre-modification of nouns: e.g. that red ball
Two years eight months			Compound sentences: e.g. 'The dog bit the cat and then he ran away'
Two to three years	Refer to all members of category as the same: e.g. all flowers as flower		

(continued overleaf)

Table 18.1 Continued.

Age	Phonological development	Sense relations	Vocabulary	Morphological development	Syntactic development	Discourse development
Two years nine months						Greater precision of articulation in self-repairs, increased volume and use of contrastive stress: e.g. 'It was *on* the chair!' (not under it)
Three years					Post-modified phrases: e.g. 'the picture of Lego town'. Complex sentences	Can cope with non-situated discourse
Two years four months to three years eight months						Embedded requests: 'Can I have big boy shoes?'
Three years eight months to four years						Conversation consists largely of initiation/response (I/R) exchanges
Four years						Elaborate oblique strategies: 'We haven't had any sweets for a long time'

Four years to four years seven months	Acquisition of auxilliary verbs (might, may, could) and negation. Child's response itself increasingly becomes R/I
Four years seven months to four years ten months	Greater ability to encode justifications and causal relationships allows for longer exchanges
Four to five	Spontaneously use category names: e.g. rose or daisy
Four years six months	Coordination with ellipsis: e.g. 'The dog bit the cat and ran away'
Three years eight months to five years seven months	Advanced embedding: 'Don't forget to buy sweets'
Six years old	Average vocabulary understood = 14,000 words. Average spoken vocabulary = 6,000 words

Speaking and listening in educational policy and practice

Prior to the 1960s the idea that talk should be an important part of the English curriculum would have been greeted with some scepticism. However, in the 1960s, educational researchers became increasingly interested in the idea that learning could be enhanced by careful consideration of the role of talk. Andrew Wilkinson's work resulted in him coining the new word 'oracy' as a measure of how important he thought talk was, a fact confirmed by the *Oxford English Dictionary* which lists Wilkinson's text historically as the first time the word was used in print:

> **1965** A. WILKINSON *Spoken Eng.* 14 The term we suggest for general ability in the oral skills is *oracy*; one who has those skills is *orate*, one without them *inorate*.

The establishment of a new word is perhaps the most fitting sign of Wilkinson's legacy. The work of Wilkinson and other educationists resulted in speaking and listening becoming part of the National Curriculum programmes of study for the subject English.

Although the speaking and listening requirements of the National Curriculum remained statutory from 1997 onwards, the implementation of the National Literacy Strategy meant that in practice speaking and listening was neglected due to a powerful focus on reading in particular, and writing to a lesser extent. It was not only the fact that speaking and listening programmes of study were not addressed by the NLS Framework for Teaching but the teaching methods that were strongly advocated by the NLS also resulted in weaker oral work as a series of strong research studies has shown. English *et al.* (2002) found that there was a conflict between the achievement of short-term lesson objectives that are a feature of the NLS Framework for Teaching and the fostering of extended pupil contributions. In 2006, an attempt was made to address the absence of speaking and listening by including strands of objectives for speaking and listening in the new literacy framework. In view of the discussion about the importance of oracy the title *literacy* framework when describing the inclusion of speaking and listening objectives seems nonsensical.

Few would argue that speaking and listening is not an important feature of early years and primary teaching and learning but there are still a number of questions that need to be asked. One of the key questions concerns the balance between speaking and listening, reading, and writing. To answer this question there is a need to separate the content to be covered from considerations of teaching style. It seems to us that most of the debates about oracy and the recent considerations of talk in teaching and learning have more to do with teaching style than a careful consideration of programmes of study. If national curricula are present, as they are in England, then it is appropriate that they should specify

the content of the curriculum. This can apply to commu
listening just as it can apply to reading and writing and
curriculum. However, there is a need for clear thinking abo
should be. We would argue that if teachers' practice more rc
things like exploratory talk and dialogic teaching (Alexander
be appropriate to reduce the overall content of the progran
speaking and listening. This would require renewed thinking
content should be and might lead to more of a focus on some   ~ kinds of
language exploration quite rightly advocated by the Language in the National
Curriculum (LINC) project of the 1980s.

By examining the stages of language acquisition and beginning to understand the theories of how and why this process takes place, it becomes clear
that pre-school experience is an important factor in the child's language
development. The significance of the way that adults interact with the child
at this time should not be underestimated. It has been acknowledged that adults
provide a number of important conditions for the child as they do the
following:

- provide access to an environment where talk has high status;
- provide access to competent users of language;
- provide opportunities to engage in talk;
- provide responses which acknowledge the child as a competent language
  user.

(Wray *et al.*, 1989: 39)

In addition, adults model (in an unplanned way) the conventions of language;
provide feedback on the effectiveness of a child's ability to communicate by
responding to them; scaffold the child's language learning; and enable the child
to test their current hypotheses about how language works. The ability of the
adult to take into account the limited abilities of the child and adjust their
language accordingly so that the child can make sense of them is intuitive for
most parents.

The degree to which a rich language environment assists language development has been well documented. Two examples of relevant studies here are
those of Tizard and Hughes (1984) and Wells (1986). Both document the
influence of language experiences on a child's ability to use language and communicate effectively. Wells's study, for example, found a correlation between
the amount of conversation experienced with parents and other members of
their family circle and children's rates of progress in language learning.

Even though most of the language acquisition process is complete as children
enter school, there is much that the teacher can do in the early years to consolidate and develop these skills. Littleton *et al.* (2005), in their work with 6- and 7-
year-old children, suggest that exploratory talk is particularly desirable and
something that teachers should encourage:

exploratory talk demonstrates the active joint engagement of the children with one another's ideas. Whilst initiations may be challenged and counter-challenged, appropriate justifications are articulated and alternative hypotheses offered . . . Progress, thus emerges from the joint acceptance of suggestions.

(ibid.: 173)

Children's language acquisition is likely to be stronger if they are encouraged to become active participants in conversation, if they are encouraged to be questioning (despite how frustrating this can be for some adults to deal with), to hypothesise, imagine, wonder, project and dream out loud, to hear stories and to tell stories to others, experiencing a range of telling techniques which illustrate the potential power of the spoken word. The social and cultural aspects of language development are equally important at this time, as children learn, through talk, to place themselves within a specific social context, and in this way the development of language and identity are closely linked.

The quality of social experience and interaction will vary greatly between children, and, during the early years, teachers need to be aware that some children will arrive at school appearing to be confident, articulate users of the English language, whereas others seem less comfortable language users. However, teachers should beware deficit models and remember that it is too easy to label a child's spoken language as 'poor', or even to say that they have 'no language', without sufficient thought. Bearne, for example, offers a transcription of a discussion including Sonnyboy, a 6-year-old boy from a Traveller community, demonstrating his ability to 'translate' language for other children:

Emily:	I loves them little things.
Sonnyboy:	Yeah . . . I loves the little said things – that tiny wee spade . . . And this little bucket . . .
Teacher:	Do you think it would be a good idea to ask Cathy to get some? (*Cathy runs a playgroup for the Traveller children on their site.*)
Emily:	What for?
Teacher:	So that you'd have some at home.
Sonnyboy:	And who'd pay for them? Would Cathy pay?
Teacher:	No, it would be part of the kit.
Emily:	I don't know what you mean. Kit – who's Kit? Me Da's called Kit – would me Da have to pay?
Sonnyboy:	Not your Da – it's not that sort of kit, Emily. It's the sort a box with things in that you play with . . . like toys and things for the little ones.

(Bearne, 1998: 154)

It is important then that teachers understand about language diversity and the ways in which judgements are made about speakers in the classroom. From this perspective it is equally important that teachers recognise their own histories and status as language users, and resist the temptation to impose their own social criteria on the child's ongoing language development. As Bearne goes on to point out:

> Language diversity is . . . deeply involved with social and cultural judge-ments about what is valuable or worthy . . . Judgements are often made about intelligence, social status, trustworthiness and potential for future employment on the basis of how people speak – not the content of what they say, but their pronunciation, choice of vocabulary and tone of voice. Such attitudes can have an impact on later learning.
>
> (ibid.: 155)

Language development and the Foundation Stage

Siraj-Blatchford (Siraj-Blatchford and Clarke, 2000: 20) argues that 'language involves more than learning a linguistic code with which to label the world or to refer to abstract concepts; language also involves learning how to use the code in socially appropriate and effective ways'. From a very early age children are learning through language, they are learning to use language and they are learning about language. In the early years setting, children do the following:

- Develop their knowledge and understanding about how language works.
- Develop a range and variety of vocabulary to use.
- Develop awareness of their audience – the people they are speak to. (There is some evidence to suggest that by the age of 4, children have learned to adjust their speech according to different audiences.)
- Think about the appropriate language to use according to the circumstances of the situation.
- Learn to speak coherently and with clarity to make themselves understood.
- Learn to speak with confidence.

All these features are part of the expectations of the Early Years Foundation Stage (EYFS) requirements. The EYFS is a single framework for care, learning and development in all early years settings for children from birth to five. The EYFS replaced the Curriculum Guidance for the Foundation Stage. One of the main changes in emphasis was to create more overt links between speaking and listening and reading and writing, putting forward the argument that:

> As children develop speaking and listening skills they build the foundations for literacy, for making sense of visual and verbal signs and ultimately for reading and writing. Children need varied opportunities to interact with others and to use a wide variety of resources for expressing their

understanding, including mark-making, drawing, modelling, reading and writing.

(DfES, 2007)

The EYFS has more strongly stated 'requirements' than the previous guidance:

Communication, Language and Literacy Requirements
Children's learning and competence in communicating, speaking and listening, being read to and beginning to read and write must be supported and extended. They must be provided with opportunity and encouragement to use their skills in a range of situations and for a range of purposes, and be supported in developing the confidence and disposition to do so.

(DfES, 2007)

Communication, Language and Literacy is divided into six areas of learning: Language for Communication; Language for Thinking; Linking Letters and Sounds; Reading; Writing; Handwriting. The strong influence of the Rose Report (Rose, 2006) can be seen here in the priority given to the learning of letters and sounds (which is listed before 'reading') and the view that language learning is a direct precurser to literacy learning.

Language for Communication and Language for thinking are described as follows:

Language for Communication – is about how children become communicators. Learning to listen and speak emerges out of non-verbal communication, which includes facial expression, eye contact and hand gesture. These skills develop as children interact with others, listen to and use language, extend their vocabulary and experience stories, songs, poems and rhymes.

Language for Thinking – is about how children learn to use language to imagine and recreate roles and experiences and how they use talk to clarify their thinking and ideas or to refer to events they have observed or are curious about.

(DfES, 2007)

Purposeful language situations must be planned in order for children to practise their language skills and become aware of what is appropriate or suitable for a specific context. Children need to learn to take turns, negotiate, share resources, listen to and appreciate another person's point of view and function in a small group situation. Opportunities for purposeful language situations are many; in role-play areas, for example, or round a talk table. Collaborative interaction can be encouraged round the water and sand trays. If there are two chairs by the computer, one child can discuss with another the program they are using and children can also learn to wait for their turn (the use of a sand timer to make the waiting time fair can help). The practitioner can skilfully draw children into various activities and discussions in the setting, both indoors and outdoors.

Children need to know that the setting is a place where emotions can be expressed but that there may be undesirable consequences for expressing emotions in particular ways. It is the ability to manage some of these emotions through talk that is the challenge both for the individual child and the practitioner. For example, young children experience an intense sense of injustice if they feel they have been wronged. Consider the scenario where one child hits another who immediately responds by hitting back. The practitioner must aim to support the child to use language as a tool for thinking by encouraging the child to ask the following kinds of questions: Why did they hit me? Did I do anything to provoke or upset them? Why am I upset? How should I respond to being hit? What should I do if this happens again? A strong early years setting will provide guidelines for children to follow or appropriate support systems if they find themselves in this kind of situation.

Non-verbal language such as facial expression, effective eye contact, posture, gesture and interpersonal distance or space is usually interpreted by others as a reliable reflection of how we are feeling (Nowicki and Duke, 2000). Mehrabian (1971) devised a series of experiments dealing with the communication of feelings and attitudes, such as like-dislike. The experiments were designed to compare the influence of verbal and non-verbal cues in face-to-face interactions, leading Mehrabian to conclude that there are three elements in any face-to-face communication: visual clues, tone of voice and actual words. Through Mehrabian's experiments it was found that 55 per cent of the emotional meaning of a message is expressed through visual clues, 38 per cent through tone of voice and only 7 per cent from actual words. For communication to be effective and meaningful, these three parts of the message must support each other in meaning; ambiguity occurs when the words spoken are inconsistent with, say, the tone of voice or body language of the speaker.

Young children are naturally physically expressive, for example, when tired, upset or happy, yet they do not always understand straightaway the full meaning another child is conveying. In a situation of conflict, for example, it can be useful when practitioners point out the expression on a 'wronged' child's face to highlight the consequences of someone else's actions. Conversely, if a child is kind to another child and that child say stops crying or starts to smile, then this too can be highlighted.

Similarly, the practitioner needs to be aware of the messages they are sending out to a child via their use of non-verbal language. It is important to remember that whenever we are around others we are communicating non-verbally, intentionally or not, and children need to feel comfortable in the presence of the adults around them. According to Chaplain (2003: 69), 'children are able to interpret the meaningfulness of posture from an early age'. Even locations and positions when talking can be important. For example, it is beneficial when speaking with a young to converse at their physical level, sitting, kneeling or dropping down on one's haunches alongside them. This creates respectful and friendly demeanour and communicates genuine interest in the child and what they are doing.

The way practitioners communicate with children is therefore a very important part of their role. Some pointers include:

- Talking with children so that they feel that you respect them, are interested in them and value their ideas.
- Giving children your full attention as you talk with them; using direct eye contact to show that you are really listening.
- Finding ways of encouraging children to talk in a range of contexts.
- Using specific positive praise such as 'I really liked the way that you waited patiently for your turn on the computer.'
- Smiling!

The EYFS guidance puts the development and use of communication and language at the heart of young children's learning. It targets the importance of supporting children to become skilful communicators from an early age, arguing that learning to speak and listen begins from birth, emerging out of non-verbal language. It differs from the previous curriculum guidance in that it creates more overt links between speaking and listening and reading and writing, putting forward the argument that effective speaking and listening skills 'build the foundations for reading and writing' (p. 42).

The premise behind this approach is the recognition of the importance of the development of speaking and listening skills which, as they become more refined, provide children with key skills with which they can build the foundations for reading and writing. This is on ongoing process which moves through several stages beginning with early reading skills and mark making and ending with the ability to read and write conventionally. The ability to communicate verbally is therefore seen as a central crucial element to a child's overall progress.

Speaking and listening in the National Curriculum

At Key Stage 1 the National Curriculum conceptualises work in Speaking and listening (En1), Reading (En2) and Writing (En3) as part of the subject 'English'. Children's use of language is now deemed sophisticated enough to incorporate relevant and appropriate knowledge to extend their metalanguage for English. There are four main areas of speaking and listening to be addressed: children should learn how to speak fluently and confidently; listen carefully and with due respect for others; become effective members of a collaborative group; and participate in a range of drama activities. There is a further emphasis on the importance of using spoken Standard English and some thought is given to language variation. However, the emphasis of language variation seems to be the functional linguistic emphasis of language in different contexts more than learning centred on topics such as accent and dialect, language and identity, language and culture, etc.

In 2003 the Qualifications and Curriculum Authority (QCA) published a resource called *Speaking, Listening, Learning: Working with Children in Key Stages 1 and 2*. The pack is designed to support the teaching of speaking and listening in primary schools and consists of a set of materials which reflect National Curriculum requirements in English. A teachers' handbook provides an overview, first, emphasising the fact that children need to be taught speaking and listening skills, and acknowledging that those skills develop over time and as children mature. It puts forward an argument as to why speaking and listening is so important, linking it with children's personal and social development. The handbook describes the value of talk in helping children to organise their thoughts and ideas. It is pointed out that speaking and listening should not be seen as part of the subject English alone but as extending to all curriculum areas, acknowledging that different types of talk will be appropriate in different subject areas. The interdependency of speaking and listening, reading and writing is discussed and finally, approaches to assessment.

Another booklet in the resource breaks down speaking and listening object-ives term by term from Year 1 to Year 6 and offers suggestions for teaching sequences including activities and approaches to effective assessment. A sup-porting video exemplifies teaching of objectives by showing speaking and listen-ing techniques and activities from Year 1 to 6. A set of A3 posters look at the four main areas of speaking and listening as laid out in the National Curriculum, providing a rationale for each area, useful starting points for class-room techniques and summarising key teaching points. A final A6 poster sets out progression from Year 1 to Year 6, thus providing teachers with a clear idea of how KS1 objectives feed into KS2.

One of the central issues that is raised by the progression from the Found-ation Stage curriculum into the National Curriculum at Key Stage 1 is the competing terms that are used to describe talk. *Language* for Communication and Thinking at the Foundation Stage becomes *English* in the National Curric-ulum which is subdivided as *speaking and listening* but covered by the PNS *literacy* Framework. Although language is at the heart of early years practice it is also highly significant at Key Stage 1 and beyond. However, the title 'language' wouldn't suitably describe reading and writing, which is an increasing focus as children get older. Speaking and listening remains a phrase that hints unnecessarily at formal language use more than the everyday interaction of talk. For these reasons we would suggest that future curriculum documentation at all stages should be united under the main title English. Arguments about the extent to which the use of the word English implies a formal subject in the early years curriculum should not preclude this title because the word English carries with it many associations which can be clarified in explanatory text. What is currently called speaking and listening in the National Curriculum or 'language for communication' and 'language for thinking' at the foundation stage should be changed and titled *language* for all phases of statutory education.

Practice points

- The way that you interact with children is one very important part of supporting their development of language.
- Talk needs systematic planning similar to the way that other subjects in the curriculum do.
- Drama work can be one of the most rewarding features of teaching language.

Glossary

Lexical – relates to the words or vocabulary of a language, i.e. the lexicon.
Phonological development – development of understanding of sounds (phonemes) and ability to use phonemes as part of speech or recognise them when reading.

References

Alexander, R. (2006) *Towards Dialogic Teaching*, 3rd edn. Dialogos.

Bearne, E. (1998) *Making Progress in English*. London: Routledge.

Bruner, J. S. (1983) *Child's Talk: Learning to Use Language*. Oxford: Oxford University Press.

Chaplain, R. (2003) *Teaching Without Disruption in the Primary School*. London: RoutledgeFalmer.

Department for Education and Employment (DfEE) (1998) *The National Literacy Strategy Framework for Teaching*. London: HMSO.

Department for Education and Employment/Qualifications and Curriculum Authority (DfEE/QCA) (1999) *The National Curriculum: Handbook for Primary Teachers in England: Key Stages 1 and 2*. London: DfEE/QCA.

Department for Education and Skills (DfES) (2007) 'The Early Years Foundation Stage: areas of learning and development'. Retrieved 21 May 2007, from http: www.standards.dfes.gov.uk/eyfs/site/4/4.htm

English, E., Hargreaves, L. and Hislam, J. (2002) 'Pedagogical dilemmas in the National Literacy Strategy: primary teachers' perceptions, reflections and classroom behaviour', *Cambridge Journal of Education*, (32) (1): 9–26.

Littleton, K., Mercer, N., Dawes, L., Wegerif, R., Rowe, D. and Sams, C. (2005) 'Talking and thinking together at Key Stage 1', *Early Years*, (25) (2): 165–180.

Mehrabian, A. (1971) *Silent Messages*. Belmont, CA: Wadsworth.

Messer, D. (2006), 'Current perspectives on language acquisition', in J. S. Peccei (ed.) *Child language: A Resource Book for Students*. London: Routledge.

Nowicki, S. and Duke, M. (2000) *Helping the Child who Doesn't Fit In*. Atlanta, GA: Peachtree.

Peccei, J. S. (2006) *Child Language: A Resource Book for Students*. London: Routledge.

Qualification and Curriculum Authority (QCA) and Department for Education and Skills (DfES) (2003) *Speaking, Listening, Learning: Working with Children in Key Stages 1 and 2*. London: DfES.

Rose, J. (2006) *Independent Review of the Teaching of Early Reading*. Nottingham: DFES Publications.

Siraj-Blatchford, I. and Clarke, P. (2000) *Supporting Identity, Diversity and Language in the Early Years*. Buckingham: Open University Press.

Tizard, B. and Hughes, M. (1984) *Young Children Learning*. London: Fontana.

Wells, G. (1986) *The Meaning Makers: Children Learning Language and Using Language to Learn*. London: Hodder and Stoughton.

Wray, D., Bloom, W. and Hall, N. (1989) *Literacy in Action*. Barcombe: Falmer.

Annotated bibliography

Bearne, E. (1998) *Making Progress in English*. London: Routledge.
    While this is not purely a book about speaking and listening, it contains wonderful examples of children's talk (often with teachers) and provides keen insight into the way in which this talk is related to reading and writing development.
    L2 **

Dawes, L. and Sams, C. (2004) *Talk Box Speaking and Listening Activities for Learning at Key Stage 1*. London: David Fulton Publishers.
    A helpful practical guide to a particular approach to speaking and listening.
    L1 *

Norman, K. (ed.) (1992) *Thinking Voices: The Work of the National Oracy Project*. London: Hodder & Stoughton.
    A collection of voices which includes children, teachers, project coordinators, LEA advisers, academics and researchers, combining to present a readable and comprehensive introduction to speaking and listening issues.
    L2 **

Qualification and Curriculum Authority (QCA) (2003) *New Perspectives on Spoken English in the Classroom*. London: QCA Publications.
    There is a series of excellent contributions to this publication which summarised various kinds of work on speaking and listening.
    L3 **

Chapter 19

Accent, dialect and Standard English

The emphasis in this chapter is on accent and dialect ☞ as rich resources of the English language. A discussion on Standard English ☞ flags up the political factors that are at work. We conclude with some thoughts on language and identity.

> The Jay makes answer as the Magpie chatters;
> And all the air is filled with pleasant noise of waters.
> (Wordsworth, 1807: 270)

William Wordsworth's regional accent meant that water would have been pronounced 'watter' in the extract above; chatter' and 'water' represent a natural rhyme. Many poets have embraced the wonderful variation and authenticity that come from accent and dialect. The study of accent and dialect is an important part of knowledge about language (➡ Chapter 16)

One of the reasons why the English language is considered to be so rich is because of the many intriguing and fascinating variations it has to offer. These variations reveal themselves in many ways including through accent and dialect. While there are many people in society who regard accents and dialects as a rich source of language, there is sometimes a tendency to treat them differently in schools. Some teachers feel that they are obliged to correct children's 'mispronunciations' because of the National Curriculum's insistence on the use of Standard English. It is not difficult to become confused about the differences between accent, dialect, Standard English, Queen's English, etc. The whole business of the child's language can seem like a linguistic minefield. A strong understanding of some of the terms can help you to know when it is appropriate to correct a child and when it may be inappropriate.

All speakers of English use a dialect. Dialect refers to a specific vocabulary and grammar which is influenced by geographical factors. It does not refer to the ways in which words are pronounced. Regional dialect includes particular words that are special to the locality. For example, a flat, circular slice of potato cooked in a fish and chip shop has a large range of names across the country: in Warrington it is a *scallop*, in South Wales it is a *patty*, in Liverpool it is a *fritter*, in West Bromwich it is a *klandike* and in Crewe it is a *smack*. Dialect also contains grammatical differences: for example, in Stoke the phrase 'Her's not coming until tomorrow' is an example of the ways in which regional dialect alters the grammatical structure of the sentence while maintaining meaning.

Just as all speakers of English are users of dialect, all speakers of English use an accent. Accent is the way in which the language is spoken. Some accents are geographical, others are related to social characteristics, but in all cases accent refers to the ways in which the language sounds. Some accents have character-istic inflections and pronunciations which typify them and allow the listener to make guesses about the speaker's geographical origin. You cannot guess this about speakers who use received pronunciation.

Received pronunciation (RP) ☞ is sometimes referred to as 'the Queen's English' or 'BBC English'. It is the 'posh' accent which we have come to associ-ate with public schools, 'high society' and radio broadcasters from 50 years ago. It is different to other accents because it denies the listener any indication of the speaker's geographical origin. It is primarily a socially influenced accent rather than a geographically influenced one, and it locates the speaker in a particular social group.

Standard English

The question of spoken 'Standard English' is one that has also been particularly influenced by political factors. It is a complex issue that is centrally about the social context of language use, and it is bedevilled by prejudice and misunder-standing. The Cox Report contained a sensible discussion of the issue (DES, 1989) and the 1990 National Curriculum orders required only that older primary pupils should have opportunity to use spoken Standard English 'in appropriate contexts' (DES, 1990: 25) and that knowledge should rise out of the pupil's 'own linguistic competence' (DES, 1989: 6.11). The 1995 National Curriculum highlighted the issue of Standard English in a separate section which included the misleading requirement that 'To develop effective speaking and listening pupils should be taught to use the vocabulary and grammar of Standard English' (DFE, 1995: 2, 3) but otherwise left the Cox approach intact. The statement is misleading because effective speaking and listening develops in all dialects not just Standard English.

The following note accompanies the statement on Standard English:

> Standard English
> 5) Pupils should be taught the grammatical constructions that are character-istic of spoken Standard English and to apply this knowledge appropriately in a range of contexts.

Teacher: You think the bottom ... well, have a close look at the bottom horns. What is the snail doing with the bottom horns?
Susan: He is feeling along the ground.
Teacher: He's feeling along, so what would you call the bottom horns, Jason?
Susan: Arms? No ... sort of ...
Emma: Legs?
Teacher: You think they're legs, you think they're arms. What do you think they are Jason, if he's feeling with them?
Jason: Feelers?

(ibid.: 2)

From these transcripts several learning points are clear:

- The children are unafraid to hypothesise ('I think it's moisture').
- The children generate more creative, descriptive and insightful observations *without* their teacher.
- The children operate as a group, they share their ideas, they listen to one another and they respond positively to new suggestions.
- They look for opportunities to draw one another into the task, typically using 'tag' questions (☞).

Although the teacher probably has the best of intentions, there are a number of ways that talk is less productive in the second extract than in the first.

- Typically, the teacher asked closed questions which necessitated single word, 'correct' answers.
- The teacher was keen to draw in all members of the group (especially Jason). It would appear to the teacher that following their discussion, Jason has learned the word 'feelers', but Susan already used the word in context in the previous transcript.
- The structure of the discussion shifts when the teacher arrives so that short questions are followed by short answers which lead to further short questions.
- The existence of exploratory, supportive and hypothetical talk becomes non-existent as a response to the teacher's questioning.

These extracts serve as a reminder that direct instruction and intervention can only achieve so much. It is important to remember that the teacher's ability to plan exciting learning opportunities and to sometimes *leave* children to talk is an important skill in itself. Guidance often stresses the need for teachers to model features of speaking and listening, but it is important to remember that there are times when good teaching also consists of planning which allows children to explore and interact.

Classroom strategies

Given that children are capable of using high-order language skills in their discussions and debates, it is the responsibility of the teacher to plan for opportunities where these skills can be exploited to the full. One simple way of encouraging collaboration – and therefore talk – is to insist that if there is a written outcome for a talk session it should be on a single shared piece of paper. If there is a single written outcome, then the children involved are pushed towards a period of negotiation and agreement, aiming for a document which ideally will reflect all the findings, feelings and ideas of the group. Just like similar adult discussion contexts the person or people who do the writing have a role which will tend to involve less speaking than those who are free to give their ideas. Nomination of someone to write can be done strategically by the teacher who will be aware of group members who might dominate the discussions.

Planning for talk can quite often be helped by knowing about organisational strategies that are likely to lead to a different kind of talk to the norm in the classroom. Numerous talk activities were identified by the National Oracy Project including drama activities (➡ Chapter 21, 'Drama') and these have been successfully used over the years. Here is a brief selection.

Twos to fours

The teacher sets a particular problem for a pair to discuss. After discussion, the pair meet with another pair who have been given *exactly the same task* in order to compare and elaborate on their findings. This is a good idea to use with maths and science problems.

Envoying

When working in groups, one member of each group is allocated the role of envoy. The envoy has the responsibility of gathering further information and resources as required, reporting progress to the teacher and seeking further clarification for the group. This is a particularly effective way of managing practical group activities as the teacher can focus attention on a much smaller number of children in order to maintain progress.

Jigsawing

This technique is a straightforward idea which is complicated to explain, but which offers considerable learning opportunities. Children are organised into 'home' groups (of four to six children) to begin to solve a particular problem or to work on a collaborative activity. Each child in the group then has the responsibility of finding out more about one particular aspect of the problem.

These children gather together in 'expert' groups in order to gather as much information as possible to then take back and share with their 'home' group. Once each child in the group has given their expert opinion to their home group the problem solving continues until an end point is reached.

Children as researchers

The opportunities for children to make real choices over their curriculum is currently very restricted indeed. In the past, one area where genuine choice could be offered was when children were encouraged to research an area of their choice. There are a number of advantages to this way of working. First of all it can be a good way to motivate children. Second, peer-to-peer learning takes place because children present the outcomes of their research to each other. This could be through a class book, through a display, and/or through presentations. This kind of dissemination of the outcomes of the children's research means that it is more likely that there will be genuine interest because each presentation will offer substantially new information.

A variation on this is to build in opportunities for working groups to diverge from the central core of study and begin a period of collaborative research. For example, if the children are studying Roman Britain, there will be core content that the teacher plans to cover with all the class. Beyond this, groups of children could be offered opportunities for further study of an area within this subject which particularly interested them. If necessary, the teacher could control the pool of suggested topics, so in the example above, optional study areas could be law, food, housing, stories, art, and so on. Each group of children could be given the task of researching their chosen subject in detail, and the outcome might be a mini-lesson given to their peers.

Each group is encouraged to use resources and materials they can find to enhance their lesson. This would then be followed up with an activity devised and delivered by the group which they would administer and mark. The kind of work might include a cloze (☞) procedure, or a comprehension (☞) passage for example. The benefits of this way of working are that:

- The children feel some ownership over their area of study and are consequently better motivated.
- The teacher has the potential to focus in more closely on particular groups of children because they are working independently.
- The work demands a high level of negotiation and cooperation.

By doing this the teacher sacrifices the exciting range of topics that can emerge when children are given open choices for a more in-depth examination of the curriculum through controlled choice.

Note!

1 He is not very tall so he can't reach the number 19 on the lift control buttons.

Practice points

- Talk-based activities require specific planning just as reading and writing activities do.
- The absence of a written outcome can sometimes result in a higher level of learning.
- Talk activities inevitably result in a noisier working environment, but this is often the product of a high level of engagement and thought.

Glossary

Cloze – activities that involve filling in missing sections of text, usually words.

Comprehension – a series of questions centred around a particular text extract.

Lateral thinking – a way of thinking that involves people establishing creative, imaginative and alternative solutions to problems. Popularised by Edward de Bono.

Tag questions – questions that are added onto the end of a statement, e.g. '. . . isn't it?' or '. . . aren't they?'

References

De Bono, E. (1967) *The Use of Lateral Thinking*. London: Penguin Books.

Grugeon, E., Dawes, L., Smith, C. and Hubbard, L. (1998) *Teaching Speaking and Listening in the Primary School*. London: David Fulton.

Annotated bibliography

Baddeley, G. (1992) *Learning Together Through Talk*. London: Hodder & Stoughton.
Pack that includes a range of classroom strategies in text and video. Another influential project from the National Oracy Project.
L1 *

Department for Education and Skills (DfES) and Qualifications and Curriculum Authority (QCA) (2003) *Speaking, Listening, Learning: Working with Children in Key Stages 1 and 2. Handbook*. London: DfES Publications.
This pack includes video extracts of speaking and listening work in classrooms. Booklets include a handbook for teachers and a sequence of objectives for teaching speaking and listening. Detailed planning examples include teaching sequences and explanations of language features that are being addressed.
L1 *

Mercer, N., Dawes, L., Wegerif, R. and Sams, C. (2004) 'Reasoning as a scientist: ways of helping children to use language to learn science', *British Educational Research Journal*, 30(3): 359–377.
This research shows the importance of talk in supporting reasoning and scientific thinking. The effect of an experimental teaching programme is examined.
L3 **

Chapter 21

Drama

Reasons for teaching drama are outlined. Drama is linked to play in the early years and to story across the primary curriculum. A theoretical model of the 'building blocks of drama' is provided and some practical ideas are presented as starting points.

The importance of drama in its own right and as a tool for learning has been formally recognised since its inclusion, in 1999, as a separate section in the speaking and listening requirements of the National Curriculum. Some teachers feel a lack of confidence about drama, claiming that drama is like teaching without a 'safety net', others find it the most liberating and invigorating part of their job. Drama sessions can provide some of the most memorable, challenging, enjoyable and rigorous moments of the child's time at school, yet for some this potential is reduced to a predictable and pedestrian Christmas nativity play.

Drama can be overlooked for a variety of reasons: lack of suitable space, inability to book hall times, the sense of not feeling 'arty' enough, etc. Similarly, a lack of teacher confidence and the sense of a 'loss of control' in teaching situations tend to dissuade some teachers from taking risks with the subject. Effective primary teachers understand the risks but recognise that these are actually key features of drama teaching. Good drama teaching acknowledges the shifts in control and the changing nature of knowledge during the sessions. It builds on positive relationships and trusting interaction between teachers and learners.

Why teach drama?

- Drama promotes an awareness of the self which is difficult to achieve in any other area of the curriculum.
- Drama helps children to understand their world more deeply and allows them an opportunity to find ways to explore and share that understanding.
- Drama helps children to cooperate and collaborate with their peers. It

encourages them also to see themselves in a wider social context and should help them become more sensitive to others.

- Relationships between the teacher and the child through their shared language are different in drama sessions. Expectations change, negotiated progress is a more prominent feature and there is a greater sense of active participation for the child.
- Drama creates direct links across the curriculum into other areas of study. Drama can be highly motivating for children and highly productive for teachers as learning becomes a more dynamic process.
- Drama offers the primary teacher a route into language study that is not covered by any other form of teaching.
- Drama offers an element of negotiation and unpredictability in an increasingly rigid curriculum
- Drama is an art form which has played a central part in our cultural heritage.
- It encourages self-expression and focuses the child on the art of communication.

There are two broad schools of thought concerning the promotion of drama in the primary classroom. For some, the priority is to make links with other subjects of the National Curriculum in order to integrate drama. Winston and Tandy (1998), for example, offer carefully designed drama sessions that link in with science (materials and their properties), history (Anglo-Saxon settlements) and geography (the coming of a reservoir). Cremin *et al.* (2006) show how drama can invigorate children's writing.

Others offer the argument that drama is important for its own sake, and that it should be taught in primary schools as such. The National Curriculum moved towards this position by prescribing drama as a separate section in the speaking and listening requirements. The welcome increased emphasis on drama means that both schools of thought are important, opening up a form of language-based study which is beneficial for the child not just educationally, but also spiritually, morally and socially. Teachers should plan accordingly, encouraging children to use the richness of the experience in a multitude of ways.

The early years

When children first come to school they are not bound by the formal conventions of learning, and for them play is an intrinsic part of the process by which they come to know about the world and by which they then come to refine and communicate their knowledge. Early years teachers recognise the importance of play and provide a wealth of opportunity for the child to explore a variety of roles and social situations. This should never be perceived as 'mere' play. Role-play areas for dressing-up, for playing shop, and many other possibilities offer children crucial opportunities to enact, to imitate, to imagine, to confront, to review and to understand the social world they inhabit. Good drama teaching builds on this understanding, acknowledging that play is part of the way in which children come to make sense of their world.

Early drama teaching builds on the child's natural inclination for play and usually develops into two areas. First, there are a variety of drama games which often involve walking and clapping, mime and movement activities often through the use of songs and music. These activities introduce some structure to drama times and establish the position of the teacher within a specific exploratory context. Second, and more importantly, there is a movement towards the provision of structured imaginative play, allowing the teacher to plan more carefully and encouraging the child to use their intrinsic sense of participation to explore some issues in greater detail.

Story regularly provides a natural and productive initiation for more detailed drama sessions. Story is a familiar and important feature of early years classrooms, and there are clear links between the thematic features of children's stories (finding/losing, friends/enemies, deception, hiding, escaping, etc.) and early explorations into movement and drama. Stories also serve as a perfect medium through which the teacher can begin to introduce the productive language associated with drama: What would happen if? Let's suppose that . . . , Perhaps there might be . . . . By using familiar characters and story settings a new discourse opens through which children can explore possibilities. These can be discussed, debated, transformed into a turn-taking game with the teacher controlling the narrative and children providing dialogue, or re-enacted using class toys.

Airs and Ball (1997), for example, use established children's stories such as *Golddocks* and Janet and Allan Ahlberg's *Burglar Bill*, to investigate a range of dilemmas through drama. Using the familiar story of the *Three Little Pigs*, the authors suggest that children work on a different ending, where the pigs have constructed 'Fortress Pork' and the wolf retires to the forest only to discover a bag containing a walking stick, a grandmother's shawl and a skirt (left over from another story). Using the 'Grandma' disguise, the wolf now has all kinds of new possibilities which children can structure, discuss, practise, re-enact and finally reflect upon, assessing the wisdom of 'judging by appearances'.

Understanding drama

The movement towards more formally planned drama work with older children needs to be capable of being both spontaneous and well structured. Brian Woolland suggests that the building blocks for music are *pitch, melody, harmony, tempo, rhythm* and *texture*, and asks 'What are the raw materials of drama?' His answer begins to indicate a conceptual route for intending drama teachers:

- **Role or character**
  Acting as if you were someone else.
  Placing yourself in another situation.
- **Narrative**
  Ordering a sequence of events or images in such a way that their order creates meaning.
- The way in which the drama is moved forward – withholding information; sudden turn of events; surprise ending or beginning, etc.
- **Language**
  Verbal (This may include: naturalistic dialogue; a formal, heightened style of language such as a proclamation, or the beginning of a ritual; a direct address to an audience; characters talking to themselves; choral speech.)
  Non-verbal (This may include symbols; body language; facial expression; the use of space; ritual.)

Finally, Role or character, Narrative and Language all operate within a particular context:

- **Context**
  Where does the action of the drama occur?
  Is it set in a particular historical period?
  What are the relevant social/political conditions?

(Woolland, 1993)

Teachers therefore need to know how to use these 'building blocks' to construct meaningful and valuable drama. One method which is cited by almost all drama books is that of *teacher-in-role*. At its most basic, this involves the teacher adopting the role of another person (typically historical, fictional or imagined) for the purposes of questioning and answering. Often this is a technique used to explore the motivation of historical figures or to generate debate about current (perhaps local) social issues. More importantly, as Bolton (1992: 32) argues, 'The main purpose of Teacher-in-Role is to do with ownership of knowledge.' While the teacher (in this simplified version) is potentially in control at all times, the nature and origin of knowledge begin to shift, so that children become instrumental not only in generating new understandings, but also (and most importantly) in understanding the process of social interaction. As children learn how to interact within this context, they, of course, become capable of reversing roles and assuming the 'mantle of the expert'. This is a term originally devised by Heathcote and Bolton (1995) with its origins firmly in drama and which is experiencing something of a renaissance as part of early years and primary practice.

Practice points

- Drama often requires large spaces although 'pushing back the desks' in the classroom is sometimes necessary and important.
- Use children's natural creativity by giving them the chance to invent their own collaborative drama at times.
- Use the observation of drama experiences as an opportunity to plan for new skills/subject matter.

References

Airs, J. and Ball, C. (1997) *Key Ideas: Drama*. Dunstable: Folens.

Bolton, G. (1992) *New Perspectives on Classroom Drama*. Hemel Hempstead: Simon & Schuster.

Cremin, T., Goouch, K., Blakemore, L., Goff, E. and Macdonald, R. (2006) 'Connecting drama and writing: seizing the moment to write', *Research in Drama Education*, 11(3): 273–291.

Heathcote, D. and Bolton, G. (1995) *Drama for Learning: Dorothy Heathcote's Mantle of the Expert Approach to Education*. Portsmouth, NH: Heinemann.

Winston, J. and Tandy, M. (1998) *Beginning Drama 4–11*. London: David Fulton.

Woolland, B. (1993) *The Teaching of Drama in the Primary School*. Harlow: Longman.

Annotated bibliography

Airs, J., Wright, J., Williams, L. and Adkins, R. (2004) 'The performing arts' in R. Jones and D. Wyse (eds) *Creativity in the Primary Curriculum*. London: David Fulton.
A powerful reminder that drama is and should be a political act. An important message in view of the increasing control of the curriculum taken by politicians.
L2 **

Cremin, T., Goouch, K., Blakemore, L., Goff, E. and Macdonald, R. (2006). 'Connecting drama and writing: seizing the moment to write', *Research in Drama Education*, 11(3): 273–291.
A detailed analysis of the possibilities for enhancing children's writing through drama. Particularly persuasive about the advantages of spontaneous writing emerging from drama work.
L3 **

Heathcote, D. and Bolton, G. (1995) *Drama for Learning: Dorothy Heathcote's Mantle of the Expert Approach to Education* Portsmouth, NH: Heinemann.
This book concerns itself primarily with the study and promotion of

drama. It provides an excellent link between theories of drama education and their application in primary education.
L3 ***

Winston, J. and Tandy, M. (2001) *Beginning Drama 4–11*, 2nd edn. London: David Fulton.
Usefully structured for the non-specialist. Offers advice for developing drama across the curriculum.
L2 **

Chapter 22

Assessing talk

The chapter starts by outlining some features of talk then offers guidance on principles for the assessment of talk. The chapter concludes by examining ways in which these principles may be put into practice with the help of a transcribed conversation between a teacher and pupil. This chapter should be read in conjunction with Chapter 10, 'Assessing reading' and Chapter 17, 'Assessing writing', as some strategies – such as diaries of observations – are applicable to all three modes and other strategies are specific to one mode.

There are practical problems when attempting to assess talk in the primary classroom mainly because it is more difficult to *record* than other curriculum areas. In order to assess talk, a number questions need to be thought about: What criteria am I going to apply? What contexts for talk will I include? How will I record the talk? How will I ensure that my assessments are fair?

Assessment of talk serves two primary functions. First, it allows the teacher to make judgements about the development of talk itself. Second, it affords the teacher an opportunity to assess other forms of understanding which are communicated through that talk:

> A child who feels confident with her or his knowledge in a particular area is more likely to be fluent, at ease, capable of communicating information, making explanations or being persuasive, than a child who has no particular expertise in that area. On the other hand, a child might know a great deal yet not wish to voice that knowledge publicly, or show the ability to use particular talk strategies on any given occasion.
>
> (Bearne, 1998: 174)

So, different forms of assessment are needed at different stages of development and in order to record different features of talk. According to Grugeon *et al.* (2005: 137), in the early years, the assessment of talk usually takes the form of observable features such as:

- Does the child initiate and carry on conversations?
- Does the child listen carefully?
- Can the child's talk be easily understood?
- Does the child describe experiences?
- Does the child give instructions?
- Does the child follow verbal instructions?
- Does the child ask questions?
- Can the child contribute to a working group?
- Does the child 'think aloud'?
- Does the child modify talk for different audiences?

At later stages, other features of talk will take on greater significance in the assessment process. Teachers will find that they begin to look for evidence where the child is seen to be hypothesising, imagining, directing, exploring, practising, recalling, developing critical responses, explaining and sustaining talk.

It is essential to understand that talk is very much dependent on the context of its occurrence. For example, when early years teachers observe children in play contexts they often see a very different language user. Some children, freed of the pressures of performance in front of the teacher, begin to demonstrate skills as language users and a preparedness to explore and experiment which teachers would otherwise never witness. Experienced teachers at Key Stage 2 will be only too ready to add that this kind of evidence is equally applicable among older children who perceive themselves as poor users in the classroom, yet seem to be perfectly articulate and imaginative when outside at play. The point here is that teachers who intend to assess talk and who grow concerned about a child's development in this area should look at that same child at play for further evidence of language use.

The National Oracy Project (NOP) established six aspects of assessment that were applicable to speaking and listening:

- *Planning* – the groupings, the activities, the learning environment.
- *Observing and gathering information* – through notes, children's talk-diaries, file-cards, hand-held tape recording, etc.
- *Recording* – on observation sheets, audio and video tape, to build evidence of talk cumulatively for each child.
- *Summarising* – by reviewing the collected evidence and considering the main areas of achievement and needs.
- *Making judgements* – about the progress of each child, linked closely to your summaries.
- *Reporting* to parents, to children, to the school.

(Baddeley, 1992: 65)

The Primary National Strategy recommendations suggest that you build the assessment of speaking and listening into curriculum planning by adopting the following:

- *Focusing on two or three children each week* (to ensure systematic coverage of the whole class).
- *Using objectives for whole class monitoring* (developing whole class lists of which children meet specific teaching objectives).
- *Integrating speaking and listening assessment with other records* (possibly building a page-per-pupil record which incorporates talk).
- *Termly checks* (looking for patterns, omissions, etc.).
- *Annual review* (to provide feedback for children, target setting and future planning).

> (Department for Education and Skills (DfES) and Qualifications and Curriculum Authority (QCA), 2003: 31)

A short case study

The example below is an extract from a fully transcribed conversation between a teacher and a Year 4 child called Stephen. The teacher was a newly qualified teacher and inexperienced in the significance, development and the assessment of talk. Stephen was a boy who wrote very little and, over the previous three months, had offered the teacher little evidence of his ability. The task set by the teacher was to investigate 'What is a poem?', and a number of questions had been established to focus ideas along the lines of 'what colour is a poem?', 'what season is a poem?', etc. Stephen arrived late for the lesson after a visit to the dentist and missed the focused introduction. He discussed the task with some of his peers, worked for some 20 minutes and then arrived at the teacher's desk with an indecipherable piece of writing. The teacher was taping a conversation with another child as Stephen arrived (as part of an Oracy Project investigation) and the tape was left running as Stephen began to explain his ideas.

The extract below begins to indicate that the teacher's initial assessment of the child's reasoning and language skills were inadequate. Yet it also indicates the ways in which Stephen began to sharpen and consolidate his ideas in response to the teacher's inexperienced questioning. It is clear that Stephen had not been intimidated by the challenging nature of the task, nor by his lack of ability in writing. The extract shows that he had clear ideas and wanted to be able to clarify and communicate them effectively:

Teacher: Let's find out what you've got. What colour is a poem?
Stephen: I put 'white and innocent' because it's ready for your thoughts to . . . (inaudible) the paper.
Teacher: I'm sorry, Stephen, it's for your thoughts to what the paper?
Stephen: Sweep. Or dazzle.
Teacher: That's a nice picture in my mind. Why did you use the word 'sweep'?

Stephen:	Well, I just thought it sounded right. It does sweep across the paper really. As you write it. It just goes across the paper. That's what I think.
Teacher:	How did you answer 'What does a poem taste like?'?
Stephen:	I put 'It tastes like a lemon because when you bite into it, it stings.' Like when you get into the actual poem it tingles in your head. Sometimes it stings. Sometimes it makes you go all excited.
Teacher:	So how is that like a lemon?
Stephen:	Well the lemon stings and the poem kind of stings.

At this point, there is already clear evidence that Stephen has responded thoughtfully to the task, that he is still clarifying his responses (he is unsure whether to use 'sweep' or 'dazzle'), but that he is engaged in a challenging process of sifting through his own ideas, searching for the most appropriate responses. It is interesting that sometimes he thinks about the physical comparisons he is drawing, and at other times he is thinking carefully about the *sounds* that the words make; in both cases providing evidence of poetic thought at a high level. However, he went on to develop a larger idea he had been developing:

Teacher:	What was the next question?
Stephen:	'What season is a poem?'
Stephen:	I put 'winter' because it's hibernating in your head until you write it down. Then it becomes spring.
Teacher:	Oh! After it's written down it becomes spring. Why do you think that is?
Stephen:	Because in spring everything comes out new, and with a poem it's brand new to everybody else.
Teacher:	That's a really nice way of thinking about it.
Stephen:	The next question was 'What sound is a poem?' and that is to do with winter as well, because in winter it's muffled.
Teacher:	Why does it sound muffled?
Stephen:	Because it's in a deep sleep.
Teacher:	The poem is?
Stephen:	Yes, until it comes out you don't hear it that well in your mind. Then it's been unblocked. Or unmuffled.
Teacher:	'Unmuffled'! What a lovely word. What's the next question?
Stephen:	'Where is a poem?' Again it's in the mind of the author until it's written down, and then it starts to grow up.
Teacher:	Say that again slowly.
Stephen:	A poem is in the mind of the author until you get it written down, and then it starts to grow up.
Teacher:	Why does a poem start to grow up once it's written down?
Stephen:	Well, it's like a human, because when a human leaves home it's kind

of like a sign of growing up and finding it's own way around in the world by itself. Stuff like that.

Stephen went on to develop his ideas throughout the conversation and was extremely pleased with his results.

If you compare this case study with the NOP assessment framework at the beginning of this chapter you will see that this description addressed four of the categories:

- Planning – the poetry activity.
- Observing and gathering information – noting that Stephen arrived late and that he asked his peers about the activity.
- Recording – literally, on a tape-recorder.
- Summarising – revealed by our analysis in this section.

There is sufficient evidence in these short extracts to indicate that had Stephen's talk not been part of an ongoing assessment process, the teacher would not have been able to establish valid statements about Stephen's language abilities. Space restricts further extracts, but an examination of the full transcription ☞ would indicate that Stephen *does* think aloud, he *does* ask questions, he continually modifies his idea using talk as a vehicle, he tests the ways that words sound out loud, he thinks about his audience, he is confident in his own ability, he is prepared to take chances with words he has invented to communicate his ideas. It is worth repeating that this is a child whose prior language assessments had been meagre to say the least.

Practice points

- Give children opportunities to explain their ideas fully without feeling hurried.
- Look for opportunities to build written assessment of talk into other areas of the curriculum (e.g. collaboration during a group science experiment).
- Use high-quality assessment of children's language to positively challenge impressions that you might have from informal assessment.

Glossary

Transcription – the written form of a recorded conversation.

References

Baddeley, G. (ed.) (1992) *Learning Together through Talk: Key Stages 1 and 2.* London: Hodder & Stoughton.

Bearne, E. (1998) *Making Progress in English*. London: Routledge.

Department for Education and Skills (DfES), and Qualifications and Curriculum Authority (QCA), (2003) *Speaking, Listening, Learning: Working with Children in Key Stages 1 and 2. Handbook*. London: DfES Publications.

Grugeon, E., Hubbard, L., Smith, C. and Dawes, L. (2005) *Teaching Speaking and Listening in the Primary School*, 3rd edn. London: David Fulton.

Annotated bibliography

Department for Education and Skills (DfES) and Qualifications and Curriculum Authority (QCA) (2003) *Speaking, Listening, Learning: Working with Children in Key Stages 1 and 2. Handbook*. London: DfES Publications.
The official guidance on speaking and listening work in primary schools.
L1 *

Grugeon, E., Hubbard, L., Smith, C. and Dawes, L. (2005) *Teaching Speaking and Listening in the Primary School*, 3rd edn. London: David Fulton.
Excellent book which gives a thorough and perceptive overview of the teaching of speaking and listening.
L2 * *

Mercer, N., Dawes, L., Wegerif, R. and Sams, C. (2004) 'Reasoning as a scientist: ways of helping children to use language to learn science', *British Educational Research Journal*, 30(3): 359–377.
A very good example of the use of talk in a different curriculum context. Research found that children can be enabled to use talk more effectively as a tool for reasoning.
L3 * * *

Part V

General issues

Chapter 23

Planning

The extent to which children and teacher have control over the planning of the curriculum are one of the main concerns of this chapter. Examples of QCA and PNS units of work are explored and critiqued.

One of the most welcome features of the PNS Framework was the belated move away from one-off lessons linked to short-term objectives towards sequences of lessons planned as part of units, sometimes lasting a number of weeks. However, there are a number of critical questions that you should ask about any planning that is offered as exemplar material: to what extent are children's choices taken into account? Are children likely to be motivated by the suggested activities? Will the planning have a positive or negative effect on learning? What scope is there for your interests and professionalism to be developed?

So with the first question in mind let us begin by thinking about the child's experience:

> Sally arrives for another day at school. She's had a bad night because her little sister who sleeps in the same room has a terrible cough and was crying. Mum and dad were hassling them to hurry up, get dressed and eat breakfast. Just as Sally was really getting into a wonderful drawing of a fish on a multicoloured symmetrical pattern background dad loses his rag and shouts at the children to 'Hurry up!' The school morning always starts with the literacy hour followed by the daily mathematics lesson. School is a bit boring when it is the same every day but sometimes something really interesting happens. Like on Pancake day when all the class got to make a pancake and eat it or when they do PE or when the teacher tells stories about her cat.

Children are not particularly interested in lesson plans, objectives, differentiation, assessment. Their main thought will be: 'Is this activity interesting?' If the answer to this question is 'yes', then you have tapped into their natural motivation, and learning is more likely to take place. Think back on your own education both in school and out of it. Can you think of occasions when you were really fired up about something and the intensity of learning was strong? One way to find out what interests children is to ask them directly: questions like 'Are you enjoying this activity?', 'What's your favourite subject?', 'What would you like to learn about?' are all ways of getting feedback from children. A more informal approach is to be aware of the kinds of things that they talk about and to encourage them to bring things to school and to use them as part of the curriculum.

There are many ways to find ideas for activities. The best way is for you to think about what you want your children to learn and then to create a suitable activity. If you create it yourself you usually get a much closer match between the activity and your assessment of the children's needs. This creative process can of course involve you 'pinching' ideas from all kinds of sources: colleagues; the internet; published materials, etc.

It can be very tempting to overuse published worksheets. Sometimes, these materials can save you a bit of time but there are considerable weaknesses. The main problem is that the writers of the materials cannot possibly know about the learning needs of your class. Because of this, the activities that they suggest often aim for the needs of an average child of a particular age. When you create activities and resources yourself you go through a process of development which includes having teaching objectives that are closely matched with the needs of your class. Too often, even commercially successful published schemes contain poor activities and generally their use, without adaptation, is not regarded as 'good practice'.

Examples of planning

Planning is commonly described in three levels: short-term, medium-term and long-term. Short-term planning is usually daily or weekly and includes the lesson plans that you will need to do as part of your course. Medium-term refers to planning for terms and half-terms. Long-term planning tends to mean planning for a year or more; the PNS Frameworks are an example of long-term planning.

As an example of medium-term planning it is useful to look at one of the Qualifications and Curriculum Authority (QCA) schemes of work:

Art and design at Key Stages 1 and 2 (Year 1/2)
Unit 2A Picture this!:
Section 1: Exploring and developing ideas (1)

Objectives
Children should learn:

- to record from first-hand observation and explore ideas

Activities
- Ask the children to pretend to be a camera. Give the children view-finders and ask them to walk around the classroom looking through the viewfinder with one eye closed as though they were looking through a camera's viewfinder.
- Encourage the children to explore what happens when they move closer to something or further away and when they hold the viewfinder vertically or horizontally.
- Ask the children to frame something in their viewfinder that interests them. Ask them to make a drawing of this – about the size of a colour print – noticing whether their frame is wider (landscape) or taller (portrait). Ask them to draw everything they see in their frame. Ask them to take a photograph of what is in the drawing, keeping to exactly the same angle and proportions.

Outcomes
- Compare the drawing with the photograph.
- Frame and record an interesting viewpoint in a drawing and a photograph.
- Identify similarities and differences between the drawing and the photograph.

Points to note
- Make sure children hold the viewfinder in front of their eye so that it successfully frames what they see.
- This 'framing' technique can be used in many art and design activities as a way of encouraging children to be more selective about what they want to include in their work.

(Qualifications and Curriculum Authority (QCA), and
Department for Education and Skills (DFES), 2005)

Up until the time of writing the idea that national documentation might be critiqued in government-sanctioned public arenas was unheard of. So it was quite refreshing to see that the QCA schemes of work were being subject to such a process. The QCA website includes examples of the ways in which teachers have adapted the schemes of work. The following example explains how a teacher changed the 'Picture This!' unit shown above.

How did the changes improve children's learning?
The aim of helping all the children, including those who speak English as an additional language, to develop an art vocabulary relating to shape, colour, pattern and composition was achieved. The children not only produced interesting and authentic artwork, they also developed descriptive vocabulary that enriched their literacy work.

Changing the starting point
Starting off with the story of Cinderella helped to shape the whole
sequence of activities in the unit.

Changing the resources
The children were really taken by the illustrations and excited by the pros-
pect of making books.

Adjusting the activities
Giving the children experience of looking at, touching, drawing and
photographing the objects from the story and acting out scenes was vital to
the success of this unit. Many of the children had not used a camera before.
When the teachers introduced this part of the unit, they had additional
teaching support and worked with small groups of children. They explained
the functions of different parts of the camera and showed the children how
to hold the camera correctly, frame a view and take a photograph of their
group of objects. However, some children needed more time just to experiment with using a viewfinder. Reflecting on the different techniques and
media used in the unit, children were asked to make decisions about what
might be included in a range of books. This involved them all in discussions
about various approaches to book illustration and in thinking about the
relationship between words and images, and about how ICT could be used
effectively. Their experience of developing a painting reinforced earlier discussions in the unit about styles of illustration. Using ICT to combine
words and images has a lot of potential. The links made with ICT added to
the success of the unit.

Changing the outcome
Making the books produced very good results. The children were keen to
share their books with the other classes in the year group, which reinforced
their literacy work.
(Qualifications and Curriculum Authority (QCA) and Department for
Education and Skills (DFES), 2005)

It is not just in the Foundation subjects that it has been realised that the models
need considerable change. The Literacy and Numeracy Strategies have offered
more and more guidance on planning. In 2006/2007, the introduction of the
PNS Frameworks resulted in another round of considerable change. The following discussion focuses on an example from the Year 5 PNS planning unit on
narrative.

PNS planning

The first thing to say about the electric resources offered by the PNS Framework is their scale. The main features are:

- a separate link to information about communication, language and literacy in the early years framework;
- guidance papers on issues such as phonics;
- specific information about early reading including phonics;
- the learning objectives which can be viewed by strand or by year group;
- general statements about assessment;
- planning.

The planning link starts with general advice on how to use the planning guidance. Each year group is detailed separately and features sections on narrative; non-fiction; poetry and planning guidance. The example we focus on here is the narrative one. When you click on the narrative link you are taken to a timetable which suggests the number of weeks to spend on topics such as, 'Novels and stories by significant children's authors (4 weeks)' or 'Instruction (3 weeks)'. The first thing to say about the guidance is that there is so much of it. An informed, intelligent professional really does not need this level of prescription.

Let us now turn to the detail of the recommended teaching. The narrative unit at Year 5 covers traditional stories, fables, myths and legends. This is potentially a very exciting aspect of the curriculum. When teaching this our priorities would be to acquire as many examples of these kinds of stories as possible and to read them daily to our class, if possible on more than one occasion each day. We would want to encourage the widest possible personal response from the children and would want to build on that response as we fashioned our own curriculum. Through democratic means such as voting we would find out what the class's favourite stories were. One of these would be chosen for more extended analysis and as the basis for cross-curricular work. Very early on we would encourage the children to begin drafting their own stories inspired by our story tellings. But these would be entirely their own ideas. Our work with the children on their early drafts would lead to specific lessons in order to help them improve their writing. These might include a look at structure but would also focus on how the children could generate stories that were genuinely original but which also linked appropriately to the existing stories that had contributed to them. The final drafts of the stories would be prepared for a class book and or other ways of presenting them including drama.

The guidance highlights a different approach in which there is a heavy emphasis on analysis of genre:

Phase 1

Read and analyse features of the text-type. Make comparisons between different versions of the same legend.

Phase 2

Children continue familiarisation with the text-type. Discuss and investigate the effect of different techniques used by the author. Work in a group to explore and empathise with characters through drama activities. Children use a reading journal to record inferences and demonstrate understanding of characters by writing in the first person.

Phase 3

Make comparisons between oral and written narratives. The teacher demonstrates effective note-taking techniques. Children make notes on visual and oral performances before working in small groups to prepare and present an oral retelling of the legend of Robin Hood for an audio or digital video file.

Phase 4

Children evaluate their oral performances against agreed success criteria. The teacher demonstrates how to write a legend, transferring oral storytelling skills into writing. Children work collaboratively to write the legend, exploring how to transfer the visual and oral text to a written narrative.

Even more detailed specification is offered for each of these phases. The legend of Robin Hood is suggested as a possible topic for analysis. This is a good idea which is likely to be of interest to many children but unfortunately it is weighed down by the dominant influence of pedagogies used for non-fiction writing based on analysis of genre structures. Instead of encouraging teachers and children to analyse writing in progress to see if the sentence structure can be redrafted to better represent the children's intentions, the *Grammar for Writing* resource is recommended resulting in unnecessary decontextualisation.

Finally, in phase 4, after 15 days of text study, the children are encouraged to do some extended writing: collaborative writing for a tourist leaflet based on the legend. Collaborative writing is a very useful technique; throughout the phases of this unit there are many other good ideas such as activities on empathising with characters, the use of drama to explore texts, and comparison of oral and printed versions. But where is the individual voice and enthusiasms of the child in this, and where is the voice of the teacher?

Practice points

- Consider your children's interests and enthusiasms as you think about planning.
- Be confident to develop your own curriculum and pedagogy in the classroom including your approach to planning.
- Carefully critique any suggested planning including that from government.

References

Qualifications and Curriculum Authority (QCA) and Department for Education and Skills (DFES) (2005) *Schemes of Work*. Retrieved May 25, 2005, from http://www.standards.dfes.gov.uk/schemes3/

Annotated bibliography

Boyle, B. and Bragg, J. (2006) 'A curriculum without foundation', *British Educational Research Journal*, 32(4): 569–582.
Research that shows the narrowing of the curriculum that has resulted from the intense focus on literacy and numeracy in the past ten years.
L3 **
Department for Education and Skills (DfES) (2007) '*Primary National Strategy: Primary Framework for Literacy and Mathematics*. Retrieved 22 January, 2007, from http://www.standards.dfes.gov.uk/primaryframeworks/
The official view of literacy teaching. Very useful for finding ideas for activities and up-to-date resources from government.
L1 *
Medwell, J. (2006) 'Approaching short-term planning', in J. Arthur, T. Grainger and D. Wray (eds) *Teaching and Learning in the Primary School*. London: Routledge.
Complements this chapter's focus on medium- and long-term planning.
L2 **

Chapter 24

Home–school links

Some of the differences between learning at home and learning at school are discussed. The setting of homework is related to home-reading and home–school agreements. The chapter concludes with some ideas from research on working with families.

Throughout the history of education in England there has been a tendency by some to think that children are like 'empty vessels' who know nothing until they are filled with knowledge by schools. This attitude can result in parents and children feeling powerless to engage in ways that would benefit both schools and their communities. As early as 1975 the Bullock Report signalled that a change in such attitudes was necessary:

> No child should be expected to cast off the language and culture of the home as he [sic] crosses the school threshold, nor to live and act as though home and school represent two totally separate and different cultures which have to be kept firmly apart. The curriculum should reflect many elements of that part of his life which a child lives outside school.
>
> (DES, 1975: S20.5)

In order to turn the fine words of the Bullock Report into practice, many schools continue to work hard to involve parents more in their children's education. However, the ever-increasing documentation that accompanies the primary curriculum runs many risks, one of which is the alienation of parents who may feel that they have nothing to offer in such a complex world. Nothing could be further from the truth.

Learning at home and at school

Direct evidence of the importance of the home environment in supporting children's learning comes from a range of research. Barbara Tizard and Martin

Hughes's early work looked at the differences between talking and thinking at home and at school. They argued forcefully that the home was a 'very powerful learning environment' (1984: 249) and that school nurseries were not aware of this:

> Our observations of children at home showed them displaying a range of interest and linguistic skills which enabled them to be powerful learners. Yet observations of the same children at school showed a fundamental lack of awareness by the nursery staff of these skills and interests. There is no doubt that, in the world of the school, the child appears to be a much less active thinker than is the case at home. We do not believe that the schools can possibly be meeting their goals in the most efficient manner if they are unable to make use of so many of the children's skills.
>
> (ibid.: 264)

Later work by Hughes looked again at some of the issues. Greenhough and Hughes (1999) suggested that the 'conversing' ☞ of parents may be weaker than the conversing of teachers. They tentatively suggested that there might be a link between the amount of meaningful conversation about books at home, and the child's reading progress at school. One part of their research was an illustration of the different ways that four schools tried to improve the level of conversing in the home: (1) a workshop for parents; (2) a modified version of the home–school reading diary; (3) introductory talk by the class teacher and a modified diary; (4) use of a 'visitors' comments' book for each reading. They conclude that these strategies only had limited success and argue that changing parents' approaches with their children may be similar to changing teacher's practice; often a gradual and sophisticated process. One aspect that Greenhough and Hughes did not seem to address was the child's own perspective. It is possible that some children might have wanted a different kind of reading experience at home – such as 'just' listening to a story – after a day at school that was full of a high level of conversing.

As far as reading is concerned there are two particularly powerful studies that showed the positive influence of parents. In 1966, Durkin carried out some research in America and published it in a book called *Children Who Read Early*. These were the things that were common to the children's experiences:

- Parents had read to their children frequently, and had also found time to talk with them and answer their questions.
- Real books were more commonly read by the children than typical school textbooks or reading scheme books.
- Whole-word learning had been used more than letter-sounds for reading, although letter-sounds had been used to help writing.
- Print in their everyday surroundings was of interest to the children.
- Many of the children had been interested in writing as well as reading.

A year later Clark published a very similar study in England. She said that although the child's natural abilities were important, 'the crucial role of the environment, the experiences which the child obtained, their relevance to his interest and the readiness of adults to encourage and to build upon these, should not be underestimated' (1976: 106).

And here are the factors that were common to the children in Clark's study:

- At least one parent, often the mother, had a deep involvement with their child and their progress.
- Parents welcomed the opportunity to talk to their children.
- Non-fiction and print in the home and local environment were mentioned as much as the reading of storybooks.
- Most of the children used the public library.
- Parents would happily break off from other activities and tell their child what words said if the child couldn't work them out independently from the context.
- Very few parents taught their children the letter-sounds. If they did, this was to help with writing more than reading. More children learned the letter names first.
- The children had a range of strategies for working out difficult words if their parent wasn't available to supply the word.
- Many of the children were interested in writing as well as reading.

There was very little evidence that systematic instruction in reading, including phonics, was part of these children's pre-school experiences, yet they all learned to read before they started school. Socio-economic differences were not a significant factor in the research which showed that children from a range of family backgrounds learned to read. The implications for teachers are: (1) a range of approaches to reading is beneficial; (2) support for children should be based on understanding of home experiences; (3) other parents may benefit from guidance in the kinds of approaches that the parents in the two studies used. Wyse (2007) offers guidance to parents on supporting their children, not just in reading but also in writing because of the mutual benefits that occur from looking at both.

Sending 'work' home

One of the most common strategies to support home/school links has been through 'bookbag' schemes. Each child has a durable bag that contains books, often a reading scheme book and a free choice book, and the child takes this home on a regular basis. A reading diary accompanies the books, and parents are expected to note the date, title of the book and to make a comment about their child's reading. Table 24.1 shows an example of a parent's comments.

The idea of bookbags was extended by the Basic Skills Agency who set up a National Support Project to promote 'storysacks' throughout England and Wales. These have proved very popular and are widely used. Storysacks, containing a good children's book and supporting materials, are designed to stimulate reading activities. The sacks and the soft toys representing the book characters can be made by parents and other volunteers. which can be a good way to involve parents in the school community. Other related items such as an audio tape, language game and other activities, can be used by parents at home to bring reading to life and develop the child's language skills.

Since September 1999 all schools had to have 'home–school agreements'. The Secretary of State believed that all agreements should cover: the standard of education, the ethos of the school, regular and punctual attendance, discipline and behaviour, homework, the information schools and parents will give one another, and matters raised during the consultation process. Bastiani and Wyse (1999) looked beyond the legal requirement (that such an agreement must be in place) to the hard work that is involved in setting up a meaningful home–school agreement. One of the interesting points they make is that parents are not obliged to sign such agreements nor should there by any punitive consequence if they do not. It is suggested that if parents have reservations, these should be used as a basis for discussion and a possibility for greater understanding of families' needs. They also stress the vital importance of genuine consultation.

> A key ingredient in the process of consultation with parents, which is a formal requirement in the introduction of agreements, is genuineness. Unfortunately educational practice is littered with the debris of glossy rhetoric ☞, phoney consultation and unfilled promises. Schools may, for example, consult but only hear what they want to hear; they may listen to some parents and ignore others; they may hear, but do nothing.
>
> (ibid.: 10)

Most home–school agreements include statements about homework. The government recommendation is that children as young as 6 should do 1 hour a week of homework and that children in Years 5 and 6 should do 30 minutes a day. The idea that children of 9 should be required to do 30 minutes a day

Table 24.1 A parent's comments on a child's reading

Date	Book	Comments
7/5	Roll over	Well read.
14/5	Better than you	Fluent reading.
17/5	Big fish	Well read. Why no punctuation, i.e. question marks, speech marks? Esther commented on this. [Teacher:] I don't know. I will check.
21/5	Sam's book	Well read.
28/5	Lion is ill	Well read.

is highly questionable and seen by some as an infringement of their family's freedom to engage with their children in ways that are more interesting than the kind of homework that schools are likely to send home. Nevertheless, popular opinion would seem to suggest that homework is a good thing and that parents' concerns are more about how they can help rather than whether it should be done.

As schools are required to set homework, it is important that they encourage children to engage in interesting activities. For example, one of our children's teachers suggested that they phone up a grandparent and ask them about the time when they were children. This activity inspired Esther to write one of her longest pieces of writing at home:

> My grabad [grandad] and gramar didn't have a tely. they did hav a rabyo [radio]. they had a metul Ian [iron]. they had sum bens [beans] and vegtbuls. thee wa lots ov boms in the war. the shoos were brawn and blac Thay had long dresis. Thay had shun trawsis and long socs.

There is always the danger that the pressures of time for teachers can result in photocopied homeworksheets that are uninteresting and of questionable value. As is the case with many things in teaching it is better to organise a limited number of really exciting homework tasks, that are genuinely built on in the classroom, than to set too many tasks where it is difficult for the teacher to monitor them all.

Working with parents in the classroom

The PNS clearly recognises the importance of community and parental involvement in raising standards of literacy. As a teacher you are likely to have the opportunity to work with parents who have volunteered to help in the classroom. These parents volunteer to support schools in their own time and are a precious resource. Schools are also increasingly employing assistants who work in a variety of ways with teachers. The workforce reforms are also resulting in teachers having more responsibility for managing other adults who work with them, something which continues to be very important in early years settings.

One of the most important things to remember is that schools and teachers need to offer guidance to people who are supporting literacy in the classroom. The PNS Framework includes complex ideas which teachers will need to help the adults that they work with be clear about. Parental help is often invaluable in the group work section of the literacy sessions. They can also support struggling readers either individually or in groups, but again it should be remembered that this is a skilled task and they will require the chance to discuss how things are going and how they can best help the children.

Knowsley local education authority carried out a project that included the recruitment and training of large numbers of adult volunteers who helped primary pupils with their reading on a regular basis. An evaluation by Brooks *et al.* (1996: 3) concluded that the training for parents and other volunteers was one of the most important components of the project and 'it seemed to make the most significant difference to raising reading standards'. The idea of training parents is one that the Basic Skills Agency has also been involved in. The main purpose of their family literacy initiatives was to raise the basic skills of both parents and children together. For parents the emphasis was mainly on helping them to understand more about what happened in schools and how they could support this. The children's sessions involved hands-on motivational activities. Joint sessions were also held where parents were encouraged to enjoy a natural interaction with their children during joint tasks. Brooks *et al.* (1999) found that these family literacy programmes – with some modifications – worked as well for ethnic minority families as for other families. The most notable extension of family literacy programmes in England has been the *Surestart* initiative which has involved significant investment by government in supporting the families of young children, not just in education but across all the areas of the *Every Child Matters* legislation.

Practice points

- Involve and support parents who work in your classroom as much as possible.
- Talking to the parents of children who have special education needs should be one of your priorities.
- Genuinely seek information from parents about their views of their child's development and progress.

Glossary

Conversing – a broad range and high quality of talk related to a book or other text.

Rhetoric – literally the skills of speech used for particular effects, but in this case fine-sounding words not reflected by the day-to-day reality.

References

Bastiani, J. and Wyse, B. (1999) *Introducing Your Home-School Agreement.* London: Royal Society of Arts (RSA).

Brooks, G., Cato, V., Fernandes, C. and Tregenza, A. (1996) *The Knowsley Reading Project: Using Trained Reading Helpers Effectively.* Slough: The National Foundation for Educational Research (NFER).

Brooks, G., Harman, J., Hutchison, D., Kendall, S. and Wilkin, A. (1999) *Family Literacy for New Groups.* London: The Basic Skills Agency.

Clark, M. M. (1976) *Young Fluent Readers*. London: Heinemann Educational Books.

DES (Department of Education and Science) (1975) *A Language for Life (The Bullock Report)*. London: HMSO.

Greenhough, P. and Hughes, M. (1999) 'Encouraging conversing: trying to change what parents do when their children read with them', *Reading*, 24(4): 98–105.

Tizard, B. and Hughes, M. (1984) *Young Children Learning: Talking and Thinking at Home and at School*. London: Fontana Press.

Wyse, D. (2007) *How to Help Your Child Read and Write*. London: Pearson/BBC Active.

Annotated bibliography

Bastiani, J. and Wyse, B. (1999) *Introducing Your Home-School Agreement*. London: RSA.
A useful guide to introducing home-school agreements. Informed by good practice in secondary schools but relevant to all phases.
L1 *

Greenhough, P. and Hughes, M. (1998) 'Parents' and teachers' interventions in children's reading', *British Educational Research Journal*, 24(4): 283–398.
A fuller version of the research that we refer to in this section. This was included in a special edition of the journal where all the articles are concerned with 'families and education'.
L3 ***

Tizard, B. and Hughes, M. (1984) *Young Children Learning: Talking and Thinking at Home and at School*. London: Fontana Press.
An important text that asks awkward questions about schools' approaches to parents. Interesting comparison with Hughes's more recent work.
L2 **

Wyse, D. (2007). *How to Help Your Child Read and Write*. London: Pearson/BBC Active.
As this book was written for parents it may offer a useful source of information to support your discussions with parents who often ask how they can help their child with reading and writing.
L1 *

Chapter 25

Information and communication technologies (ICTs) and multimedia

The growth of ICTs is one of the most significant areas of change in modern society. This chapter looks at some of the issues that the new technology raises for teachers. The significant role of image media, the internet and applications software form the main focus for discussion.

The establishment of the World Wide Web marked a very important development in the history of human communication: as significant as the printing press. However, the interactivity of educational sites and their capacity to support learning have been much more modest than was at first hoped, but the internet more generally has extended interactivity. For example, the *Second Life* site allows people to create a character (called an avatar) and engage in a cyber world, so real that the first real millionaire was created in 2006.

Although true interactivity on the internet is restricted to a limited number of sites, its role as a vast library of knowledge continues to astonish. The launch of *Google Earth* is a good example, providing as it does images from almost every place on earth, including most children's houses. *Wikipedia*'s innovative democratic knowledge base is both a useful source of information and a very interesting concept. It also raises the question of how knowledge is authenticated. It is perhaps this that children need most help with in relation to the knowledge available through the internet. How do they (and you) know that what they are reading is accurate and valid?

Technological developments like the web and many less significant ones frequently attract claims of revolution in many spheres of life including educational ones. Since 1997 significant amounts of public money have been expended on ICT in schools in the belief that it would have a dramatic effect on raising standards. Nearly all schools now have dedicated rooms with suites of computers which are connected to the internet. Interactive whiteboards (IWBs) are a feature of most primary classrooms. ICT has been built into the PNS Framework for literacy.

Following the changes in schools we now also have the benefit of research which has looked at the role of ICT. As far as the important, but narrow, question of effectiveness of ICT the indications from research are not particularly promising. One of the most recent reviews was a systematic review of the effectiveness of different ICTs in the teaching and learning of English (written composition) (Andrews *et al.*, 2005). It was found that in the field of ICT, research was very much in its infancy. Key definitions such as ICT, literacy and English were not clear enough, and the relationship between them was not well understood. Although there were some reasonably good research studies which looked at effectiveness, they were not sufficiently similar to make useful generalisations:

> As in previous reviews in the field (see Andrews, 2004, for an account of reviews undertaken by the English Review Group between 2001 and 2003), one of the main implications for policy is that we must move away from a belief that ICT will act as a panacea for the successful learning of literacy. It is clear from the present review, and from previous reviews, that ICT should be seen as a range of technologies that can have particular effects on particular parts of the English syllabus. These effects vary according to the age and ability of learners, and very much in relation to the readiness of teachers to incorporate ICT into their understanding of the subject and thus into their lessons.
>
> (Andrews *et al.*, 2005: 38)

The prime importance of the role of the teacher and their pedagogy, not the technology, has been understood for a long time. Miller and Olson's (1994) research found that the personal pedagogy of teachers could not be easily separated from the use they made of ICT and that ICT did not seem to drive practice, if anything, previous practice determined the nature of ICT use. This is important because it suggests that 'revolutions' are unlikely but nevertheless ICT is an important part of the development of learning and teaching. You should view ICTs as useful tools which, with the appropriate pedagogy, can enhance learning and teaching.

There are typically long phases when ICTs are used in parallel with more traditional tools prior to the replacement of old technology. For example, we would imagine that very few people now use a typewriter rather than a word processor. Email and text messaging dominate communication in a way that not so long ago was impossible. Yet paper letters continue to be important, in fact in many ways have a higher status due to their rare use and the necessity to use them in many legal decisions. The death of the book has been predicted many times yet book sales continued to grow. At the same time interactive electronic texts slowly improve. Rollable screens allowing downloading and reading of electronic texts are currently at the forefront of book technology.

The question of whether and when electronic tools will replace traditional ones remains unclear.

One of the features of ICT is the increasing need for specialisation. People's jobs and interests are served by specialist knowledge in an increasing diverse range of hardware and software. This is also true of children who usually have knowledge of the particular ICTs that they are interested in far beyond the knowledge of their teachers. For example, at age 10, Dominic's son Olly was regularly playing *Runescape*, an online adventure game. This involves frequent reading of instructions and rules, and interaction with other online players through use of the computer keyboard. Sometimes friends that he knew in the real world (some who ironically lived a few minutes away!) would appear in *Runescape* for a conversation. Another example of his computer use started with him resurrecting some relatively old technology (his *Gameboy Advance*), using the eBay site to buy some software, and locating a site which explained 'cheats' for *Super Mario*, one of the games that he had bought online. In all of this Dominic took an interest but his level of knowledge far exceeded mine. On the other hand there were specific packages which I use frequently, mainly for work, that he knows nothing about. The main implication of this is that teachers should take an interest in their pupils' ICT use out of school. Occasional opportunities to present to their peers information about ICTs that they use and are interested in could have a number of positive consequences.

The example of Olly's use of technology illustrates that the separation between ICT and multimedia ☞ is far from clear-cut. Print media and image media, both moving image and still image, are created and enhanced by using ICTs.

Moving image media

In order to emphasise the significance of moving image media we will return briefly to examples from our children. At the time that the *Lord of the Rings* films were released Olly asked again and again to see them. Having watched the DVD of the first film, he saw the next two films in the cinema. The experiences led to a rich seam of development for him: role-play using his bow and arrows from York's Jorvik centre and his Harry Potter sword with sound effects; dramatic re-enactment with toy models of the characters; defeat of Orcs, Uruk-Hai and other unpleasant monsters on the Sony PlayStation *Lord of the Rings* game; and all of these in the context of sustained motivation, interest and determination. Oliver also made a very good attempt (for a 7-year-old) to read *The Fellowship of the Ring*. Although it was really too difficult he did enjoy skimming and scanning to find his favourite bits. Dominic's own interest in the book had been rekindled along with a slight guilt that he still hadn't read one of the great pieces of literature, so he tried again, and was transfixed. Many interesting conversations followed where father and son compared their understandings of the film version and their different readings of the *Fellowship*. Oliver's factual knowledge of characters and particular details remained higher than his dad's but because he didn't read all of the *Fellowship* he had less specific evidence of where, for example, the film differed from the books. A case in point is the chapter about Tom Bombadil, which doesn't appear in the film.

Russell's daughter Sophie had also become entranced by *The Fellowship of the Ring* DVD although her response to this text was quite different. Having watched the film she returned to the scene of Bilbo's 111th birthday party and spent an afternoon learning Frodo's dance, rewinding the film and joining in with the festivities. From there, she completed her usual ritual of selecting sections of dialogue to memorise by heart and then re-enacting them with her own toys. This began with the opening:

> 'You're late Gandalf!'
> 'A wizard is never late and neither is he early. He arrives precisely when he means to.'

and continued through to the complicated scenes prior to the start of the quest, where she spent several days memorising lines and re-enacting them in a clear attempt to grasp and control narrative structure and character motivation. Several questions along the lines of 'Dad, why do they all have more than one name?' reflected her desire for accuracy and appropriateness within her re-enactments.

The many aspects of creativity and learning in these episodes came about due to the excitement and interest generated by a film. The significance of film for both children was one important element of the creativity but without another element, the freedom to develop their own interests, there would not have been the same level of engagement nor arguably the same level of learning. The anecdote serves to remind us that in the twenty-first century a film and even a video game are just as much a 'text' as a book is.

Given the central role of moving images in children's lives it was a disappointment to see that the promising early draft of the PNS Framework which quite strongly emphasised multimedia work was very much diluted in the final version. In fact we could not see a direct mention of films in the objectives. Instead a guidance document explains the following:

> DVD and video texts are increasingly being seen as part of the reading repertoire and offer good opportunities for evaluating purposes and viewpoints. Discussion of the ways that film texts are put together, for example decisions made by the director about camera angles, where to use a close-up, middle- or long-distance shot can greatly aid the process of evaluating the effect of a text on the reader or viewer and offer a focus for sharing impressions of the overall effects on a text on the reader. DVDs can be easily paused and re-viewed to analyse how directors (and so writers)

construct narratives. Discussions like these, based on film, transfer very readily to discussions about authors' intentions and points of view and give pupils a frame for discussing response to books.

(Department for Education and Skills (DfES) and Primary National Strategy (PNS), 2006: 4)

The recommendation that digital video cameras might be used to 'create and shape' texts with moving images is not made, and the emphasis is on electronic forms of print more than the images.

The British Film Institute (BFI) strongly advocates film work and has produced some suggestions for structured teaching. Pilot work for the teaching resource *Story Shorts* (British Film Institute, 2001) involved teachers and others from Birmingham LEA; Bristol and Lambeth EAZ; Bristol Watershed Media Centre; and Warwickshire Arts Zone. Some of the teachers' comments show their excitement about the work: 'I have been more surprised by the children's reactions to the films than anything else I have ever seen'; 'Using the film *Growing* stimulated the strongest poetry ever written by the children.' The resource consists of a series of films which are about five minutes long. The films are all interesting and the length means that they can be used more easily in literacy lesson than a feature film. However, this does raise some issues. Some of the best work with film can come from using films that are current and that relate closely to children's interests. Although these are feature-length films, DVD technology means that they can be viewed in short sections (called 'chapters'). This means that teachers can design activities which do not require children to see the whole film each time.

Story Shorts suggests a set of opening questions that can be used to stimulate discussion: the '3 Cs' are Camera; Colour; Character; and the '3 Ss' are Story; Sound; Setting. So, for example, with regard to *Lord of the Rings* you might ask: What is the motion of the *camera* just before we see an Orc being born from the filth of the earth? Or, what kinds of *colours* do you see after Gandalf's death as the fellowship emerge from the Mines of Moria? Or, what kinds of *sounds* make the black riders so terrifying? Following whole group discussion supported by the Cs and Ss questions there are suggestions for how the films can be used to stimulate other more extended activities which take speaking and listening into writing and drawing.

Story Shorts is more about using film as a stimulus for reflection than actually getting involved with creating films but there are many examples where the skills learned could be applied to such work. Although it steers an uneasy path through the competing demands of the objectives in the NLS Framework for Teaching and the institute's own agenda for greater knowledge about the techniques of filmmaking, it was an important development in the context of working with film to support the teaching of English at primary level.

Parker (1999) suggested that there is a positive link between moving image media and literacy development. His research featured a project that involved

Year 3 children adapting Roald Dahl's story *Fantastic Mr Fox* into an animated film. One aspect of the programme of study involved some children working towards a simplified version of the book for younger children, and others were getting ready to use the animation package on the computer. Parker felt that some of the children's first person writing to support the script had particularly strong visual characteristics:

1   'I saw some metal in the moonlight night.'
2   'All I can see is the 4 walls. Brown, dim and muddy like a pison.' [prison].
3   'I can see the opening to our den. Its daytime the light light is coming in.'

(ibid.: 31)

David Buckingham has done much work on the influence of television, and more recently has written about multimedia technologies. He suggests that society – and ironically the media – tend to take up two main positions: either that new technologies are a very good thing or that they are dangerous. He points out that neither position is satisfactory as the real picture is much more complex. Buckingham's (1999) research has included a focus on computer games and creative use of multimedia. In contrast to public concerns he found that games playing was very much a social activity. Although games were played alone, they were also played collaboratively. The games also provided a topic for much discussion that included swapping games, sharing cheats and hints, and discussion about the wider world of games playing such as TV programmes about the subject, games shops, games arcades and magazines. Buckingham also added a cautionary note that a great deal of the discussion was influenced by consumerism. This perhaps adds further justification for helping children to become critical consumers of media messages so they are not unfairly influenced by advertising messages.

In another piece of research Buckingham tried to find out 'to what extent, and how, were children using computers for digital animation, design work, sound or video editing, or for what is sometimes called "multi-media author-ing"'. Some of this survey's results mirrored the previous piece of research, for example, overall he found that 'boys were generally more interested and involved' in the area than girls. He also found that although many of the children claimed to be involved in multimedia authoring, it was rarely a creative process. For example, although some of the children thought that they had made animations, they confused their own input with examples that were already available on the computer. The lack of creativity was caused by parents' lack of skill and therefore ability to help their children, the children's view that computers were mainly to be used for 'messing about' when they were bored, and the lack of meaningful audiences for their work. This kind of work at home is an area that teachers can actively address.

Applications software

As a teacher your emphasis in relation to ICT should be on *composing* and *creating* using a range of application packages, not on the overuse of skills-building software. The scope for the 'spiral' development of knowledge, skills and understanding using applications packages is vast. Applications are tools that allow us to carry out various jobs quicker and more efficiently. Examples include: word processing, desktop publishing, spreadsheets, web authoring packages, databases, and a range of multimedia packages.

The biggest area of expansion in recent years has been in multimedia applications. Children can now make films by filming moving image sequences, editing them with packages like Apple iMovie, composing music for soundtracks, inserting editing effects, and 'burning' DVDs. This kind of project requires extended regular periods of time to bring together the different sources to create a satisfying outcome. We feel that the learning that is possible through such projects is very promising indeed.

Word processing software continues to become more and more sophisticated. It offers the chance to compose from first draft and to go through several editing stages. Spell checkers are particularly useful, grammar checkers less so because they are very poor at understanding the context for the words and phrases being used. Documents created in word processors can easily be saved as web pages and published on school websites. Integration of images is straightforward, helped by the use of tables to organise documents. One of the biggest limitations of word processing software is that use of the keyboard is slow if you do not learn to type. Given that voice recognition software is still slower than fluent typing, and because of the difficulties you find if not in a quiet environment, the keyboard is likely to be used for the foreseeable future. For that reason children should be taught how to type properly. We found a very cheap but good quality typing package, called *Master Key*, online.

Desktop publishing (DTP) packages started a trend which reached new heights in web authoring packages. DTP encourages children to 'publish' texts by creating pictures using art packages or by scanning in their own artwork, and combining these with texts that they have created. These packages primarily make the organisation and layout of pages much easier than if you tried to achieve the same result using a word processor.

The software that enables children to design web pages has the added facility to include moving images and sound. The other significant difference that this software has is the ability to link different texts by clicking on an icon, picture or piece of text using hyperlinks. These packages challenge us to think about what a 'text' really is. If children are encouraged to record their own sounds, create their own images, develop their own writing, and establish their own links, this really can lead to exciting learning outcomes.

The government's drive from the late 1990s onwards to ensure that all schools had a higher level of ICT capability was in many ways welcome, but, it would perhaps have been better if this had been driven more by curriculum need and pedagogy rather than aspirations for particular technologies. In the light of some significant research on the impact of such technology it was hoped that lessons might have been learned. However, it appears that once again technological aspirations are driving the government's agenda.

According to Becta, the government's e-strategy sets the expectation that:

- by spring 2008 every pupil should have access to a personalised online learning space with the potential to support an e-portfolio (provided by their local authority);
- by 2010 every school should have integrated learning and management systems (a comprehensive suite of learning platform technologies).

A learning platform brings together hardware, software and supporting services to enable more effective ways of working within and outside the classroom. They can vary considerably, but every learning platform should provide a range of ICT-based functions.

Practical benefits to teachers

What do these benefits mean in practice for teachers? An effective learning platform will enable teachers to do the following:

- create and share teaching materials which can be accessed online, printed out or used with an interactive whiteboard;
- put their resources online page by page, lesson plan by lesson plan, so colleagues can access them both in school and from home;
- access a wide variety of learning materials that they can customise for the exact needs of their pupils;
- access lesson plans from colleagues to support supply cover;
- assess, monitor and track individual and group progress;
- receive submissions of work from pupils in one area that is easy to manage;
- manage their timetables, diary, email and discussions within personal desktop space;
- increase their ICT competence and confidence.

Practical benefits to pupils

An effective learning platform will enable pupils to do the following:

- access learning materials created by their teachers and others, outside lesson time and from locations such as the library and home;

- store work and notes online for use in assignments, homework and revision, outside normal school hours;
- work at their own pace and with a wider choice of learning styles, through a more personalised curriculum;
- create an online portfolio, including digital photos and videos of performance as well as text;
- improve their ICT skills and online management of materials;
- submit homework and assignments for marking and assessment;
- communicate by email and participate in live discussions and forums with other students and teachers.

Practical benefits to parents

An effective learning platform will enable parents and carers to do the following:

- play a greater part in children's learning, where they have access to the learning platform from home;
- support children in any learning which takes place outside school;
- access their child's personal home page to keep track of their work and the curriculum;
- view reports, attendance data and scores in assessment activities;
- communicate effectively with teachers, school administrators and others supporting their child's learning;
- engage with wider school issues through online communication tools;
- become active partners with the school.

Practical benefits for administration and management

An effective learning platform will enable administrators and managers to do the following:

- provide up-to-date management information on attendance and attainment;
- track the progress of individuals and groups of children;
- collate summative and formative assessments;
- reduce the administrative burden on teachers by using transferable data;
- enable communication within school and beyond, on a one-to-one, one-to-many, or many-to-many basis;
- increase communication with parents.

(Becta, 2007, online)

It remains to be seen if this approach to ICTs will bring real benefits for teaching and learning.

Practice points

- Use ICTs as tools that naturally extend your pedagogy.
- Critically evaluate all software and ask tough questions about its effectiveness for helping pupils learn more.
- Emphasise active creation and composition more than the more passive aspects of ICTs.

Glossary

Multimedia – texts that use a range of media in their production including text, pictures, links, moving images, sounds.

References

Andrews, R., Dan, H., Freeman, A., McGuinn, N., Robinson, A. and Zhu, D. (2005) *The Effectiveness of Different ICTs in the Teaching and Learning of English (Written Composition), 5–16.* London: EPPI-Centre, Social Science Research Unit, Institute of Education, University of London.

Becta (2007) 'What are the main benefits of a learning platform?' Retrieved 24 January, 2007, from http://schools.becta.org.uk/index.php?section=re&rid=12889

Buckingham, D. (1999) 'Superhighway or road to Nowhere? Children's relationships with digital technology', *English in Education*, 33(1): 3–12.

British Film Institute (2001) *Story Shorts: A Resource for Key Stage 2 Literacy.* London: British Film Institute.

Department for Education and Skills (DfES) and Primary National Strategy (PNS) (2006) *Multimodal – Ict Digital Texts.* Retrieved 26 January, 2007, from http://www.standards.dfes.gov.uk/primaryframeworks/literacy/Papers/learningandteaching/

Miller, L. and Olson, J. (1994) 'Putting the computer in its place: a study of teaching with technology', *Journal of Curriculum Studies*, 26(2): 121–141.

Parker, D. (1999) 'You've read the book, now make the film: moving image media, print literacy and narrative', *English in Education*, 33(1): 24–35.

Annotated bibliography

Burn, A. and Leach, J. (2004). *A Systematic Review of the Impact of ICT on the Learning of Literacies Associated with Moving Image Texts in English, 5–16.* London: EPPI-Centre, Social Science Research Unit, Institute of Education, University of London.

Makes the important point that pupils should *produce* moving image texts. This kind of work should be regarded as a form of 'writing' and should not just be a feature of the reading curriculum. There are also cross-curricula benefits for use of moving image texts.
L3 ***

Marsh, J. (2004) 'The primary canon: a critical review', *British Journal of Educational Studies*, 52(3): 249–362.

Marsh's work on popular culture including multimedia is excellent. This paper offers further evidence of the marginalisation of multimedia.

L3 ***

Mercer, N., Fernandez, M., Dawes, L., Wegerif, R. and Sams, C. (2003) 'Talk about texts: using ICT to develop children's oral and literate abilities', *Reading, Literacy and Language*, 37(2), 81–89.

Mercer and colleagues' work on interaction and ICT is excellent.

L2 **

Teachers Evaluate Educational Multimedia (TEEM)http://www.teem.org.uk/).

Very useful site that includes teacher evaluations of packages to support the teaching of English and literacy and most areas of the curriculum.

L1 *

Chapter 26

Supporting black and multilingual children

The importance of supporting all languages at children's disposal is empha-sised in this chapter. Although classroom practices that are part of multi-cultural teaching are recommended, it is argued that support for black and multilingual children requires teachers to be aware of issues to do with race ☞ and culture, particularly in predominantly white schools.

Over two hundred languages are spoken by children in British schools and the number of young bilingual speakers continues to rise. Underachievement (for a variety of reasons) is a recurring factor for many children from minority ethnic background (Gillborn and Gipps, 1996), although this is a highly prob-lematic relationship that should not be read simplistically. Contemporary arguments have claimed that deprivation, disadvantage and child poverty are the key indicators of underachievement (Brettingham, 2007) but of course it is often the case that these are experienced disproportionately by many minority ethnic children, meaning that teachers need to be highly skilled in the ways that they adapt and devise language work to genuinely support and encourage the academic potential of all pupils. All teachers are necessarily involved in the promotion and development of language work in schools, but some remain unfamiliar with the particular needs of the multilingual ☞ child. It is extremely important that all children become competent and confident users of the Eng-lish language as soon as possible in order to maximise their life chances through examinations and assessment processes (which are primarily carried out in English). However, this should never mean that the teacher expects children to surrender their own first languages in order to achieve academic success. A large-scale study of emergent bilingual pupils in America clearly showed the importance of supporting all pupils' languages:

> Non-English speaking student success in learning to read in English does not rest exclusively on primary language input and development, nor is it solely the result of rapid acquisition of English. Both apparently contribute to students' subsequent English reading achievement . . . early literacy

experiences support subsequent literacy development, regardless of language; time spent on literacy activity in the native language – whether it takes place at home or at school – is not time lost with respect to English reading acquisition.

(Reese *et al.*, 2000: 633)

The potential of linguistic diversity in the multilingual classroom can easily be overlooked by those who insist on the exclusive use of English in their language work. Multilingual children are experts in handling language and in many ways could be more proficient than the teacher. As such, these children have considerable language skills on which the teacher can build, and they are likely to have much to offer others, particularly with regards to the subject of language study. Having said this, even if the child may be skilled in language use, he or she will still need particular support and guidance to develop greater proficiency in the use of English at school.

The language development of multilingual children often highlights a considerable gulf between the rate of oral language acquisition and the equivalent in reading and writing. In a study carried out with 2,300 11-year-olds in London, Strand (2005) found that

EAL pupils at the early stages (1–3) of developing fluency had significantly lower KS2 test scores in all subjects than their monolingual peers. However, EAL pupils who were fully fluent in English achieved significantly higher scores in all KS2 tests than their monolingual peers.

(ibid.: 275)

Consequently, the beginning teacher needs to be aware of the need to apply greater sensitivity to these children; on the one hand, the child should be encouraged to use spoken English at every possible opportunity, on the other, the teacher needs to employ teaching strategies which ensure that the same child does not begin to lose confidence in their language use because they perceive themselves as failed readers and writers.

Beginning teachers also need to understand that it is unhelpful to conceive of 'multilingual children' as some kind of homogeneous group. Some children will have been born in this country and their parents may have insisted on a different first language in order to retain the child's sense of ethnic identity and community (this is sometimes the case with Italian families, for instance). It is important to acknowledge that there are social and cultural differences which have direct relevance for the teacher of English. British Black and Asian parents may have different perceptions of their relationship to and role within the 'host' white community. Some will encourage their children to embrace British customs, language, codes, etc., as fully and as unproblematically as possible, others will seek to resist such moves and instead promote and defend their own cultural beliefs, languages and practices in order to maintain their cultural identity as distinct within British society. It would be unwise for the beginning teacher to begin to enter into a debate which meant that one side or another would be seen as preferable; it is more important to acknowledge that the child's own role within this can be difficult to negotiate. It is professionally important, therefore, to be aware of the child's set of cultural beliefs, to make every effort to understand and respect the position of the parents and to ensure that the child is not placed in a position whereby he or she is required to make unhelpful comparisons between the school and the home.

Standard English is the required language form of the National Curriculum, but teachers should be wary of promoting this to the detriment or exclusion of the multilingual child's first language. To adhere rigidly to Standard English with multilingual children is to deny those children aspects of their own identity, their skills as language users and their access to self-expression. It affects their confidence, their perception of themselves as speakers, listeners, readers and writers, and therefore has a potentially negative effect on the child's self-esteem. As one writer points out:

> If English is to replace rather than add to the languages of the children we teach, we must ask what is the effect of such a programme on their cultural identity, their self-esteem and sense of place in the community.
>
> (Blackledge, 1994: 46)

There is evidence to show that the least successful way to deliver English teaching to a multilingual child with a poor grounding in English is to remove them from the classroom setting and provide short sharp bursts of tuition in isolation. More effective is the practice of resourcing the multilingual classroom with bilingual texts (including big books), dual language CD-ROMs, stories taped (often by parents) in other languages, etc. Teachers who develop practices which ignore or exclude the needs of bilingual pupils in order to serve a perceived need of the white majority in the class should be aware of research into this area which reported the success of 204 'two-way bilingual' schools, demonstrating through achievement data that all pupils benefited from such approaches and not, as might be expected, only the bilingual children themselves (Thomas and Collier, 1998).

Classroom approaches

Many teachers find themselves developing their own resources in response to the challenge of multilingual children. While this may initially stem from a lack of suitable resources, more effectively it stems from the teacher's overt recognition of the child's needs, and the production of such materials helps to consolidate the positive approach to language work that the child will need to develop. Such materials also communicate an equally positive message to parents, who can be encouraged to use them either in the school or at home.

It has been pointed out that dual language books are not always as immediately helpful as may be presumed (Gravelle, 1996). One language may be given greater status than another, cultural subtleties in translation are not always successful and there are difficulties when written languages which are read from right to left are placed next to English as the starting points for the child could become confusing. However, the construction of dual language books are a popular way forward in many multilingual classrooms as children often find the process supportive and beneficial. Language issues should be less problematic when children are allowed to create dual language books for themselves, and when parents are encouraged to take part in this process. Walker *et al.* (1998: 18) offers particularly interesting and intricate designs for dual language book making, and it should be remembered that once these books are made, they can serve the purpose of recording the child's personal development and later provide an immediate and personal starting point for other children who need similar support.

Cross-curricular and thematic approaches in primary classrooms often offer opportunities to acknowledge multicultural dimensions to study. Teachers can acknowledge consciously the monocultural ☞ way in which many primary school themes are conceived, and open this planning up to more accurately reflect a multicultural society. Themes such as 'Ourselves', 'Food', 'Shelter', 'Sacred Places' and 'Journeys' all offer links across the National Curriculum and possibilities for multicultural work to emerge (Hix, 1992).

Story telling can be another particularly successful method of encouraging the multilingual child to negotiate between more than one language. There is evidence that story telling has been a particularly important strategy with bilingual learners in the early years (MacLean, 1996). All cultures have their own histories, myths, legends and stories which are passed on through generations of children. These stories cross cultural boundaries; some are recognisably similar with subtle shades of difference, others will be particular within a specific cultural context. In either case, the story itself becomes a powerful, shared experience and the telling, the retelling, the writing and reading of the range of possible stories open a rich vein of language study for the teacher to exploit. Again, parents should be seen as a valuable and authoritative resource in this area.

As far as the potential for ICT to support children with EAL, Low and Beverton (2004) found that there need to be sufficient computers for children to work on and that the work should be part of normal classroom teaching but tailored to the specific needs of the children. There were indications that collaborative computer work could be valuable and that although computer work could be motivational, it should not be done to extreme as, for example, in the case of word processing, some pupils composed better on the computer and some composed better with pen and paper.

It is important to recognise that the black or Asian child whose first language *is* English may still need particular support. It should hardly need stating that if the black, Asian or multilingual child is isolated in a predominantly white context, it is important that they are not perceived in any way as a novelty. Research repeatedly reports that teachers have different relationships with children from ethnic minorities. For example, it has been claimed that teachers spend less individual time with ethnic minority children, they are more likely to misinterpret black boys' language use as aggressive or confrontational (Nehaul, 1996; Sewell, 1997) and statistics have shown that in some parts of the country black boys are 15 times more likely to be expelled than their white peers (Thornton, 1998). Other research indicates significant discrepancies in the ways in which white teachers are prepared to deal with issues of race in general, and ethnic minority children in their classes in particular (Jones, 1999). This kind of evidence needs exploration in greater depth than this space allows, but it is clear that black and white children in British schools experience quite different relationships with the education system that serves them. Recommendations relating to successful practices and strategies for the support of black and multilingual children in British schools have been published to guide teachers in these areas (Blair and Bourne 1998; Jones 1999).

Practice points

- Be particularly aware of the bilingual child's first few weeks in the classroom. Look for opportunities to display your respect for their language through dual language notices and opportunities to share new words and phrases together.
- Make a particular point of learning to pronounce unfamiliar names accurately both as a mark of respect and as a model for the rest of the class.
- Acknowledge that you are unlikely to know everything about every child's culture, but in so doing acknowledge also that it is your responsibility to understand the lives of *all* the children in your class, not just those who share your own cultural background.

Glossary

Multilingual – referring to a child who speaks two or more languages.
Monocultural teaching – teaching that fails to recognise the multicultural nature of society.
Race – a heavily disputed concept that refers to ethnic identity and origin.

References

Blackledge, A. (ed.) (1994) *Teaching Bilingual Children*. Stoke-on-Trent: Trentham Books.
Blair, M. and Bourne, J. (1998) *Making the Difference: Teaching and Learn-*

ing Strategies in Successful Multi-Ethnic Schools. London: Department for Education and Employment (DfEE).

Brettingham, M. (2007) 'Race is not key to poor results', *TES*, 16 March 2007.

Gillborn, A. and Gipps, C., Office for Standards in Education (OFSTED) (1996) *Recent Research on the Achievements of Ethnic Minority Pupils*. London: HMSO.

Gravelle, M. (1996) *Supporting Bilingual Learners in Schools*. Stoke-on-Trent: Trentham Books.

Hix, P. (1992) *Kaleidoscope: Themes and Activities for Developing the Multi-cultural Dimension in the Primary School*. Crediton: Southgate.

Jones, R. (1999) *Teaching Racism or Tackling it?* Stoke-on-Trent: Trentham Books.

Low, G. and Beverton, S. (2004) *A Systematic Review of the Impact of ICT on Literacy Learning in English of Learners between 5 and 16, for whom English is a Second or Additional Language*. London: EPPI-Centre, Social Science Research Unit, Institute of Education.

MacLean, K. (1996) 'Supporting the literacy of bilingual learners: storytelling and bookmaking', *Multicultural Teaching*, 2: 26–29.

Nehaul, K. (1996) *The Schooling of Children of Caribbean Heritage*. Stoke-on-Trent: Trentham Books.

Reese, L., Garnier, H., Gallimore, R. and Goldenberg, C. (2000) 'Longitudinal analysis of the antecedents of emergent Spanish literacy and middle-school English reading achievement of Spanish-speaking students', *American Educational Research Journal*, 37(3): 622–633.

Sewell, T. (1997) *Black Masculinities and Schooling: How Black Boys Survive Modern Schooling*. Stoke-on-Trent: Trentham Books.

Strand, S. (2005) 'English language acquisition and educational attainment at the end of primary school', *Educational Studies*, 13(3): 275–391.

Thomas, W. P. and Collier, V. P. (1998) 'Two languages are better than one', *Educational Leadership*, 55: 23–26.

Thornton, K. (1998) 'Blacks 15 times more likely to be excluded', *Times Educational Supplement*, 11 December.

Walker, S., Edwards, V. and Leonard, H. (1998) *Write Around the World: Producing Bilingual Resources in the Primary Classroom*. University of Reading: Reading and Language Information Centre.

Annotated bibliography

Department for Education and Skills (DfES) and Primary National Strategy (PNS) (2007) *Rationale for Planning for Children Learning English as an Additional Language*. Retrieved 25 January, 2007, from http://www.standards.dfes.gov.uk/primaryframeworks/downloads/PDF/EAL_Planning.pdf

Helpful statement about basic principles for planning for the needs of children with English as an additional language.

L1 *

Edwards, V. (1998) *The Power of Babel: Teaching and Learning in Multi-lingual Classrooms*. Stoke-on-Trent, Trentham Books.
A particularly helpful text in terms of its sensitivity to new arrivals in school and its guidance for teachers with limited experience of children from a range of cultures. Practical advice for the production of dual language cassettes, books, displays, etc.
L1 **

Jones, R. (1999) *Teaching Racism or Tackling it?* Stoke-on-Trent: Trentham Books.
A book aimed in particular at white teachers working in predominantly or exclusively white classrooms.
L3 ***

Kennedy, E. (2006) 'Literacy development of linguistically diverse first graders in a mainstream English classroom: connecting speaking and writing', *Journal of Early Childhood Literacy*, 6(2): 163–189.
Argues that teachers' understanding of home and school languages is still an issue and that this understanding has an impact on multilingual children's learning.
L3 ***

Chapter 27

Gender and the teaching of English

> Following some introductory general remarks about gender and education this chapter focuses on the issue of boys and attainment. We conclude with a look at an excellent study of the work of one school.

Exploration of issues like gender is fraught with difficulties for teachers. In particular this is because stereotypes and preconceptions are rife in society. The danger of preconceptions is that they can lead to low expectations of children's capabilities. It is very difficult to collect 'objective' evidence because characteristics of gender are shared across men and women in subtly different ways. One example of a gender characteristic is preference for reading fiction as opposed to non-fiction. In general it is argued that women and girls tend to prefer fiction whereas men and boys prefer non-fiction. However, there are many qualifications that need to be made to such an idea. The characteristic does not mean that *all* boys prefer non-fiction or all girls prefer fiction. Therefore in every class of children while it may be true that the characteristic is generally accurate, there will still be boys and girls who do not conform to the stereotype. There is also a developmental angle. The youngest children tend to have a particularly strong relationship with story, nursery rhymes, and songs. There is less of a distinction for them between fiction and non-fiction. As pupils get older, non-fiction forms tend to take on more importance as part of school work but the texts that children select themselves to read at home will not necessarily follow this pattern. It is probably also true to say that most people read a wide variety of texts hence it may be difficult to classify someone as mainly a fiction reader or mainly a non-fiction read. So, the statement about boys' and girls' reading habits needs to be carefully qualified by the factors raised above. Before a judgement could be made about your class you would have to analyse the reading habits of all the children. If you involve the children and parents in such a survey, it could provide helpful information for teaching and provide an opportunity for children to learn more about gender.

This strategy of opening up investigation and discussion is one very good way to practically address gender issues in the classroom.

Even if there is evidence to show gender differences there is still the question of how the knowledge should affect our teaching. For example, if we accept that girls prefer fiction, then we could look at this in at least two ways: (1) there is a potential problem that they are not accessing non-fiction texts which becomes increasingly important in secondary schooling and later life, therefore we should take steps to encourage them to access non-fiction; or (2) we want to relate our teaching to girls' interests and want to motivate them so we will expose them to even more fiction. We think that a combination of (1) and (2) is probably a sensible way forward. Another practical way to address gender differences is the use of in-class single sex groupings.

In a systematic review of studies on classroom practice Francis *et al.* (2002) concluded that different kinds of classroom groupings could be effective in helping to reduce children's stereotypical gender constructions. For example, the use of some in-class single sex grouping could do the following:

- increase the self-confidence of girls and/or encourage their experimentation with non-gender-traditional activities; or
- provide a setting for boys to tackle aspects of traditional forms of masculine attitudes and behaviours.

(ibid.: 2)

But overall the authors were struck by how little research had been carried out in the area, the predominance of small-scale studies, and how the issue of boys' attainment had become an area of concern.

Boys and attainment

Concern about boys' attainment in the statutory tests had been growing for some years when in 2004 the United Kingdom Literacy Association and the Primary National Strategy (PNS) launched some research to look at the issue. Their research found that

- The project has impacted not only on standards of boys' achievements in writing but on teachers'/practitioners' professional development and capacity.
- The planning and teaching model with the integration of drama and/or visual approaches was successful in promoting marked and rapid improvements in standards of boys' writing.

(The United Kingdom Literacy Association (UKLA), 2004: 2)

A survey which measured pupils' perceptions about writing, carried out as part of the research, included the question: 'Is there anything you don't like about writing?' Although there is a lack of clarity about the number of pupils who answered this question in relation to the number of statements they made, before and after the project the pupils' main dislike was, 'Technical: spelling, handwriting, use of grammatical devices, particular text types' (ibid.: 14). The first three items in this list are consistent with other research which has shown the demotivating effects of an undue emphasis on the transcription elements of the writing process. The fourth item is particularly interesting in that the technical analysis of text types has not previously been mentioned as a demotivating factor. An emphasis on analysis of text types has been a key feature of literacy teaching since 1997.

Overall, the research makes very strong claims in favour of the approach to writing that was adopted. However, the methodological design of the study has a number of factors which mean we have to be cautious about accepting the findings at face value. It is possible that the impact on standards of writing in the project could have been a result of the emphasis on a new approach rather than the specific teaching methods that were tried. No control groups were used. The teaching methods used were not the only aspect of the change in practice: for example, the projects involved a series of review and evaluation meetings. This opportunity to reflect and discuss could have been a key factor in attainment gains.

The claimed gains in writing standards were unusually large. On average the boys progressed one-third of a National Curriculum level in one term. However, the validity of this assessment needs some investigation. Teachers assessed their target pupils using local authority guidance that sub-divided National Curriculum levels into assessment statements. No examples are included in the report of the different scales that the three different authorities used. Although we are informed that moderation meetings were held there is very little detail about the ways that pupils' writing was assessed; the nature of the samples that were collected or how attainment across different text types was accounted for.

Despite the caveats about the methodology of the research the practices used by the teachers are interesting. The teaching was generally planned in three-week blocks concentrating on one type of text. Electronic and print-based forms of texts were used. Reading, writing and speaking and listening were integrated. Drama techniques were used to enhance understanding of texts. Although these approaches are interesting the report does not explain why they might benefit boys in particular. It is probable that girls would benefit from such an approach as well. The approach used in the research seemed to anticipate the methods of the PNS Framework in 2006, and was similar to a DfES study which found the following:

> We would suggest that gains can be made in primary literacy, particularly in the levels achieved by apparently under-achieving boys, when:

- a variety of interactive classroom activities are adopted, with a 'fitness for purpose', so that both short, specific focused activities and more sustained, ongoing activities are used, as and when appropriate
- acknowledgement is given to the central importance of talk, to speaking and listening as a means of supporting writing
- the advantages to be gained through companionable writing with response partners and through group work are recognised
- teachers are prepared to risk-take to bring more creativity and variety to literacy
- more integrated use is made of ICT so that quality presentation can be more easily achieved, and drafts amended with more ease.

(Younger *et al.*, 2004: 10)

The work of one school

Trisha Maynard's study looked at the issue of gender from the perspective of one school who decided to address the problem of boys underachievement. Very early on in her book Maynard makes it clear that in spite of renewed concerns about boys' achievements it was not a new phenomena. As long ago as 1868 girls outperformed boys and had more positive attitudes to learning. At that time the issue was defined as a problem for *girls* because they were in danger of 'overstrain':

> Girls' excessive conscientiousness and their almost morbid obsession with learning were castigated as unhealthy and contrasted with boys 'breezy attitude' towards life. Cohen comments that boys' poor academic performance and their negative attitudes towards school and school-work were tolerated – even admired – as natural expressions of their rebellious and superior intellect.
>
> (Maynard, 2002: 17)

Maynard also raises the issue of narrative vs. non-narrative texts. As we show in Chapter 11, in the 1980s claims were made that there was too much story writing going on in primary schools. Maynard says that her data showed that boys were particularly reluctant to write stories. Some of the teachers at the school claimed that this was due to the attitude of the boys rather than their ability. The teachers felt that the boys often had very imaginative ideas during whole class discussion but were reluctant to put their ideas down on paper. Other chapters in the book shed more light on boys' motivation for writing. One of the teachers describes a child who was usually motivated by practical science work but when asked to write up the results would say: 'Why do I have to write it down? . . . There's no need . . . I know it.' There is also convincing evidence in the book that boys preferred action in their stories and tended to include more violence, which is often regarded by teachers as inappropriate.

This does present a dilemma. Schools do not want to encourage violence in any way. But it should not be the inclusion of violence in stories *per se* that is the problem. If violence is included, one of the question should be, is it written about in a way that is powerful, meaningful, consequential, etc.? In other words is it good writing whatever the subject? Maynard observes:

> What is so wrong with the inclusion of ideas gained from the visual medium of television and computer games? ... Should we take more account of boys' popular cultural interests when planning children's literacy work ... And are we clear why the development of narrative through dialogue and passages of description is considered preferable to a more episodic, visual narrative style?
>
> (Maynard, 2002: 66)

The most powerful chapter in the book features the children's own thoughts. The children identified issues that transcended the gender question. The monotonous use of story planning sheets received short shrift:

G: The planning sheet ... that's the worst part of the story.
TM: Why?
G: Because it takes up too much time.
B: I write it and then I forgets it.
B: It worns you out.
B: I don't reckon there's any point in doing it because we only rush through it ... and then don't even look at it ... I bet you any money that everybody who uses a planning sheet they don't even look at it ... they just write it to keep the teacher happy and then put it in the bin.
B: That's what I does. I writes on it then puts it to one side and carries on ... I don't bother with the planning sheets ...
G: It's a waste of time.
B: Say Miss gives us an hour to do it all, it takes us nearly an hour to fill in the planning sheet and we don't have time to write the story.
B: He's exaggerating.
G: I would prefer to use a rough book ... just jot things down.

(Maynard, 2002: 101)

The children also didn't like other techniques that teachers used to help them structure their writing. This was powerful evidence and not surprising. The mantra of 'shared reading; teacher demonstration; scribing; supported composition'; ... finally followed by *independent* writing can so easily become an inflexible model. It can also signal low expectations based on the idea that all children are incapable of writing unless their writing is scaffolded. You should assume that children will have interesting ideas for their writing and that they are able to write well with your support. If they are unable to for whatever reason then you can offer them more structured support.

> I hate writing stories in school. If we were allowed to choose our own titles it would be all right. When I go to bed I don't go to bed . . . I put my lamp on and writes stories.

> I prefer writing my own stories because you've got a free mind . . . You don't have to put down what Mrs G says.

(ibid.: 99)

At the end of the period of study the teachers in the school had tried out a number of strategies to tackle the gender problem and had been encouraged to reflect on these. The teachers realised in the main that there were no easy solutions but some were frustrated that they couldn't 'solve the problem'.

Gender as a subject needs to be an explicit part of the curriculum in order to help boys and girls understand more about themselves and their peers and to combat discrimination. Approaches have to be chosen which allow self-determination for learners and which allow them to pursue their own interests. As this chapter has shown, there are no simple solutions to addressing gender and attainment. First and foremost teachers need to collect evidence about boys' and girls' learning rather than rely unduly on anecdotal evidence. Involving children in study of and discussion about gender issues is both a necessary part of education and a good way to start to address gender in the classroom. The use of single gender groups as a regular part of classroom organisation can help girls and boys access curricula that is more closely tailored to their needs. Teachers also need to find out about boys' and girls' interests and use this information to provide a curriculum that is relevant to their different needs. Giving pupils opportunities to make choices, for example, over reading material and writing topics is also an important way to support the preferences of girls and boys and gives the sensitive teacher a deeper understanding of the pupils that they teach.

Practice points
- Use evidence about your class as the basis for decisions in terms of the needs of girls and boys.
- Organise your classroom for occasional use of single gender groups. This can work well in collaboration with another colleague.
- Give opportunities for pupils to make choices as part of their English learning.

References

Francis, B., Skelton, C. and Archer, L. (2002) 'A systematic review of class-room strategies for reducing stereotypical gender constructions among girls and boys in mixed-sex UK primary schools', *Research Evidence in Education Library* Retrieved 28 January, 2007, from http://eppi.ioe.ac.uk/cms/

Maynard, T. (2002) *Boys and Literacy: Exploring the Issues*. London: RoutledgeFalmer.

United Kingdom Literacy Association (UKLA) and Primary National Strategy (2004) *Raising Boys' Achievements in Writing*. Royston: UKLA.

Younger, M., Warrington, M., Gray, J., Ruddock, J., McClellan, R., Bearne, E., *et al.* (2004) *Raising Boys' Achievement*. London: Department for Education and Skills.

Annotated bibliography

Barrs, M. and Pidgeon, S. (eds) (1998) *Boys and Reading*. London: The Centre for Language in Primary Education.
An early examination of boys' underachievement which features case studies of teachers showing the strategies they use to address the issues.
L1 *

Jackson, S. and Gee, S. (2005) ' "Look Janet", "No you look John" ': constructions of gender in early school reader illustrations across 50 years, *Gender and Education*, 17(2): 115–128.
Shows that gender stereotypes are still a feature of reading schemes.
L3 **

Maynard, T. (2002) *Boys and Literacy: Exploring the Issues*. London: RoutledgeFalmer.
A powerful and in-depth exploration of the issues relating to boys and literacy.
L2 **

Teacher Training Resource Bank (TTRB) Available at: http://www.ttrb.ac.uk
See a review of the United Kingdom Literacy Association/Primary National Strategy (2004) project on Raising Boys Achievement in Writing.
L2 **

Chapter 28

Poetry

The significance of poetry in the primary classroom is discussed and we suggest that it can be a highly motivational method of developing work in language and literacy. Some examples of different approaches to the teaching of poetry are outlined.

Poetry offers degrees of intensity, subtlety and artistry which are unique to the English curriculum. However, in many primary classrooms poetry is underused as a tool for language development and for learning. It is important look back to the early years to see where children's relationships with language develop. Story is an important early influence, but poetry exists as an even earlier feature of many children's first steps towards language acquisition. Nursery rhymes are an early introduction to many features of the English language. They are self-contained, offering the child a (typically humorous) snippet of language that is worth remembering and through repetition the child learns to share the poetic structure with others. Children learn to invest rhyme with emphasis, for example 'Ring-A-Ring-Of-Roses' ends with the phrase 'all fall DOWN', which the child learns to accentuate by intonation and by literally falling down. Similarly, the rhyme:

> Round and round the garden
> like a teddy bear
> one step, two step
> and TICKLE HIM UNDER THERE

teaches the child anticipation, turn-taking, humour, and the joy of another shared fragment of language. There are close links here with communal songs and stories, but poetry has the particularly important feature (at this stage) of brevity: it is manageable and memorable.

Parents of young children know how advertisements and jingles from the radio and television become embedded in much the same way. The child learns that (for whatever reason) this piece of language is worth holding on to, and that it is worth the investment of time and effort needed to capture and then control it. Once sufficient examples are mastered, the child has a common language reserve that can be shared with other children and adults even if they are complete strangers. Children often arrive at school with a myriad of such examples of captured language under their belts. These become supplemented with skipping games, chants, songs learnt in assembly (typically), and the repertoire grows accordingly.

Beyond the early years

One typical poetry starting point is to create associations with colours. The American writer Kenneth Koch did used this and many other simple memorable techniques with inner city children in America (Koch, 1970). Often the results are along the line of 'Red is Santa at Christmas, Red is the colour of my blood . . .', but with careful encouragement from the teacher the child can bring more imaginative and sensitive descriptions to the task and begin to expand each line to incorporate personal and more detailed observations. Using a theme can be a worthwhile process, and moving away from the more predictable limitations of colours, teachers can initiate work on a much wider range of possible starting points such as spells, tortures, animals, and so on. However, poetry need not be restricted to the 'exotic'. Michael Rosen has regularly promoted the concept of 'memorable speech', and suggested that teachers should look to children's everyday contact with language as starting points for their writing: 'Everything we remember, no matter how trivial: the mark on the wall, the joke at luncheon, word games, these like the dance of a stoat or the raven's gamble are equally the subject of poetry' (Rosen, 1989: 11).

Some teachers begin poetry writing by simply asking children to collect together the language they come across (verbal and written) and use these as starting points for poems about their lives.

Using specific poetic forms based on syllabic patterns (such as the haiku ☞ or the cinquain ☞) helps children work within particular confines, and returning to such small tasks several times helps them develop self-criticism and the discipline of redrafting. Regular rhythmic patterns such as the limerick provide similar opportunities for children to work within specific poetic structures that are light-hearted and offer reasonably quick returns for their linguistic investment, although like many classic forms this takes time to master. Other poetic devices such as alliteration ☞ can be enjoyably explored (*Sesame Street* uses this concept all the time – 'Wanda the Wicked Witch Went to the Well on a Wednesday') and once these devices are learnt they become tools for the child to use in future writing.

Book-making, class anthologies and open readings are particularly well received ways of enhancing the profile of poetry. Parents are invariably appreciative of such opportunities to see their child's work 'in print' or to hear them perform. Children should always have audiences in mind for their work, and these kinds of opportunities to share their work with others helps to encourage further reflection on the impact and meanings of their poetry. It should be remembered that regular opportunities to browse through a large range of poetry books, to find favourites and to return to these, sometimes as performance requires your school to prioritise poetry books as a resource.

Extraordinary observations

The temptation to move into 'what does the poet really mean?' should be resisted as this is not the point of poetry. A better approach is 'what are the different ways that we all *read* this poem?' It should also be remembered that poetry is meant to be *heard*, and children need opportunities to develop the specific skills required to listen to the relationship between the sounds of the words in poetry. Teachers should also be wary of believing that poetry should always be 'fun': for many people it can be a way of coming to terms with complex emotions.

Writing poetry can be a liberating and challenging experience for those children who respond to investigative study. Some see the skills of poetic inference ☞ and deduction as comparable to scientific processes such as the experimental, trial and error nature of much writing being analogous to scientific enquiry:

> In writing, we as teachers should aim to bring the precision of poetry – that unrelenting, largely conscious search for the right word, and the largely unconscious search for the appropriate sounds, in terms of rhyme, rhythm, assonance and alliteration – to the emotion, the excitement of science.
>
> (Sedgwick, 1997: 2)

Children are capable of extraordinary observations and often make startling conceptual links between what they see, hear, feel, know and imagine and how they compare those understandings. Working on the Northumbrian coastline, a group of children studied one village's fading relationship with the sea. One child looked at the slight film of oil on the surface of the water and wrote:

> Anchored kittiwakes bob calmly
> on the vinegar water
> A bitter scent lingers in the air.
> Sweet shards of crystal nuzzle
> into the knotted rocks.
> A lilted tongue tilts to its side
> whispering
> tish
> tish

The child's perception of the water's surface is something that would have been difficult to predict, and responses such as these become crucial starting points for creative writing as they allow metaphors to be played with, expanded and explored linguistically. At another stormier part of the coast other children variously described the sea as a cobra, a lion, a porpoise and a wolf, developing animal metaphors and similes which were often insightful and occasionally surprising. Waves were variously described as 'carelessly turquoise', 'hypnotising', 'pearl diamonds' and 'silk sheets'. The noise of the water became a lullaby, a quarrel, a whisper, a growl, a lisp and a roar. Observations such as these offer powerful starting points for discussion and for further investigations into poetry. They also provide a forum for reading aloud, opportunities for which should be supported and frequently provided by teachers.

As primary teachers typically spend longer periods of time with the same children it is possible for them to develop methods of writing which build on shared previous experiences. After a period of working on the development of new images to describe observations one of the authors arrived at school one morning after a particularly heavy frost. He took his Year 3 class into some woodland adjacent to the playground and one girl wrote:

> Sour frost swirls through the air,
> mist killing the sun.
> A solid surface
> protecting the undergrowth.
> The ice crumbles on frozen puddles, spikes on branches
> frozen
> like fingers trying to crack the air.
> Sun beaming through a line
> of gleaming frost,
> lost
> in a crystal clear desert of ice.
> Cracked and empty.

The child's conceptual connection between the frozen twigs and 'fingers trying to crack the air' was an entirely natural process. Once a sense of trust is established between teacher and child in a supportive language environment children can be encouraged to capture observations on paper along with associated thoughts, dreams, imaginings and connections, making it possible to arrive at a raw palette of words and ideas which can then be mixed, combined and developed in a variety of ways for poetic ends.

The PNS Framework

The PNS Framework has detailed guidance on poetry. There are two or three poetry units per year each lasting one or two weeks. The topics of the units can be seen in Table 28.1.

In addition to the planning guidance there is also a progression paper on poetry which only loosely seems to relate to the teaching sequences of the poetry units. The Year 6 guidance from the progression paper is shown in Table 28.2.

Year 6 unit two is called 'Finding a Voice'. The teaching sequence in the PNS Framework is summarised as follows:

Year 6 Poetry – Unit 2
Finding a voice (1 week)
This is a relatively free-standing poetry unit, and could be taught at any stage of the school year. However, its learning develops from that in Year 6 poetry unit 1, which therefore needs to precede it. Whenever this unit is taught, the level of reading and writing expected and the word-level and presentation skills integrated within it must clearly build on from previous learning and towards end-of-year expectations. The content of the poems (both read and written) could be linked to other curriculum areas if desired.

Phase 1
Children explore an issue meaningful to them, and at the same time read, respond, analyse and evaluate a range of poems about that issue.

Phase 2
Children write their own poems in response to the issue. In the course of this, a way of working, involving playing with language and then forming and shaping ideas, is further developed, modelled and practised. ICT may

Table 28.1 Poetry units in the PNS Framework

Year	Unit 1	Unit 2	Unit 3
Y1	Using the senses	Pattern and rhyme	Poems on a theme
Y2	Patterns on the page	Really looking	Silly stuff
Y3	Poems to perform	Shape poetry and calligrams	Language play
Y4	Creating images	Exploring form	
Y5	Poetic style (word-play, rhyme, metaphor, word choice)	Classic/narrative poems	Choral and performance
Y6	The power of imagery	Finding a voice	

Table 28.2 Year 6 guidance from progression paper on poetry

Year	Strands 2, 5, 6 and 7 Reading Poetry:	Strands 1 and 6 Performing Poetry:	Strands 8–12 Creating Poetry:
	• subject matter and theme • language use; style • pattern	• use of voice • presentation	• original playfulness with language and ideas • detailed recreation of closely observed experience • using different patterns
Year 6	• interpret poems, explaining how the poet creates shades of meaning; justify own views and explain underlying themes • explain the impact of figurative and expressive language, including metaphor • comment on poem's structures and how these influence meaning	• vary pitch, pace volume, rhythm and expression in relation to the poem's meaning and form • use actions, sound effects, musical patterns, images and dramatic interpretation, varying presentations by using ICT	• use language imaginatively to create surreal, surprising, amusing and inventive poetry • use simple metaphors and personification to create poems based on real or imagined experience • select pattern or form to match meaning and own voice

be used to provide a visual or aural stimulus and/or to develop and present the poems.

Phase 3
Outcomes from the whole unit are shared and evaluated against pre-agreed criteria for effective communication with the reader and then performed and/or published in some oral, paper or electronic form.

If any of the genres covered by the PNS Framework were likely to offer the opportunity for children to find their 'voice', you would hope poetry could do this. So it is with some dismay that we find that children, even after all the poetry work that is prescribed throughout their primary school life, still do not get the chance to exercise real choice over the topic and form of their poetry. Instead the suggestion seems to be that a topic of general interest to the class is chosen (such as the environment, for example) and children are expected to find their voice within the constraints of the class topic and the constraints of the poems that are chosen by the teacher for analysis to precede the poetry writing.

Poetry writing should most of all be about searching for things that genuinely matter to the writer. These things are personal to individuals. When young people experience this process it can change their lives. As Ted Hughes said, 'Almost everybody, at some time in their lives, can produce poetry. Perhaps not very great poetry, but still, poetry they are glad to have written' (1967: 33).

Practice points

- Plan regular use of a large selection of varied poetry books for choosing, reading, learning and performing.
- Mix structured poetry writing activities with opportunities for free poetry writing where children make genuine choices.
- Experiment with poetry work that combines drama, music, dance and visual artwork and always look for opportunities for children to publish or perform their work.

Glossary

Alliteration – phrases that include words that begin with the same phoneme.
Cinquain – American originated poetry form with five lines, 22 syllables in a 2, 4, 6, 8, 2 pattern.
Haiku – Japanese poetry form with three lines, and 17 syllables in a 5, 7, 5 pattern.
Inference – the knowledge of textual meanings – beyond the literal or 'obvious'.

References

Hughes, T. (1967) *Poetry in the Making*. London: Faber and Faber.
Koch, K. (1970). *Wishes, Lies, and Dreams: Teaching Children to Write Poetry*. London: Harper and Row.
Rosen, M. (1989) *Did I Hear You Write?* London: Andre Deutsch.
Sedgwick, F. (1997) *Read My Mind: Young Children, Poetry and Learning*. London: Routledge.

Annotated bibliography

Brownjohn, S. (1980) *Does it Have to Rhyme?* London: Hodder & Stoughton.
Brownjohn, S. (1982) *What Rhymes with 'Secret'?* London: Hodder & Stoughton.
Two small books packed full of interesting ideas to develop an ongoing approach to poetry writing in the primary school. Each section is richly supported by examples of children's work.
L1 *

Carter, D. (1998) *Teaching Poetry in the Primary School*. London: David Fulton.

Detailed provision of links between planning, assessing and the study of poetry and planning for the National Literacy Hour.

L2 *

Styles, M. (2004) 'Poetry', in P. Hunt (ed.) *International Companion Encyclopedia of Children's Literature*, 2nd edn., Vol. 1. London: Routledge.

Styles has made a very significant contribution to academic work on children's literature. This chapter surveys the history of poetry for children.

L3 **

Wilson, A. (2005) 'The best forms in the best order? Current poetry writing pedagogy at KS2', *English in Education*, 39(3): 19–31.

Explores the importance of content and form in poetry. Includes analysis of four influential writers on teaching poetry including Sandy Brownjohn (see above).

L2 **

Appendix

Methodology used to determine stages of development in reading and writing

The aim of the study was to document and analyse the reading and writing development of Dominic's two children Oliver and Esther. The aims were:

1   To analyse previously published case studies of reading and writing development in order to establish generalisable characteristics.
2   To establish developmental stages based on the analysis of generalisable characteristics.
3   To explicitly build an analysis of new case study data on the developmental stages.
4   To identify significant aspect of development.

The analysis of new data spanned the age of Oliver from one year and 10 months (1.10) to 5.6 and the age of Esther from 3.10 to 7.6. Data collection methods included a research diary where the children's mother and father noted what were felt to be significant moments in the children's develoment. Approximately 90 per cent of the diary observations were made by the father.

Diary methods are a common feature of this kind of case study work, however, one of the ways the study extended the data of previous studies was through the use of video evidence. 120 video clips ranging from between approximately 1 minute and 15 minutes were collected on eleven 45-minute video tapes. The video camera was used by both parents to capture different events from the diary as well as triangulating by method to explore significant moments. The video evidence included moments when one or other of the parents was interacting with the children on literacy activities such as reading a book or helping with drawing and writing and also included times when the children were playing together.

The other data set was one large size level-arch file for each child of examples of their mark-making and writing. In addition to informing the analysis of writing generally, the file also supported a specific focus on writing genres. The different genres of writing that the children wrote at home were tabulated and a frequency count established.

The selection of data was guided by moments that the parents felt were significant in relation to the children's development. My knowledge of published case studies and other research concerning the development of reading and writing influenced the selection of data that I considered to be significant. The other factors in the selection of data were time and opportunity. There were short periods when the collection of data was not possible because events in daily life were such that the energy and time of the parents were dominated by these events. It could be argued that this relatively unsystematic approach to data collection is a limitation in the methodology, however, its advantage is that it allows the researcher to accommodate a wide range of influences on development and to avoid an inappropriately narrow focus. The approach has been commonly used in studies of this kind.

Data organisation and analysis initially involved a systematic analysis of previous research. This served two purposes: first, it enabled the data to be managed and categorised efficiently and, second, it established a picture of common developmental characteristics. The analysis of previous work focused upon published research which reported longitudinal evidence of developmental progression in reading and writing. The final selection of studies was as follows: Baghban (1984), Bearne (1998), Bissex (1980), Campbell (1999), Centre for Language in Primary Education (CLPE) (1989), Chall (1983), Ehri (1995), Fadil and Zaragoza (1997), Kamler (1984), Lass (1982), Minns (1997), Payton, (1984), Perera (1984), Schmidt and Yates (1985), Wyse (1998), Wyse and Jones (2001).

Initially, the language mode, age range and key conclusions of the studies were documented. Subsequently, concentrating on the developmental progression evidence, four new developmental levels were established: Prior to Beginning Level (<B); Level B; Level 1; and Level 2. The levels were initially established by analysing the studies that described development in stages which were conceptual rather than age-related and which were derived from larger groups of children (Bearne, 1998; Chall, 1983; CLPE, 1989; Wyse, 1998; Wyse and Jones, 2001). The developmental evidence from age-related studies including individual child case studies was then located in the levels through a consideration of 'best fit'.

Evidence of progression of reading development reported in research studies was tabulated by placing it within the four levels in one of two categories: 'contextual' and 'phonological' development. Contextual evidence was defined as reading development that was primarily text-level and sentence-level, including semantic and syntactic development. Phonological evidence was defined as evidence concerned with the development of understanding at word-level, in particular, knowledge of the relationship between phonemes and graphemes and the developing ability to decode words.

Evidence of progression of writing development reported in previous research studies was tabulated by placing it within the four levels and in one of five categories: composition, grammar, spelling, punctuation and handwriting. Composition was defined as writing development that was primarily text-level and focused on communicative intent and the semantic aspects of the writing process. Grammar mainly referred to develoment of sentence structure. Evidence of spelling, punctuation and handwriting development was also tabulated.

Once the initial analysis of evidence had been tabulated, an additional table was created which listed general characteristics for each level. These were a series of summary statements describing typical development at that level. An initial set was drafted and each characteristic was critically assessed for the extent to which the research evidence from the initial analysis of published studies strongly, moderately or weakly supported the statement. Quantitatively this analysis recorded the number of incidences of evidence related to the statement. Qualitatively the analysis judged the significance of the developmental evidence reported in the different studies and the extent to which it provided support for the statement. This was an assessment of whether there was multiple and significant evidence from the studies to support the general characteristics. The focus was on developmental characteristics that might be generalisable to larger groups of children. If the link between the research evidence and the characteristic was judged to be too weak, it was rejected.

The process of linking the different studies with the levels was a difficult one which involved judgement. Personal preference and bias were inevitably present because of the judgements required in order to synthesise the diverse range of evidence. However, the subsequent development of sets of general characteristics for each level enhanced the validity due to a focus on the most common features represented by the research studies. Once the four levels were established, they provided the conceptual focus for the analysis of Esther and Oliver's development. A decision was made to initially concentrate on levels B, 1 and 2 because this enabled the research to reflect upon the implications for formal early years education although the final outcome included the establishment of Summary tables for age 4, 7 and 11.

The video evidence was selected as the priority data source in view of its lack of use in previous case studies. All videos clips were viewed in order to establish a catalogue documenting time, date, duration and summary of content. The clips were then repeatedly viewed in order to select those which were conceptually related to the general characteristics of the three levels. Finally a series of clips of no more than five minutes in total for each reading and writing level were selected for further analysis. The selected video clips were transcribed using the following coding system:

/x/ – phonological representation of speech based on *Longman English Dictionary* pronunciation scheme;

(.) short pause;

(n) pause of approximately n seconds;

(?) inaudible word; (??) inaudible phrase;

Capital letters to represent spoken letter names unless indication of participants' names: E – Esther; O – Oliver; F – Father; M – Mother;

(cut) cut in film as part of editing process.

The video cataloguing and analysis was supported by the use of Apple iMovie
software.

The analysis of video evidence led to the locating of texts that were being
written or read as part of the video extracts. For reading, the particular books
that the children were reading were located. If these were reading scheme books
(i.e. basal readers) they were borrowed from the children's school. For writing,
the files of examples were searched to locate the writing/mark-making that
featured on the video. The evidence from the videos was then triangulated with
the diary evidence, and the evidence from texts, and reduced to developmental
progression statements which were added to the tables of reading and writing
development which had been built from previous studies. After this the statements of general characteristics were rechecked, and amended if appropriate,
by considering the significance of the new data. Triangulation of the different
data sets was facilitated by the design of an HTML page which featured a series
of hyperlinks used to group examples of the different data sets at the three
levels of reading and writing. This systematic linking of the data sets enabled
quick access to the most significant data and facilitated further checks on the
validity of the emerging findings.

References

Baghban, M. (1984) *Our Daughter Learns to Read and Write: A Case Study
 from Birth to Three*. Newark, DE: International Reading Association.
Bearne, E. (1998) *Making Progress in English*. London: Routledge.
Bissex, G. (1980) *GNYS AT WORK: A Child Learns to Read and Write*.
 Cambridge, MA: Harvard University Press.
Campbell, R. (1999) *Literacy from Home to School: Reading with Alice*.
 Stoke-on-Trent: Trentham Books.
Centre for Language in Primary Education (CLPE)/Inner London Education
 Authority (ILEA) (1989) *The Primary Language Record Handbook for
 Teachers*. London: Centre for Language in Primary Education.
Chall, J. S. (1983) *Stages of Reading Development*. New York: McGraw-Hill
 Book Company.
Ehri, L. C. (1995) 'Phases of development in learning to read words by sight',
 Journal of Research in Reading, 18(2): 116–125.
Fadil, C. and Zaragoza, N. (1997) 'Revisiting the emergence of young child-
 ren's literacy: one child tells her story', *Reading*, 31(1): 29–34.
Kamler, B. (1984) 'Ponch writes again: a child at play', *Australian Journal of
 Reading*, 7(2): 61–70.

Lass, B. (1982) 'Portrait of my son as an early reader', *The Reading Teacher*, 36(1): 20–28.

Minns, H. (1997) *Read It to Me Now!: Learning at Home and at School.* Buckingham: Open University Press.

Payton, S. (1984) *Developing Awareness of Print: A Young Child's First Steps Towards Literacy.* Birmingham: University of Birmingham: Educational Review.

Perera, K. (1984) *Children's Reading and Writing: Analysing Classroom Language.* Oxford: Basil Blackwell, in association with Andre Deutsch Ltd.

Schmidt, E. and Yates, C. (1985) 'Benji learns to read naturally! Naturally Benji learns to read', *Australian Journal of Reading*, 8(3): 121–134.

Wyse, D. (1998) *Primary Writing.* Buckingham: Open University Press.

Wyse, D. and Jones, R. (2001) *Teaching English, Language and Literacy.* London: RoutledgeFalmer.

Index

Note: References in **bold** are to the glossaries; b, f, and t refer to boxes, figures and tables.